Tangled Relationships

FOUNDATIONS OF SOCIAL WORK KNOWLEDGE
FREDERIC G. REAMER, SERIES EDITOR

Foundations of Social Work Knowledge

Frederic G. Reamer, Series Editor

Social work has a unique history, purpose, perspective, and method. The primary purpose of this series is to articulate these distinct qualities and to define and explore the ideas, concepts, and skills that together constitute social work's intellectual foundations and boundaries and its emerging issues and concerns.

To accomplish this goal, the series will publish a cohesive collection of books that address both the core knowledge of the profession and its newly emerging topics. The core is defined by the evolving consensus, as primarily reflected in the Council of Social Work Education's Curriculum Policy Statement, concerning what courses accredited social work education programs must include in their curricula. The series will be characterized by an emphasis on the widely embraced ecological perspective; attention to issues concerning direct and indirect practice; and emphasis on cultural diversity and multiculturalism, social justice, oppression, populations at risk, and social work values and ethics. The series will have a dual focus on practice traditions and emerging issues and concepts.

David G. Gil, *Confronting Injustice and Oppression: Concepts and Strategies for Social Workers*

George Alan Appleby and Jeane W. Anastas, *Not Just a Passing Phase: Social Work with Gay, Lesbian, and Bisexual People*

Frederic G. Reamer, *Social Work Research and Evaluation Skills*

Pallassana R. Balgopal, *Social Work Practice with Immigrants and Refugees*

Dennis Saleeby, *Human Behavior and Social Environments*

Tangled Relationships

*Managing Boundary Issues
in the Human Services*

Frederic G. Reamer

COLUMBIA UNIVERSITY PRESS   NEW YORK

COLUMBIA UNIVERSITY PRESS
Publishers Since 1893
New York   Chichester, West Sussex
Copyright © 2001 Columbia University Press
All rights reserved

Library of Congress Cataloging-in-Publication Data

Reamer, Frederic G., 1953–
  Tangled relationships : managing boundary issues in the human services /
Frederic G. Reamer.
    p. cm. — (Foundations of social work knowledge)
  Includes bibliographical references and index.
  ISBN 0-231-12116-4 (cloth : alk. paper)
  ISBN 0-231-12117-2 (pbk. : alk. paper)
  1. Social workers—Professional relationships. 2. Human services personnel—
Professional relationships. 3. Counselor and client. 4. Social service. I. Title.

  HV40.35 .R43 2001
  361.3'2—dc21

                                                                00-052360

∞

Casebound editions of Columbia University Press books
are printed on permanent and durable acid-free paper.
Printed in the United States of America

c 10 9 8 7 6 5 4 3 2 1
p 10 9 8 7 6 5 4 3 2 1

For Deborah, Emma, and Leah

Contents

Preface   *xi*

1. Boundary Issues and Dual Relationships: Key Concepts   1

   Boundary Issues in the Human Services   2

   A Typology of Boundary Issues and Dual Relationships   8

   Managing Dual Relationships   17

   Sound Decision Making   20

   The Role of Practitioner Impairment   47

2. Intimate Relationships   55

   Sexual Relationships with Clients   55

   Sexual Relationships with Former Clients   81

   Counseling Former Sexual Partners   85

Sexual Relationships with Clients' Relatives
or Acquaintances   87

Sexual Relationships with Supervisees, Trainees, Students,
and Colleagues   90

Physical Contact   92

3. Emotional and Dependency Needs   99

Friendships with Clients   101

Unconventional Interventions   104

Self-disclosure   108

Affectionate Communications   112

Community-based Contact with Clients   115

4. Personal Benefit   122

Barter for Services   122

Business and Financial Relationships   128

Advice and Services   133

Favors and Gifts   135

Conflicts of Interest   143

5. Altruism   148

Giving Gifts to Clients   148

Meeting Clients in Social or Community Settings   151

Offering Clients Favors   156

Accommodating Clients   160

Self-disclosing to Clients   166

6. Unavoidable and Unanticipated Circumstances   173

Geographic Proximity   173

Conflicts of Interest   181

Professional Encounters   189

Social Encounters   190

Epilogue   194

References   199

Index   *211*

Preface

Only recently have boundary issues become an explicit topic of conversation among human service professionals. Boundary issues occur when practitioners—including social workers, psychologists, counselors, psychiatrists, and psychiatric nurses—establish more than one relationship with clients, whether professional, social, or business. Not until the 1990s did a · critical mass of literature on the subject begin to emerge. This is the latest chapter in the evolution of the broader field of applied and professional ethics. Exploration of boundary issues also is the most recent development in my own evolving concern with professional ethics.

I first explored issues of professional ethics in the mid-1970s, at about the time the broader field of applied and professional ethics was just emerging. My inquiry started when I began to appreciate the complex ways in which human service professionals—including clinicians, community organizers, administrators, policy makers, and researchers—encounter daunting ethical dilemmas and decisions. At the time, I did not fully grasp how my nascent interest in this subject reflected a much larger phenomenon: the emergence of a new, bona fide academic field focused on professional ethics. With the benefit that only hindsight can provide, I now understand how significant that period was. What began as a fledgling interest among a relatively small coterie of scholars and practitioners has evolved into an intellectually rich, widely respected field with its own conceptual frameworks, body of knowledge, vocabulary, and academic imprimatur. Professional ethics truly has come of age.

Paralleling this phenomenon, my own understanding of ethical issues has evolved, leading up to my current interest in boundary issues—particularly those in which human service professionals become involved in "dual relationships" with clients. Up through the late 1980s, my work in the professional ethics arena focused mainly on the nature of diverse ethical dilemmas encountered by practitioners, ethical decision-making models, and the practical implications of ethical theory. During this period my colleagues and I paid relatively modest attention to boundary issues; the general subject hardly was a major focus of attention.

By the early 1990s, my own interests had broadened to include issues pertaining to what I now call ethics risk management, including concepts and strategies that human service professionals can use to protect clients' rights and prevent ethics complaints and lawsuits that allege ethics-related negligence or malpractice committed by professionals. This interest stemmed in part from my expanding service as an expert witness (to use the court's term) in a large number of lawsuits around the United States involving human service professionals as plaintiffs or defendants. Also, my emerging interest in risk-management issues has been influenced by my position as chair of a statewide committee responsible for reviewing and adjudicating ethics complaints filed against social workers. A significant portion of the court cases and ethics complaints in which I have been involved have concerned the kinds of boundary issues that I examine in this book. Also, my recent experience as chair of the committee that rewrote the National Association of Social Workers' *Code of Ethics* deepened my understanding of the complicated challenge involved in cultivating ethical standards pertaining to boundary issues.

What I have learned over the years is that, without question, boundary and dual relationship issues are among the most challenging ethical dilemmas in the field. Some dual relationships need to be prevented, such as sexual relationships with clients. Other dual relationships need to be managed carefully—for example, when professionals who practice in rural areas encounter clients in the community. Our collective understanding of these issues—the diverse forms they take, their consequences and implications—has matured greatly in recent years. This book represents my effort to organize and reflect on these complex issues and to suggest how human service professionals who face them can best protect clients and themselves.

This book contains considerable case material. In most instances, I report case-related details that I have disguised to protect the privacy of the parties involved. Some cases are a matter of public record.

Tangled Relationships

1   Boundary Issues and Dual Relationships: Key Concepts

In recent years, especially since the early 1980s, human service professionals have developed an increasingly mature grasp of ethical issues. Since then, the professional literature has expanded markedly with respect to identifying ethical conflicts and dilemmas in practice; developing conceptual frameworks and protocols for ethical decision making when professional duties conflict; and formulating risk-management strategies to avoid ethics-related negligence and ethical misconduct (Austin, Moline, and Williams 1990; Berliner 1989; Bersoff 1999; Besharov 1985; Bullis 1995; Corey, Corey, and Callanan 1997; Herlihy and Corey 1992; Loewenberg and Dolgoff 1996; Reamer 1980, 1982, 1990, 1994a, 1995a, 1998a, 1999; Rhodes 1986).

Clearly, ethical issues related to professional boundaries are among the most problematic and challenging (Congress 1996; Jayaratne, Croxton, and Mattison 1997; Kagle and Giebelhausen 1994; Reamer in press; Strom-Gottfried 1999). Briefly, boundary issues arise when human service professionals encounter actual or potential conflicts between their professional duties and their social, sexual, religious, or business relationships (St. Germaine 1993, 1996). As I will explore more fully later, not all boundary issues are necessarily problematic or unethical, but many are. My principal goal is to explore the range of boundary issues in the human services, develop criteria to help professionals distinguish between boundary issues that are and are not problematic, and present guidelines to help practitioners manage boundary issues and risks that arise in practice.

Boundary Issues in the Human Services

Human service professionals—be they clinicians (social workers, psychologists, psychiatrists, counselors, psychiatric nurses), community organizers, policy makers, supervisors, researchers, administrators, or educators—often encounter circumstances that pose actual or potential boundary issues. Boundary issues occur when practitioners face potential conflicts of interest stemming from what have become known as dual or multiple relationships. According to Kagle and Giebelhausen (1994), "A professional enters into a dual relationship whenever he or she assumes a second role with a client, becoming social worker and friend, employer, teacher, business associate, family member, or sex partner. A practitioner can engage in a dual relationship whether the second relationship begins before, during, or after the social work relationship" (213). Dual relationships occur primarily between human service professionals and their current or former clients and between professionals and their colleagues (including supervisees, trainees, and students).

Historically, human service professionals have not generated clear guidelines regarding boundaries for use in practice. This is partly because the broader subject of professional ethics—to which the topic of boundaries is closely tied—did not begin to receive serious attention in the scholarly and professional literature until the late 1970s and early 1980s. In addition, the human service field, starting with Freud, is rife with mixed messages related to boundaries and dual relationships (Gutheil and Gabbard 1993). Freud sent patients postcards, lent them books, gave them gifts, corrected them when they spoke inaccurately about his family members, provided some with considerable financial support, and on at least one occasion gave a patient a meal (Gutheil and Gabbard 1993; Lipton 1977). According to Gutheil and Gabbard,

> The line between professional and personal relationships in Freud's analytic practice was difficult to pinpoint. During vacations he would analyze Ferenczi while walking through the countryside. In one of his letters to Ferenczi, which were often addressed "Dear Son," he indicated that during his holiday he planned to analyze him in two sessions a day but also invited him to share at least one meal with him each day (unpublished manuscript by A. Hoffer). For Freud the

analytic relationship could be circumscribed by the time boundaries of the analytic sessions, and other relationships were possible outside the analytic hours. The most striking illustration of this conception of boundaries is Freud's analysis of his own daughter, Anna. (189)

These various manifestations of blurred boundaries occurred despite Freud's explicit and strongly worded observations about the inappropriateness of therapists' love relationships with patients: "The love-relationship actually destroys the influence of the analytic treatment on the patient; a combination of the two would be an inconceivable thing" (Freud 1963, cited in Smith and Fitzpatrick 1995).

Several other luminaries have provided intriguing mixed messages regarding boundaries. When Melanie Klein was analyzing Clifford Scott, she encouraged him to follow her to the Black Forest for her vacation. During each day of the vacation, Klein analyzed Scott for two hours while Scott reclined on the bed in Klein's hotel room (Grosskurth 1986; Gutheil and Gabbard 1993). D. W. Winnicott (1949) reported housing young patients as part of his treatment of them. According to Margaret Little's (1990) first-person account of her analysis with Winnicott, Winnicott held her hands clasped between his for many hours as she lay on the couch. Little also reports that Winnicott told her about another patient of his who had committed suicide and disclosed significant detail about his countertransference reactions to the patient. Winnicott also apparently routinely concluded sessions with coffee and biscuits.

Further complicating efforts to develop definitive guidelines regarding proper boundaries is the contention by a relatively small number of critics that the human service professions have mishandled their efforts to generate boundary-related guidelines and that current prohibitions are misguided. Ebert (1997), for example, argues that "the concept of dual relationship prohibitions has limited value in that it creates confusion and leads to unfair results in ethics and licensing actions. It serves little purpose because it does not assist psychologists in analyzing situations. Neither does it provide much help in assisting psychologists in deciding how to act in a particular situation, such that the client's best interest is considered" (137). Ebert asserts that many dual relationship prohibitions enforced by the American Psychological Association (APA)—especially those related to nonsexual relationships—violate practitioners' constitutional and privacy rights and are overly vague:

There are major problems with dual-relationship prohibitions. Because they are poorly defined and there is limited publication of decisions regarding nonsexual dual relationships, they are vague in the constitutional sense. Second, they tend to be overly broad in that, as written, the prohibitions tend to restrict constitutionally protected rights while also restricting nonconstitutionally protected rights. Third, they are often interpreted literally as prohibitions against all dual relationships when that was never the intent of APA. . . . Fourth, the prohibitions interfere with the constitutionally protected right to privacy. This substantive due-process right guaranteed under the 14th Amendment of the Constitution has been one often used by APA to support its position on nondiscrimination and pro-choice. Fifth, the First Amendment Right to Association is unacceptably restricted. Some policies surrounding dual relationship could be considered as gender discrimination. Finally, the way in which decisions have been handed down, the confusion regarding accepted practices, and the lack of publication of cases as well as the lack of an analytical model to be applied to ethics decisions, have created a system without adequate procedural due process. (143)

The contemporary human service literature contains relatively few in-depth discussions of boundary issues and guidelines (Corey and Herlihy 1997; Jayaratne, Croxton, and Mattison 1997; Kagle and Giebelhausen 1994; Strom-Gottfried 1999). Understandably, much of the available literature focuses on dual relationships that are exploitative in nature, such as the sexual involvement of human service professionals with clients (Olarte 1997; K. Pope 1995; Simon 1999). Certainly, these are important and compelling issues. However, many boundary and dual relationship issues in the human services are much more subtle than these egregious forms of ethical misconduct. An empirical survey of a statewide sample of clinicians uncovered substantial disagreement concerning the appropriateness of behaviors such as developing friendships with clients, participating in social activities with clients, serving on community boards with clients, providing clients with one's home telephone number, accepting goods and services from clients instead of money, and discussing one's religious beliefs with clients (Jayaratne, Croxton, and Mattison 1997; also see Borys and

Pope 1989; Pope, Tabachnick, and Keith-Spiegel 1988; Strom-Gottfried 1999). As Corey and Herlihy (1997) note,

> The pendulum of controversy over dual relationships, which has produced extreme reactions on both sides, has slowed and now swings in a narrower arc. It is clear that not all dual relationships can be avoided, and it is equally clear that some types of dual relationships (such as sexual intimacies with clients) should always be avoided. In the middle range, it would be fruitful for professionals to continue to work to clarify the distinctions between dual relationships that we should try to avoid and those into which we might enter, with appropriate precautions. (190)

To achieve a more finely tuned understanding of boundary issues, we must broaden our analysis and examine dual relationships through several conceptual lenses. First, human service professionals should distinguish between boundary violations and boundary crossings (Gutheil and Gabbard 1993). A boundary violation occurs when a practitioner engages in a dual relationship with a client or colleague that is exploitative, manipulative, deceptive, or coercive. Examples include professionals who become sexually involved with current clients, recruit and collude with clients to fraudulently bill insurance companies, or influence terminally ill clients to include their therapist in their will.

One key feature of boundary violations is a conflict of interest that harms clients or colleagues (Epstein 1994; Kitchener 1988; Kutchins 1991; Peterson 1992; K. Pope 1988, 1991). Conflicts of interest occur when professionals find themselves in a relationship that could prejudice or give the appearance of prejudicing their decision making. In more legalistic language, conflicts of interest occur when professionals are in "a situation in which regard for one duty leads to disregard of another or might reasonably be expected to do so" (Gifis 1991:88). Thus a human service professional who provides services to a client with whom he would like to develop a sexual relationship faces a conflict of interest; the professional's personal interests clash with his professional duty to avoid harming his client. Similarly, a practitioner who invests money in a client's business is embedded in a conflict of interest; the professional's financial interests may clash with her duty to the client (for example, if the professional's relationship with the client becomes strained because they disagree about some aspect of their shared business venture).

The codes of ethics of several human service professions explicitly address the concept of conflict of interest. A prominent example is the National Association of Social Workers' (NASW) *Code of Ethics* (1996):

> Social workers should be alert to and avoid conflicts of interest that interfere with the exercise of professional discretion and impartial judgment. Social workers should inform clients when a real or potential conflict of interest arises and take reasonable steps to resolve the issue in a manner that makes the clients' interests primary and protects clients' interests to the greatest extent possible. In some cases, protecting clients' interests may require termination of the professional relationship with proper referral of the client. (standard 1.06[a])

The code goes on to say that "social workers should not engage in dual or multiple relationships with clients or former clients in which there is a risk of exploitation or potential harm to the client" (standard 1.06[c]).

Some conflicts of interest involve what lawyers call *undue influence.* Undue influence occurs when a human service professional inappropriately pressures or exercises authority over a susceptible client in a manner that benefits the practitioner and may not be in the client's best interest. In legal terminology, undue influence involves the "exertion of improper influence and submission to the domination of the influencing party. . . . In such a case, the influencing party is said to have an unfair advantage over the other based, among other things, on real or apparent authority, knowledge of necessity or distress, or a fiduciary or confidential relationship" (Gifis 1991:508). The American Medical Association's *Principles of Medical Ethics with Annotations Especially Applicable to Psychiatrists* (1996) specifically addresses the concept of undue influence: "The psychiatrist should diligently guard against exploiting information furnished by the patient and should not use the unique position of power afforded him/her by the psychotherapeutic situation to influence the patient in any way not directly relevant to the treatment goals" (sec. 2, annotation 2).

In contrast to boundary violations, a boundary crossing occurs when a human service professional is involved in a dual relationship with a client or colleague in a manner that is not exploitative, manipulative, deceptive, or coercive. Boundary crossings are not inherently unethical; they often involve boundary "bending" as opposed to boundary "breaking." In principle, the consequences of boundary crossings may be harmful, salutary, or neutral

(Gutheil and Gabbard 1993). Boundary crossings are harmful when the dual relationship has negative consequences for the practitioner's client or colleague and, potentially, the practitioner him- or herself. For example, a professional who discloses to a client personal, intimate details about her own life, ostensibly to be helpful to the client, ultimately may confuse the client and compromise the client's mental health because of complicated transference issues produced by the practitioner's self-disclosure. An educator in the human services who accepts a student's dinner invitation may inadvertently harm the student by confusing him about nature of the educator's relationship with the student. *harm*

Alternatively, some boundary crossings may be helpful to clients and colleagues. Some professionals argue that, handled judiciously, a practitioner's modest self-disclosure or decision to accept an invitation to attend a client's graduation ceremony may prove, in some special circumstances, to be therapeutically useful to a client (Anderson and Mandell 1989; Chapman 1997; Reamer 1997b, 1998a, in press). A practitioner who worships, coincidentally, at the same church, mosque, or synagogue as one of his clients may help the client "normalize" the professional–client relationship. An educator in the human services who hires a student to serve as a research assistant may boost the student's self-confidence in a way that greatly enriches the student's educational experience. *benefit*

Yet other boundary crossings produce mixed results. A practitioner's self-disclosure about personal challenges may be both helpful and harmful to the same client—helpful in that the client feels more connected to the practitioner and harmful in that the self-disclosure undermines the client's confidence in the practitioner. The human service administrator who hires a former client initially may elevate the former client's self-confidence, but boundary problems will arise if the employee subsequently wants to resume his status as an active client in order to address some new issues in his life. *Mixed*

Practitioners should also be aware of the conceptual distinction in the terms *impropriety* and *appearance of impropriety.* An impropriety occurs when a practitioner violates a client's boundaries or engages in inappropriate dual relationships in a manner that violates prevailing ethical standards. Conducting a sexual relationship with a client and borrowing money from a client are clear examples of impropriety. In contrast, an appearance of impropriety occurs when a practitioner engages in conduct that appears to be improper but in fact may not be.

Let me illustrate this with a personal example. A number of years ago, I served on the governor's staff in my state. In that position, I helped formulate public policy related to low-income and affordable housing. I worked directly with the governor when important issues arose, such as when relevant bills were pending in the state legislature. After several years, I resigned that position; shortly thereafter, the governor concluded his term in office. The new governor then appointed me to the state parole board, which entails conducting hearings for prison inmates eligible for parole. After I began serving in that position, the former governor—my former employer—was indicted and charged in criminal court with committing offenses while in office (among other issues, this complex case involved financial transactions among the governor, his political campaign staff, and building contractors and other parties who sought state contracts). The former governor was subsequently convicted and sentenced to prison. When he became eligible for parole and was scheduled to appear before me, I had to decide whether to participate in his hearing or recuse myself. I knew in my heart that I would be able to render a fair decision. However, I also knew that I needed to be sensitive to the appearance of impropriety. I could not expect the general public to believe that I could be impartial, in light of my relationship with the man when he had been in office. No matter how certain I was of my ability to be fair and impartial, I had to concede that, at the very least, it would appear that I was involved in an inappropriate dual relationship. Because of the likely appearance of impropriety, I decided to recuse myself. Thus, although engaging in behaviors that only appear to be improper may not be unethical, human service practitioners should be sensitive to the effect that such appearances may have on their reputation and the integrity of their profession.

A Typology of Boundary Issues and Dual Relationships

Given the great range of boundary issues in the human service professions, practitioners need a conceptual framework to help them identify and manage dual relationships they encounter. What follows is a typology of boundary issues in the human services, based on several data sources: insurance industry statistics summarizing malpractice and negligence claims; empirical surveys of human service professionals and other professionals about boundary issues; legal literature and court opinions in litigation involving boundaries; and my experience as chair of a statewide ethics adjudication committee and expert witness in a large number of legal cases involving boundary issues.

Boundary issues in the human service professions fall into five conceptual categories: intimate relationships, pursuit of personal benefit, how professionals respond to their own emotional and dependency needs, altruistic gestures, and responses to unanticipated circumstances.

Intimate Relationships

Many dual relationships in the human services involve some form of intimacy. Typically, these relationships entail a sexual relationship or physical contact, although they may also entail other intimate gestures, such as gift giving, friendship, and affectionate communication.

Sexual relationships.   A distressingly significant portion of intimate dual relationships involves sexual contact (Akamatsu 1988; Bouhoutsos 1985; Bouhoutsos et al. 1983; Coleman and Schaefer 1986; Committee on Women 1989; Feldman-Summers and Jones 1984; Gabbard 1989; Gechtman 1989; Pope and Bouhoutsos 1986; Reamer 1984, 1992, 1994a; Sell, Gottlieb, and Schoenfeld 1986; Strom-Gottfried 1999). Although the human service professions agree that sexual relationships with current clients are inappropriate, they are not so unanimous regarding sexual relationships with *former* clients. I will discuss this debate more fully in chapter 2.

Human service professionals must also be aware of other potentially problematic sexual relationships that may involve a client indirectly. For example, current ethical standards in most human service professions prohibit sexual relationships between practitioners and a client's relatives or other individuals with whom a client maintains a close personal relationship. Typical is the NASW *Code of Ethics* (1996) standard on this issue:

Social workers should not engage in sexual activities or sexual contact with clients' relatives or other individuals with whom clients maintain a close personal relationship when there is a risk of exploitation or potential harm to the client. Sexual activity or sexual contact with clients' relatives or other individuals with whom clients maintain a personal relationship has the potential to be harmful to the client and may make it difficult for the social worker and client to maintain appropriate professional boundaries. Social workers—not their clients, their clients' relatives, or other individuals with whom the client maintains a personal relationship—assume the full burden for setting clear, appropriate, and culturally sensitive boundaries. (standard 1.09[b])

Other potentially problematic sexual relationships can occur between educators, supervisors, or trainers in the human service professions and their students, supervisees, or trainees.

Physical contact.   Not all physical contact between a practitioner and a client is sexual in nature. Physical contact in a number of circumstances may be asexual and appropriate—for example, a brief hug at the termination of long-term treatment or placing an arm around a client in a residential program who just received bad family news and is distraught. Such brief, limited physical contact may not be harmful; many clients would find such physical contact comforting and therapeutic, although other clients may be upset by it (perhaps because of their personal trauma history or their cultural or ethnic norms related to touching).

Some forms of physical contact have greater potential for psychological harm. In these circumstances, physical touch may exacerbate a client's transference in destructive ways and may suggest that the practitioner is interested in more than a professional relationship. For example, a clinician provided counseling to a twenty-eight-year-old woman who had been sexually abused as a child. As an adult, the client sought counseling to help her understand the effects of the early victimization, especially pertaining to her intimate relationships. As part of the therapy the practitioner, aiming to comfort the client, would occasionally dim the office lights, turn on soft music, and sit on the floor while cradling and talking with the client. The client was thus retraumatized because this physical contact with the clinician exacerbated the client's confusion about intimacy and boundaries with important people in her life.

The NASW *Code of Ethics* (1996) includes a standard pertaining specifically to the concept of physical touch: "Social workers should not engage in physical contact with clients when there is a possibility of psychological harm to the client as a result of the contact (such as cradling or caressing clients). Social workers who engage in appropriate physical contact with clients are responsible for setting clear, appropriate, and culturally sensitive boundaries that govern such physical contact" (standard 1.09[d]).

Counseling a former lover.   Providing clinical services to someone with whom a practitioner was once intimately, romantically, or sexually involved also constitutes a dual relationship. The relationship history is likely to make it difficult for the practitioner and the client to interact with each other solely as professional and client; inevitably, the dynamics of the prior relationship will influence the professional–client relationship — how the parties view and respond to each other — perhaps in ways that are detrimental to the client's best interests. As the American Psychological Association's *Ethical Principles of Psychologists and Code of Conduct* (1992) states, "Psychologists do not accept as therapy patients or clients persons with whom they have engaged in sexual intimacies" (standard 4.06).

Intimate gestures.   Boundary issues can also emerge when practitioners and clients engage in other intimate gestures, such as gift giving and expressions of friendship (including sending affectionate notes, for example, on the practitioner's personal stationery). It is not unusual for a client to give a human service professional a modest gift. Certainly, in many instances a client's gift represents nothing more than an appreciative gesture. In some instances, however, a client's gift may carry great meaning. For example, the gift may reflect the client's fantasies about a friendship or more intimate relationship with the practitioner. Thus it behooves the professional to carefully consider the meaning of a client's gift and establish prudent guidelines governing the acceptance of gifts. Many social service agencies do not permit staff members to accept gifts because of the potential conflict of interest or appearance of impropriety, or they permit gifts of only modest value. Some agencies permit staff to accept gifts only with the understanding — which is conveyed to clients — that the gifts represent a contribution to the agency, not to the individual professional.

The human service professions agree that friendships with current clients constitute inappropriate dual relationships. There is less clarity, however, about friendships between professionals and *former* clients. Although professionals generally understand the risk involved in befriending a former client — the possibility of confused boundaries — some professionals argue that friendships with former clients are not inherently unethical and reflect

a more egalitarian, nonhierarchical approach to practice. These professionals typically claim that emotionally mature practitioners and former clients
are quite capable of entering into new kinds of relationships after termination of the professional–client relationship and that such new relationships
often are, in fact, evidence of the former client's substantial therapeutic
progress. Later I will explore this complex debate more thoroughly.

Personal Benefit

Beyond these various manifestations of intimacy, human service professionals can become involved in dual relationships that produce other forms
of personal benefit, including monetary gain, goods, services, or useful information.

Monetary gain.   In some situations, a practitioner stands to benefit financially as a result of a dual relationship (Bonosky 1995). In one case, a
professional's former client decided to change careers and become a social
worker. After completing graduate school, the client contacted the social
worker and asked to be the social worker's supervisee (supervision was required for a state license). The social worker was tempted to take on the
supervision for a fee, in part because he enjoyed their relationship and in
part because of the financial benefit. The social worker also recognized that
the shift from the social worker–client relationship to a collegial relationship
would introduce a number of boundary issues. In another case, a client
named a counselor in his will. After the client's death and probate of the
will, the client's family accused the counselor of undue influence (the family
alleged that the counselor had encouraged the client to bequeath a portion
of the estate to the counselor).

Goods and services.   On occasion, human service professionals receive
goods or services—rather than money—as payment for their professional
services. This occurs especially in some rural communities, where barter is
a commonly accepted form of payment. In one case, a rural practitioner's
client lost his mental health insurance coverage yet still needed counseling
services. The client, a house painter, offered to paint the counselor's home
in exchange for clinical services. The counselor decided not to enter into
the barter arrangement; after consulting with colleagues, she realized that

the client's interests could be undermined should some problem emerge with the paint job that would require some remedy or negotiation (for example, if the paint job proved to be inferior in some way). In another case, a social worker received several paintings from a client—an artist—as payment for services rendered. This social worker reasoned that accepting goods of this sort was not likely to undermine the clinical relationship, whereas accepting a service might.

The NASW *Code of Ethics* (1996) now includes a specific standard on barter. The NASW Code of Ethics Revision Committee struggled to decide whether to prohibit or merely discourage all forms of barter (Reamer 1998a). On the one hand, bartering entails potential conflicts of interest; on the other hand, bartering is an accepted practice in some communities. Ultimately, the committee decided to strongly discourage barter because of the risks involved while recognizing that barter is not inherently unethical. Further, the code establishes strict standards for the use of barter by social workers:

> Social workers should avoid accepting goods or services from clients as payment for professional services. Bartering arrangements, particularly involving services, create the potential for conflicts of interest, exploitation, and inappropriate boundaries in social workers' relationships with clients. Social workers should explore and may participate in bartering only *in very limited circumstances* when it can be demonstrated that such arrangements are an accepted practice among professionals in the local community, considered to be essential for the provision of services, negotiated without coercion, and entered into at the client's initiative and with the client's informed consent. Social workers who accept goods or services from clients as payment for professional services assume the full burden of demonstrating that this arrangement will not be detrimental to the client or the professional relationship. (standard 1.13[b]; emphasis added)

The American Psychological Association's *Ethical Principles of Psychologists and Code of Conduct* (1992) conveys a similar sentiment: "Psychologists ordinarily refrain from accepting goods, services, or other nonmonetary remuneration from patients or clients in return for psychological services because such arrangements create inherent potential for conflicts, exploitation, and distortion of the professional relationship. A psychologist may participate in bartering only if (1) it is not clinically contraindicated, and (2) the relationship is not exploitative" (standard 1.18).

Useful information.   A human service professional occasionally has an opportunity to benefit from a client's unique knowledge. A counselor with a complex health problem may be tempted to consult her client who is a physician and who happens to specialize in the area relevant to the counselor's chronic illness. A psychologist who is interested in adopting a child, and whose client is an obstetrics and gynecology nurse, may be tempted to talk to his client about adoption opportunities through the client's hospital. An agency administrator who is an active stock-market investor may be tempted to consult a client who happens to be a stockbroker. A social worker with automobile problems may be tempted to consult a client who happens to be a mechanic. These situations entail the clear potential for an inappropriate dual relationship because the professional uses a portion of the client's therapeutic hour for the practitioner's own purposes, and the practitioner's judgment and services may be shaped and influenced by access to a client's specialized knowledge. The client's transference also may be adversely affected. Conversely, relatively brief, casual, and nonexploitative conversation with a client concerning a topic on which the client is an expert may empower the client, facilitate therapeutic progress, and challenge the traditionally hierarchical relationship between professional and client.

Emotional and Dependency Needs

A number of boundary issues arise from practitioners' efforts to address their own emotional needs. Many of these issues are subtle, although some are more glaring and egregious. Among the more egregious are the following examples:

- The administrator of a state child welfare agency that serves abused and neglected children was having difficulty coping with his failing marriage. He was feeling isolated and depressed. The administrator was arrested based on evidence that he had developed a sexual relationship with a sixteen-year-old boy who was in the department's custody and that he used illegal drugs with the boy.

- A psychologist in a private psychiatric hospital provided counseling to a resident who was diagnosed with paranoid schizophrenia. The psychologist, who was religiously observant, began to read biblical passages to his client in the context of counseling sessions. The client was not religiously observant and complained to other hospital staff about the psychologist's conduct.
- A psychiatric nurse in private practice provided psychotherapy services to a forty-two-year-old woman who had been sexually abused as a child. During the course of their relationship, the nurse invited the client to her home for several candlelight dinners, went on a camping trip with the client, gave the client several expensive gifts, and wrote the client several very affectionately worded notes on personal stationery.
- A social worker in a public child welfare agency was responsible for licensing foster homes. The social worker, who was recently divorced, became friendly with a couple who had applied to be foster parents. The social worker also became very involved in the foster parents' church. The social worker, who approved the couple's application and was responsible for monitoring foster home placements in their home, moved with her son into a trailer on the foster parents' large farm.

Other boundary issues are more subtle. Examples include professionals whose clients invite them to attend important life-cycle events (such as a wedding or graduation, or a key religious ceremony), professionals who conduct home visits as a meal is being served and whose clients invite them to sit down to eat, and professionals who themselves are in recovery and encounter a client at an Alcoholics or a Narcotics Anonymous meeting. Human service professionals sometimes disagree about the most appropriate way to handle such boundary issues. For example, some professionals are adamantly opposed to attending a client's life-cycle event because of potential boundary problems (for example, the possibility that the client might interpret the gesture as a sign of the practitioner's interest in a social relationship or friendship); others, however, believe that attending such events can be ethically appropriate and, in fact, therapeutically helpful, so long as the clinical dynamics are handled skillfully. Further, some professionals believe that practitioners in recovery should never attend or participate in AA or NA meetings that a client might attend, because of the difficulty that clients may have reconciling the practitioner's professional role and personal life. Others, however, argue that recovering practitioners have a right to meet their own needs and can serve as compelling role models to clients in recovery.

Altruistic Gestures

Some boundary issues and dual relationships arise from professionals' genuine efforts to be helpful. Unlike a professional's involvement in a sexual relationship or a dual relationship that is intentionally self-serving, altruistic gestures are benevolently motivated. Although these dual relationships are not always inherently unethical, they do require skillful handling, as in the following examples:

- A psychiatrist in private practice was contacted by an acquaintance — not a close friend — who was in the midst of a marital crisis. The acquaintance told the psychiatrist that she and her husband "really trusted" the psychiatrist and wanted the psychiatrist's professional help. The psychiatrist agreed to see the couple professionally but later realized that being objective was very difficult.
- A social worker in a family service agency provided casework services to a client who had a substance abuse problem. The client asked the social worker if she would like to purchase wrapping paper that the client's daughter was selling as a school fund-raiser.
- A counselor in a community mental health center provided psychotherapy services for many years to a young man with a history of clinical depression. The client asked the counselor if she would say a few words during the ceremony at the client's upcoming wedding.
- A psychiatric nurse in a small rural community provided counseling to a ten-year-old boy who struggled with self-esteem issues. In his spare time, the nurse coached the community's only youth basketball team, which played in a regional league. The nurse believed that the boy would benefit from joining the basketball team (for example, by developing social skills and new relationships).

Unanticipated Circumstances

The final category of boundary issues involves situations that human service professionals do not anticipate and over which they have little or no initial control. The challenge for the professional in these circumstances is to manage the boundary issues in ways that minimize any harm to a client or colleague. Consider the following examples:

- A social worker in private practice attended a family holiday gathering. The social worker's sister introduced him to her new boyfriend, who is the social worker's former client.
- The client of a psychotherapist in a rural community was a grade school teacher. Because of an unexpected administrative decision, the client became the teacher in the classroom in which the psychotherapist's child was a student.
- A psychologist in a community mental health center joined a local physical-fitness club. During a visit to the club, the psychologist learned that an active client also was a member.

Managing Dual Relationships

As I have discussed, not all dual relationships entail unethical circumstances, although some do. Some dual relationships are clearly self-serving and exploitative. Others, however, are ambiguous and contain features about which reasonable, thoughtful human service professionals may disagree.

As I will discuss more fully later, to protect clients and minimize the potential for harm—and to minimize the possibility of ethics complaints and lawsuits that allege misconduct or professional negligence—human service professionals should establish clear "risk management" criteria and procedures. These criteria and procedures increase the chances that a practitioner would prevail should a disgruntled client or third party allege malpractice. A sound risk-management protocol to deal with boundary issues should contain six major elements. Human service professionals should

- Be vigilant in their efforts to recognize potential or actual conflicts of interest in their relationships with clients and colleagues. Professionals should be cognizant of red flags that may signal a boundary problem. For example, clinical practitioners should be wary when they find themselves attracted to a particular client, going out of their way to extend a client's counseling sessions (facilitated by scheduling the favored client at the end of the day), acting impulsively in relation to the client, allowing the client to accumulate a large unpaid bill, and/or disclosing personal details to the client.

Inform the client and appropriate colleagues when they encounter boundary issues, including actual or potential conflicts of interest, and explore reasonable remedies.

- Consult colleagues and supervisors; relevant professional literature, regulations, and policies; and ethical standards (relevant codes of ethics) in order to identify pertinent boundary issues and constructive options. Professionals should take special care in high-risk circumstances. For example, a professional who attempts to make a decision about whether to enter a friendship with a former client should consider prevailing ethical standards, including those pertaining to the amount of time that has passed since the termination of the professional–client relationship; the extent to which the former client is mentally competent and emotionally stable; the issues addressed in the professional–client relationship; the length of the professional–client relationship; the circumstances surrounding the termination of the professional–client relationship; and the extent to which harm to the former client or others as a result of the new relationship is foreseeable (Reamer 1998a).
- Design a plan of action that addresses the boundary issues and protects clients to the greatest extent possible. In some circumstances, protecting the client's interests may require termination of the professional relationship with proper referral of the client.
- Document all discussions, consultation, supervision, and other steps taken to address boundary issues.
- Develop a strategy for monitoring the implementation of the action plan—for example, by periodically conducting assessments with relevant parties (clients, colleagues, supervisors, lawyers) to determine whether the strategy minimized or eliminated the boundary problems.

These steps can help professionals prevent ethics complaints and lawsuits alleging negligent conduct. In all the human service professions, state licensing or regulatory boards receive ethics complaints. These publicly sponsored bodies—which are established under the authority of state licensing statutes—are charged with reviewing, investigating, and, when necessary, adjudicating ethics complaints filed against professionals. When a licensing and regulatory board concludes that a professional has violated a client's boundaries or engaged in an unethical dual relationship, it may impose various sanctions and requirements for corrective action, including censure, mandated supervision, license suspension, and license revocation.

Some national professional associations also have a mechanism to adjudicate ethics complaints against members. For example, the National Association of Social Workers permits individuals to file ethics complaints against its members. Based on the concept of peer review, each state chapter of NASW has a Committee on Inquiry (COI) whose function is to review and, when necessary, adjudicate ethics complaints. If the COI accepts a complaint, it conducts a formal hearing during which the complainant (the person filing the complaint), the respondent (the person against whom the complaint is filed), and witnesses have the opportunity to testify. After hearing all parties and discussing the testimony, the COI presents to elected chapter officers a report that summarizes its findings and presents its recommendations. NASW members who are found in violation of ethical standards concerning boundaries and dual relationships may be sanctioned or required to engage in some form of corrective action. These measures may include suspension or expulsion from NASW, censure, or a requirement to obtain consultation or supervision. In some instances, the case may be publicized through local and national NASW newsletters or general circulation newspapers. Other professional associations have a similar protocol, although specific procedures vary.

In addition, individuals may file malpractice claims, or lawsuits, against human service professionals. In these instances, the plaintiff (the party who files a legal complaint or lawsuit) typically alleges that the practitioner was negligent in handling a boundary or dual relationship issue. Lawsuits and liability claims that allege malpractice are civil suits, in contrast to criminal proceedings. Malpractice is a form of negligence that occurs when a professional acts in a manner inconsistent with the prevailing standard of care, which is defined as the way an ordinary, reasonable, and prudent professional would act under the same or similar circumstances (Austin, Moline, and Williams 1990; R. Cohen 1979; Cohen and Mariano 1982; Reamer 1994a, 1995b).

Some standards of care related to boundaries and dual relationships are very clear; others are not. For example, clearly an ordinary, reasonable, and prudent professional would not engage in a sexual relationship with a client. In contrast, professionals disagree about whether barter between a professional and a client should be prohibited in all instances, and about whether friendship between a professional and a former client should always be prohibited. As we will see shortly, professionals face the greatest challenges when they encounter boundary and dual relationship issues for which no clear standards of care exist.

Ordinarily, civil suits are based on tort or contract law, with the plaintiff seeking some sort of compensation for the injury claimed.* The injury may be economic (for example, lost wages or mental health care expenses that are the result of a client's clinical depression following boundary violations), physical (for instance, as a result of being sexually assaulted by a human service professional), or emotional (for example, anxiety symptoms that may result from a therapist's inappropriate dual relationship with a client).

As in criminal cases, defendants in civil suits are presumed to be innocent until proved otherwise. In ordinary civil suits, the defendant will be found liable for her or his actions based on the standard of preponderance of the evidence, as opposed to the stricter standard of proof beyond a reasonable doubt, which is used in criminal trials (Gifis 1991).

In general, malpractice occurs when evidence exists that (1) at the time of the alleged malpractice a legal duty existed between the practitioner and the client (for example, the human service professional has a duty not to engage in an unethical dual relationship with a client); (2) the practitioner was derelict in that duty, either through an action that occurred (the practitioner had a sexual relationship with the client) or through an omission; (3) the client suffered some harm or injury (the client became clinically depressed following the termination of the sexual relationship); and (4) the harm or injury was directly and proximately caused by the practitioner's dereliction of duty (the practitioner's dual relationship with the client directly caused the client's clinical symptoms).

Sound Decision Making

The best strategy for preventing ethics complaints and lawsuits—especially when human service professionals face complex boundary issues for

---

* A tort is a private or civil wrong or injury resulting from another party's negligence or breach of duty.

which no clear standards of care exist—is to engage in a systematic, deliberate, and comprehensive series of decision-making steps. Ethicists generally agree that approaching ethical decisions in this fashion is important to ensure that all aspects of an ethical dilemma are addressed. In my experience, it is helpful for human service professionals to follow these steps when attempting to make difficult decisions related to boundaries and dual relationships (Reamer 1999):

1. *Identify the boundary and dual relationship issues, including the professional duties and obligations that conflict.* Complex boundary and dual relationship issues often entail conflicts among, or ambiguities related to, professional duties and obligations. For example, practitioners who are in recovery from alcohol abuse may face difficult decisions when they encounter a client, who is also in recovery, at an Alcoholics Anonymous meeting. Practitioners in recovery need to handle conflicts between their duty to protect clients from harm and their right to address their own recovery issues. Whether practitioners decide to participate in or leave AA meetings when a client is present depends on their views about these conflicting duties and obligations. Carefully identifying the issues and alternative ways of handling them increases the chances that the practitioner will analyze the situation thoroughly.

2. *Identify the individuals, groups, and organizations that the ethical decision is likely to affect.* In each instance, human service professionals should do their best to identify the parties that their decision may affect and the ways in which it is likely to affect them. A counselor in recovery who is trying to decide how to handle her and her client's attendance at the same AA meetings needs to think about the potential effect on the client primarily as well as the client's family and close acquaintances, the counselor herself, the counselor's employer, the counselor's malpractice and liability insurer, and the counselor's profession. Clearly, the counselor's participation in the AA meeting could affect the client and these other parties.

3. *Tentatively identify all viable courses of action and the participants involved in each, along with the potential benefits and risks for each.* Human service professionals should think through all realistic options and then engage in the conceptual equivalent of a cost-benefit analysis. In the AA example, the practitioner faces three possibilities upon seeing a client at an AA meeting: attend the meeting and speak to the group about her own recovery issues; attend the meeting without speaking about her own recovery issues; and leave the meeting. The first option offers several potential benefits. Attending the meeting and speaking would provide the practitioner with

an opportunity to address her own recovery issues. She would also serve as a role model for her client, which may enhance the client's recovery efforts. In addition, the practitioner may have greater credibility in the client's eyes because of the practitioner's personal experience with recovery issues.

However, risks are involved as well. The dual relationship may confuse the client, who may have some difficulty distinguishing between the practitioner's role as a professional counselor and as another recovering alcoholic who needs the client's support and understanding. This confusion could undermine the client's recovery efforts. In principle, the practitioner's credibility may suffer if the client concludes that a counselor who is struggling with her own recovery issues is not in a position to counsel others who are in recovery. In addition, the client's presence at an AA meeting could undermine the practitioner's recovery; the practitioner may feel self-conscious and constrained by the client's presence and may be reluctant to address personal issues that she would address in the client's absence. Thus the practitioner's earnest efforts to protect her client could interfere with the practitioner's own therapeutic progress.

The second option—attending the AA meeting without speaking—also entails costs and benefits. The practitioner's presence could be reassuring to the client and may enhance the practitioner's credibility. Participating in the group discussion, even though she chooses not to speak at this particular meeting, may enhance the practitioner's own recovery efforts. At the same time, however, this course entails potential costs. As with the first option, the client may be confused about the practitioner's role in his life, and the practitioner may feel constrained in her efforts to address her own recovery issues. The practitioner's credibility may decline in the client's opinion if the client concludes that a counselor who is struggling with her own recovery issues is in no position to guide the client effectively.

The third option—leaving the meeting—would help the practitioner and client avoid a potentially problematic dual relationship. At the same time, this would remove the possibility of any benefits that could result from the practitioner's and client's simultaneous attendance at the AA meeting and efforts to address their respective recovery issues.

4. *Thoroughly examine the reasons in favor of and opposed to each course of action, considering relevant*

a. *Ethical theories, principles, and guidelines.* As I noted earlier, in recent years—especially since the mid-1970s—interest in professional ethics has grown dramatically, particularly in relation to boundary and dual relationship issues. The remarkable emergence of the professional ethics field has been the result of various factors (Reamer 1983, 1997a, 1998b). Controversial technological developments in health care and other fields certainly helped to spark ethical debate involving such issues as termination of life support, organ transplantation, genetic engineering, and test-tube babies. Also, widespread publicity about scandals in government triggered considerable interest in professional ethics. Beginning especially with Watergate in the early 1970s, the public has become intensely aware of various professionals who have abused or exploited their clients and patients emotionally, physically, or financially. The popular media have publicized disturbing accounts of physicians, clergy, psychologists, nurses, lawyers, social workers, and other professionals who have taken advantage of the people they are supposed to help or have engaged in other forms of misconduct. Consequently, most professions now take more seriously their responsibility to educate practitioners about potential abuse and ways to prevent it.

In addition, the introduction, beginning especially in the 1960s, of such terminology as patients' rights, welfare rights, and prisoners' rights helped shape professionals' thinking about the need to attend to ethical concepts. Since the 1960s, members of many professions have been much more cognizant of the concept of rights, and this has led many training programs to broach questions about the nature of professionals' ethical duties to their clients and patients. The women's movement, which began in earnest in the 1960s, contributed to this widespread effort to protect individual rights and prevent exploitation.

Contemporary professionals also have a much better appreciation of the limits of science and its ability to respond to the many complex questions professionals face. Although for some time, particularly since the 1930s, Americans have placed science on a pedestal and widely regard it as the key to many of life's mysteries, modern-day professionals acknowledge that science cannot answer a variety of questions that are fundamentally ethical in nature (Sloan 1980).

Finally, the well-documented increase in litigation and malpractice claims, along with publicity about unethical professionals, has forced the professions to take a closer look at their ethics traditions and training. All professions have experienced an increase in malpractice claims and lawsuits against practitioners, and a substantial portion of these complaints allege some form of ethical misconduct involving boundary violations and dual relationships. As a result of this noteworthy and troubling trend, the professions—

including the various human service professions—have enhanced their focus on ethics education.

A significant by-product of these developments was the emergence in the 1980s of a critical mass of literature on ethical issues in the human services. Unlike earlier publications on ethical issues, which focused primarily on issues related to professional values and the concepts of client self-determination and confidentiality, publications in the 1980s began to explore the relevance of moral philosophy and ethical theory to ethical dilemmas that human service professionals face; similar developments occurred in nearly all the professions, such as business, journalism, law enforcement, engineering, the military, and the law (Reamer 1979, 1980, 1987a, 1989). Currently, most professional education programs acquaint students with literature and theory that can help them analyze complex ethical dilemmas (Callahan and Bok 1980; Reamer 2000; Reamer and Abramson 1982).

Briefly, pertinent ethical theories and principles concern what moral philosophers call *metaethics* and *normative ethics* (Reamer 1993, 1994a). Metaethics concerns the meaning of ethical terms or language and the derivation of ethical principles and guidelines. Typical metaethical questions concern the meaning of the terms *right* and *wrong* and *good* and *bad*. What criteria should we use to judge whether someone has engaged in unethical conduct, such as violating a boundary? How should we go about formulating ethical principles to guide individuals who struggle with moral choices related to boundary issues and dual relationships?

In contrast to metaethics, which is often abstract, normative ethics tends to be of particular interest to human service professionals because of its immediate relevance to practice. Normative ethics consists of attempts to apply ethical theories and principles to actual ethical dilemmas. Such guidance is especially useful when professionals face conflicts among duties they are ordinarily inclined to perform—what the philosopher W. D. Ross (1930) refers to as the challenge to identify one's principal duty (or actual duty) from among competing or conflicting prima facie duties (that is, duties that should be performed at first view). In the case of the AA meeting, for example, the practitioner faces a choice involving conflicting prima facie duties to her client, herself, and her profession.

Philosophers generally group theories of normative ethics under two main headings. Deontological theories (from the Greek *deontos*, 'of the obligatory') are those that claim that certain actions are inherently right or wrong, or good or bad, without regard for their consequences. Thus a deontologist—

the best-known is Immanuel Kant, the eighteenth-century German philosopher—might argue that engaging in a sexual relationship with a client is inherently wrong and that practitioners should never exploit clients in this manner. The same might be said about lying to clients, keeping promises made to colleagues, upholding contracts with vendors, obeying a mandatory reporting law related to suspected child abuse, and so on. For deontologists rules, rights, and principles are sacred and inviolable. The ends do not necessarily justify the means, particularly if the means require violating some important rule, right, principle, or law (Frankena 1973; Hancock 1974; Williams 1972).

One well-known problem with this deontological perspective is that it is often easy to argue both sides using similar language about inherently right (or wrong) actions. Thus one can imagine a deontologist's arguing that all human beings have an inherent right to experience basic mental health and that it would be immoral for a human service professional to engage in any activities that interfere with this; becoming sexually involved with a client would be morally wrong on deontological grounds, because this activity would harm the client's basic mental health. However, another deontologist might argue that practitioners have an inherent obligation to respect a client's right to self-determination so long as the actions involved are voluntary, consensual, and informed and, therefore, that it is permissible for practitioners to become sexually involved with a client.

The second major group of theories, teleological theories (from the Greek *teleios,* 'brought to its end or purpose'), takes a very different approach to ethical choices. From this point of view, the rightness of any action is determined by the goodness of its consequences. For teleologists making ethical choices without weighing potential consequences is naive. To do otherwise is to engage in what the philosopher J.J.C. Smart (1971) refers to as "rule worship." Hence from this perspective (sometimes known as consequentialism), the responsible strategy entails an attempt to anticipate the outcomes of various courses of action and to weigh their relative merits (Frankena 1973; Hancock 1974). For example, a practitioner who is contemplating a sexual relationship with a client would identify the potential and likely outcomes of this relationship and speculate about the benefits and costs for all relevant parties.

The two major teleological schools of thought are egoism and utilitarianism. Egoism typically has no place in the human services; according to this point of view, people faced with conflicting duties should maximize their own good and enhance their self-interest. Thus a practitioner contemplating a sexual relationship with a client would be concerned with only his own potential satisfaction and contentment.

In contrast, utilitarianism, which holds that an action is right if it promotes the maximum good, has historically been the most popular teleological theory and has, at least implicitly, served as justification for many decisions that human service professionals make. According to the classic form of utilitarianism—as originally formulated by the English philosophers Jeremy Bentham, in the eighteenth century, and John Stuart Mill, in the nineteenth century—when faced with conflicting duties, one should perform the action that will produce the greatest good. In principle, then, a practitioner should engage in a calculus to determine which set of consequences will produce the greatest good. Thus a counselor might argue on utilitarian grounds that the harm that may result from a sexual relationship with a former client, no matter how voluntary and consensual, outweighs any benefits. That is, the emotional harm that could result for the client—and perhaps the counselor and other parties as well—would be more substantial than any pleasure (emotional and physical) that would result from the sexual relationship.

One form of utilitarian theory is known as good-aggregative utilitarianism, according to which the most appropriate action is that which promotes the greatest total or aggregate good. According to another form, locus-aggregative utilitarianism, the most appropriate action is that which promotes the greatest good for the greatest number, considering not only the total quantity of goods produced but also the number of people to whom the goods are distributed (Gewirth 1978b). The distinction between these two forms of utilitarianism is important in the human services when one considers, for example, whether to manage boundary issues and dual relationships in a way that tends to produce the greatest aggregate satisfaction among the parties involved, without regard for how the satisfaction is distributed among the people who are affected, or produces the greatest satisfaction for the greatest number of people.

One problem with utilitarianism is that this framework, like deontology, sometimes can be used to justify competing options. For example, whereas one utilitarian might argue that a sexual relationship with a former client would result in the greatest good—considering the future pleasure—another utilitarian, who assigns different weights to the benefits and costs involved, or who might enter different variables into this complex equation, might argue that the harm involved in a sexual relationship outweighs any benefits.

Some philosophers argue that it is important and helpful to distinguish between act and rule utilitarianism (Gorovitz 1971). According to act utilitarianism, the goodness of the consequences produced *in that individual case*, or by that particular act, determines the rightness of an action. One does not need to look beyond the implications of this one instance. By contrast, rule utilitarianism takes into account the long-run consequences when one treats the case as a precedent. Thus an act utilitarian might justify a sexual relationship with a former client if it can be demonstrated that this would result in greater good for the parties involved in this particular set of circumstances. A rule utilitarian, however, might argue that the precedent established by this boundary violation would generate more harm than good, regardless of the benefits produced in this one case. That is, a rule utilitarian might argue that the precedent might undermine clients' and the public's trust in human service professionals, particularly regarding professionals' determination to protect clients from harm and exploitation, thus limiting the human services' general effectiveness as a profession.

Another illustration of the distinction between act and rule utilitarianism concerns the well-known mandatory reporting laws related to child abuse and neglect. These statutes, now found in every state in the United States, require human service professionals and other mandated reporters to notify child welfare or protective services authorities whenever they suspect child abuse or neglect. However, circumstances sometimes arise that lead practitioners to conclude that complying with a mandatory reporting law would not serve a client's best interests (for example, when the practitioner believes that the client would flee valuable treatment as a result or that the public agency's involvement in the case would make matters worse). In these instances, practitioners believe that more harm than good would result from obeying the law. What these practitioners are claiming, at least implicitly, is that violating a law is permissible when it appears that greater good would result.

This is a classic example of act utilitarianism. An act utilitarian might justify violating a mandatory reporting law if it can be demonstrated convincingly that this would result in greater good (for example, if the practitioner can show that she would not be able to continue working with the family if she reported the suspected abuse or neglect and that her continuing to work with the family offers the greatest potential for preventing further neglect or abuse). A rule utilitarian, however, might argue that the precedent that this deliberate violation of the law establishes would generate more harm than good, regardless of the benefits of this one particular violation. A rule utilitarian might argue that the precedent established by this case might encourage other human service professionals to take matters into their own hands rather than report suspected abuse or neglect to local protective services officials and that this would, in the long run, be more harmful than helpful. A key problem with utilitarianism, then, is that different people are likely to consider different factors and weigh them differently, as a result of their different life experiences, values, political ideologies, and so on.

In addition, when taken to the extreme, classic utilitarianism can justify trampling on the rights of a vulnerable minority in order to benefit the majority. In principle, a callous utilitarian practitioner could argue that the costs associated with policies and procedures designed to protect clients from a relatively small number of unethical and unscrupulous practitioners (for example, the administrative expenses required to support licensing boards and ethics committees sponsored by professional associations, the monetary value of time that volunteers donate to staff these bodies) are excessive in light of the relatively few individuals they actually protect.

Perhaps the best-known alternative to utilitarianism is presented in a book by the contemporary philosopher John Rawls, A *Theory of Justice* (1971). Rawls's theory, which has profound implications for human service professionals, assumes that individuals have a fundamental obligation to protect the most vulnerable and least advantaged. Rawls also makes a distinction that is important for human service professionals to consider: the distinction between natural duties—fundamental obligations such as helping others in dire need or not injuring other people—and supererogatory actions—actions that are commendable and praiseworthy but not obligatory. One might argue, for example, that human service professionals have a natural duty to not sexually abuse clients. Other boundary-related policies and practices might fall under the heading of supererogation, however, such as agreeing to attend a client's wedding or accepting a client's modest holiday gift.

Rawls's work highlights a concept that has become critically important in ethics and in the human services: the rank-ordering of values and ethical duties. For Rawls and many other moral philosophers, ethical decisions often are difficult judgments about what values or duties will take precedence over others. Should a professional's obligation to enhance a client's mental health—which may involve a dual relationship (for example, when a practitioner believes that terminating a clinical relationship with a client because of a dual relationship would be harmful therapeutically)—take precedence over the duty to obey standards contained in a code of ethics that prohibit dual relationships? Should a practitioner's obligation to adhere to agency policy concerning dual relationships take precedence over the practitioner's judgment about what is in the client's best interests? To use Ross's (1930) terminology, which of various conflicting prima facie duties involving boundary issues and dual relationships should take precedence; that is, which duty is one's actual duty?

Other philosophers have also offered theories about the most appropriate way to rank-order conflicting duties. The philosopher Alan Donagan argues in *The Theory of Morality* (1977) that when choosing among duties that may result in harm, one should do that which results in the least harm. Popper (1966) calls this the "minimization of suffering," and Smart and Williams (1973) call this "negative utilitarianism." According to Donagan,

> What [common morality] provides depends on the fact that, although wrongness, or moral impermissibility, does not have degrees, impermissible wrongs are more or less grave. The explanation of this is simple. Any violation of the respect owed to human beings as rational is flatly and unconditionally forbidden; but the respect owed to human beings may be violated either more or less gravely. It is absolutely impermissible either to murder or to steal; but although murder is no more wrong than stealing, it is a graver wrong. There is a parallel in the criminal law, in which murder and stealing are equally felonies, but murder is a graver felony than stealing. In general, every wrong action impairs some human good, and the gravity of wrong actions varies with the human goods they impair. Although there is room for dispute in some cases as to whether or not this action is a graver wrong than that (for example, whether theft of one's reputation is worse than theft of one's purse), when they find themselves trapped . . . in a choice between wrongs, not only do most moral agents have opinions about whether these wrongs are equally grave, and if they are not, about which is the graver; but also, if they adhere to the same moral tradition, their opinions on these questions largely agree. And, given that wrongs can differ in gravity, it quite obviously follows from the fundamental principle of morality that, when through some misdeed a man is confronted with a choice between wrongs, if one of them is less grave than the others, he is to choose it. This precept is a special application of

a more general principle which I shall refer to as the principle of the least evil, and which was already proverbial in Cicero's time: namely, *minima de malis eligenda*—when you must choose between evils, choose the least. (152)

From this perspective, then, the human service professional's obligation in cases involving complex boundary and dual relationship issues is to follow that course of action that results in the least harm (for example, to a client's mental health). This might produce a different result from a strategy that seeks to produce the greatest good (which might take into account the practitioner's pleasure and satisfaction).

In an important work entitled *Reason and Morality*, the philosopher Alan Gewirth (1978a) has offered a number of arguments that are particularly relevant to practitioners' thinking about the rank-ordering of conflicting duties (Reamer 1979, 1990). Gewirth's approach also provides a useful illustration of the ways in which moral philosophers think about ethical dilemmas. Following a series of complex—and somewhat controversial—philosophical arguments and derivations, Gewirth ultimately claims that human beings have a fundamental right to freedom (similar to practitioners' conceptualization of self-determination) and well-being and that human beings must value three core "goods": basic goods—those aspects of well-being that are necessary for anyone to engage in purposeful activity (for example, life itself, health, food, shelter, mental equilibrium); nonsubtractive goods—goods that, if lost, would diminish a person's ability to pursue her or his goals (for example, as a result of being subjected to inferior living conditions or harsh labor, or as a result of being stolen from, cheated on, or lied to); and additive goods—goods that enhance a person's ability to pursue his or her goals (for example, knowledge, self-esteem, material wealth, education). Like all moral philosophers, Gewirth recognizes that people's various duties and rights sometimes conflict and that we sometimes need to make choices among them. Gewirth argues that conflicting duties can be rank-ordered, or placed in a hierarchy based on the goods involved, with basic goods the most critical. These distinctions among basic, additive, and nonsubtractive goods are useful as we think about conflicting duties related to boundary issues and dual relationships. We may want to argue, for example, that dual relationships that threaten clients' basic goods (such as their fundamental emotional well-being or their ability to earn a living) are especially compelling, particularly when compared with dual relationships that may affect clients' and practitioners' additive goods (such as their social life or the gifts they receive at holiday time).

b. *Codes of ethics and legal principles.* Other tools to help one examine the reasons in favor of and opposed to a course of action are professional codes of ethics and pertinent legal principles. Professions typically publicize their ethical standards in the form of codes of ethics. According to Jamal and Bowie (1995:703–4), codes of ethics are designed to address three major issues. First, codes address "problems of moral hazard," or conflicts between a profession's self-interest and the public's interest (for example, whether it is ethical for a psychiatrist to refer patients to a medical laboratory in which the doctor has a financial investment). Second, codes address issues of "professional courtesy"—that is, rules that govern how professionals should behave to enhance and maintain a profession's integrity (for example, how practitioners respond to colleagues who engage in unethical conduct involving clients' boundaries). Finally, codes address issues that concern professionals' duty to serve the public interest (for example, the extent of the obligation of therapists to assist when faced with a public emergency).

Ethical standards have matured greatly in all the human service professions. Earlier versions were much more superficial and abstract than they are today. For example, the first code of ethics ratified by the National Association of Social Workers, in 1960, consisted of only fourteen broadly worded proclamations concerning, for example, every social worker's duty to give precedence to professional responsibility over personal interests; to respect the privacy of clients; to give appropriate professional service in public emergencies; and to contribute knowledge, skills, and support to human welfare programs (Reamer 1997b). First-person statements (such as "I give precedence to my professional responsibility over my personal interests" and "I respect the privacy of the people I serve") were preceded by a preamble that set forth social workers' responsibility to uphold humanitarian ideals, maintain and improve social work service, and develop the philosophy and skills of the profession.

In contrast, the current version of the NASW *Code of Ethics*, ratified in 1996, contains 155 specific ethical standards (along with more abstract ethical principles, professional values, and a mission statement for the profession) to guide social workers' conduct and provide a basis for adjudication of ethics complaints filed against NASW members. This trend, toward more detailed and specific ethical standards, has occurred in nearly all professions, reflecting the dramatic growth of knowledge related to professional ethics since the 1970s.

The codes of ethics of the various human service professions include a wide range of standards related to boundary issues and dual relationships. Excerpts from several pertinent codes follow. Although the content and substantive issues addressed by the various codes overlap somewhat, note that they have some significant differences, which reflect the professions' diverse norms and ideological perspectives. I will draw on these various standards throughout our discussion.

American Association for Marriage and Family Therapy
Code of Ethics (1998)

1.2. Responsibility to Clients. Marriage and family therapists are aware of their influential position with respect to clients, and they avoid exploiting the trust and dependency of such persons. Therapists, therefore, make every effort to avoid dual relationships with clients that could impair professional judgment or increase the risk of exploitation. When a dual relationship cannot be avoided, therapists take appropriate professional precautions to ensure judgment is not impaired and no exploitation occurs. Examples of such dual relationships include, but are not limited to, business or close personal relationships with clients. Sexual intimacy with clients is prohibited. Sexual intimacy with former clients for two years following the termination of therapy is prohibited.

1.3. Responsibility to Clients. Marriage and family therapists do not use their professional relationships with clients to further their own interests.

4.1. Responsibility to Students, Employees, and Supervisees. Marriage and family therapists are aware of their influential position with respect to students, employees, and supervisees, and they avoid exploiting the trust and dependency of such persons. Therapists, therefore, make every effort to avoid dual relationships that could impair professional judgment or increase the risk of exploitation. When a dual relationship cannot be avoided, therapists take appropriate professional precautions to ensure judgment is not impaired and no exploitation occurs. Examples of such dual relationships include, but are not limited to, business or close personal relationships with students, employees, or supervisees. Provision of therapy to students, employees, or supervisees is prohibited. Sexual intimacy with students or supervisees is prohibited.

National Association of Social Workers (NASW)
Code of Ethics (1996)

1.06. Social Workers' Ethical Responsibilities to Clients: Conflicts of Interest. (a) Social workers should be alert to and avoid conflicts of interest that interfere with the exercise of professional discretion and impartial judgment. Social workers should inform clients when a real or potential conflict of interest arises and take reasonable steps to resolve the issue in a manner that makes the clients' interests primary and protects clients' interests to the greatest extent possible. In some cases, protecting clients' interests may require termination of the professional relationship with proper referral of the client.

(b) Social workers should not take unfair advantage of any professional relationship or exploit others to further their personal, religious, political or business interests.

(c) Social workers should not engage in dual or multiple relationships with clients or former clients in which there is a risk of exploitation or potential harm to the client. In instances when dual or multiple relationships are unavoidable, social workers should take steps to protect clients and are responsible for setting clear, appropriate, and culturally sensitive boundaries. (Dual or multiple relationships occur when social workers relate to clients in more than one relationship, whether professional, social, or business. Dual or multiple relationships can occur simultaneously or consecutively.)

(d) When social workers provide services to two or more people who have a relationship with each other (for example, couples, family members), social workers should clarify with all parties which individuals will be considered clients and the nature of social workers' professional obligations to the various individuals who are receiving services. Social workers who anticipate a conflict of interest among the individuals receiving services or who anticipate having to perform in potentially conflicting roles (for example, when a social worker is asked to testify in a child custody dispute or divorce proceedings involving clients) should clarify their role with the parties involved and take appropriate action to minimize any conflict of interest.

1.09. Social Workers' Ethical Responsibilities to Clients: Sexual Relationships. (a) Social workers should under no circumstances engage in sexual activities or sexual contact with current clients, whether such contact is consensual or forced.

(b) Social workers should not engage in sexual activities or sexual contact with clients' relatives or other individuals with whom clients maintain a close personal relationship when there is a risk of exploitation or potential harm to the client. Sexual activity or sexual contact with clients' relatives or other individuals with whom clients maintain a personal relationship has the potential to be harmful to the client and may make it difficult for the social worker and client to maintain appropriate professional boundaries. Social workers—not their clients, their clients' relatives, or other individuals with whom the client maintains a personal relationship—assume the full burden for setting clear, appropriate, and culturally sensitive boundaries.

(c) Social workers should not engage in sexual activities or sexual contact with former clients because of the potential for harm to the client. If social workers engage in conduct contrary to this prohibition or claim that an exception to this prohibition is warranted because of extraordinary circumstances, it is social workers—not their clients— who assume the full burden of demonstrating that the former client has not been exploited, coerced, or manipulated, intentionally or unintentionally.

(d) Social workers should not provide clinical services to individuals with whom they have had a prior sexual relationship. Providing clinical services to a former sexual partner has the potential to be harmful to the individual and is likely to make it difficult for the social worker and individual to maintain appropriate professional boundaries.

1.10. Social Workers' Ethical Responsibilities to Clients: Physical Contact. Social workers should not engage in physical contact with clients when there is a possibility of psychological harm to the client as a result of the contact (such as cradling or caressing clients). Social workers who engage in appropriate physical contact with clients are responsible for setting clear, appropriate, and culturally sensitive boundaries that govern such physical contact.

1.13. Social Workers' Ethical Responsibilities to Clients: Payment for Services. (b) Social workers should avoid accepting goods or services from clients as payment for professional services. Bartering arrangements, particularly involving services, create the potential for conflicts of interest, exploitation, and inappropriate boundaries in social workers' relationships with clients. Social workers should explore and may participate in bartering only in very limited circumstances when it can be demonstrated that such arrangements are an accepted practice among professionals in the local community, considered to be essential for the provision of services, negotiated without coercion, and entered into at the client's initiative and with the client's informed consent. Social workers who accept goods or services from clients as payment for professional services assume the full burden of demonstrating that this arrangement will not be detrimental to the client or the professional relationship.

1.16(d). Social Workers' Ethical Responsibilities to Clients: Termination of Services. Social workers should not terminate services to pursue a social, financial, or sexual relationship with a client.

2.07. Social Workers' Ethical Responsibilities to Colleagues: Sexual Relationships. (a) Social workers who function as supervisors or educators should not engage in sexual activities or contact with supervisees, students, trainees, or other colleagues over whom they exercise professional authority.

(b) Social workers should avoid engaging in sexual relationships with colleagues when there is a potential for a conflict of interest. Social workers who become involved in, or anticipate becoming involved in, a sexual relationship with a colleague have a duty to transfer professional responsibilities, when necessary, to avoid a conflict of interest.

3.01. Social Workers' Ethical Responsibilities in Practice Settings: Supervision and Consultation. (b) Social workers who provide supervision or consultation are responsible for setting clear, appropriate, and culturally sensitive boundaries.

(c) Social workers should not engage in any dual or multiple relationships with supervisees in which there is a risk of exploitation of or potential harm to the supervisee.

3.02. Social Workers' Ethical Responsibilities in Practice Settings: Education and Training. (d) Social workers who function as educators or field instructors for students should not engage in any dual or multiple relationships with students in which there is a risk of exploitation or potential harm to the student. Social work educators and field instructors are responsible for setting clear, appropriate, and culturally sensitive boundaries.

5.02. Social Workers' Ethical Responsibilities to the Social Work Profession. Evaluation and Research. (o) Social workers engaged in evaluation or research should be alert to and avoid conflicts of interest and dual relationships with participants, should inform participants when a real of potential conflict of interest arises, and should take steps to resolve the issue in a manner that makes participants' interests primary.

American Counseling Association Code of Ethics (1995)

A.5.a. Personal Needs. In the counseling relationship, counselors are aware of the intimacy and responsibilities inherent in the counseling relationship, maintain respect for clients, and avoid actions that seek to meet their personal needs at the expense of clients.

A.6. Dual Relationships; Avoid When Possible. Counselors are aware of their influential positions with respect to clients, and they avoid exploiting the trust and dependency of clients. Counselors make every effort to avoid dual relationships with clients that could impair professional judgment or increase the risk of harm to clients. (Examples of such relationships include, but are not limited to, familial, social, financial, business, or close personal relationships with clients.) When a dual relationship cannot be avoided, counselors take appropriate professional precautions such as informed consent, consultation, supervision, and documentation to ensure that judgment is not impaired and no exploitation occurs.

A.7.a. Sexual Intimacies With Clients: Current Clients. Counselors do not have any type of sexual intimacies with clients and do not counsel persons with whom they have had a sexual relationship.

A.7.b. Sexual Intimacies With Clients: Former Clients. Counselors do not engage in sexual intimacies with former clients within a minimum of 2 years after terminating the counseling relationship. Counselors who engage in such a relationship after 2 years following termination have the responsibility to examine and document thoroughly that such relations did not have an exploitative nature, based on factors such as duration of counseling, amount of time since counseling, termination circumstances, client's personal history and mental status, adverse impact on the client, and actions by the counselor suggesting a plan to initiate a sexual relationship with the client after termination.

A.8. Multiple Clients. When counselors agree to provide counseling services to two or more people who have a relationship (such as husband and wife, or parents and children), counselors clarify at the outset which person or persons are clients and the nature of the relationships they will have with each involved person. If it becomes apparent that counselors may be called upon to perform potentially conflicting roles, they clarify, adjust, or withdraw from roles appropriately.

A.10.c. Fees and Bartering: Bartering Discouraged. Counselors ordinarily refrain from accepting goods or services from clients in return for counseling services because such arrangements create inherent potential for conflicts, exploitation, and distortion of the professional relationship. Counselors may participate in bartering only if the relationship is not exploitative, if the client requests it, if a clear written contract is established, and if such arrangements are an accepted practice among professionals in the community.

F.1.c. Counselor Educators and Trainers: Sexual Relationships. Counselors do not engage in sexual relationships with students or supervisees and do not subject them to sexual harassment.

F.1.e. Counselor Educators and Trainers: Close Relatives. Counselors do not accept close relatives as students or supervisees.

F.2.e. Counselor Education and Training Programs: Peer Relationships. When students or supervisees are assigned to lead counseling groups or provide clinical supervision for their peers, counselors take steps to ensure that students and supervisees placed in these roles do not have personal or adverse relationships with peers and that they understand they have the same ethical obligations as counselor educators, trainers, and supervisors. Counselors make every effort to ensure that the rights of peers are not compromised when students or supervisees are assigned to lead counseling groups or provide clinical supervision.

F.2.h. Counselor Education and Training Programs: Dual Relationships as Supervisors. Counselors avoid dual relationships such as performing the role of site supervisor and training program supervisor in the student's or supervisee's training program. Counselors do not accept any form of professional services, fees, commissions, reimbursement, or remuneration from a site for student or supervisee placement.

F.3.c. Students and Supervisees: Counseling for Students and Supervisees. If students or supervisees request counseling, supervisors or counselor educators provide them with acceptable referrals. Supervisors or counselor educators do not serve as counselor to students or supervisees over whom they hold administrative, teaching, or evaluative roles unless this is a brief role associated with a training experience.

American Psychological Association Ethical Principles of Psychologists and Code of Conduct (1992)

1.17. General Standards: Multiple Relationships. (a) In many communities and situations, it may not be feasible or reasonable for psychologists to avoid social or other nonprofessional contacts with persons such as patients, clients, students, supervisees, or research participants. Psychologists must always be sensitive to the potential harmful effects of other contacts on their work and on those persons with whom they deal. A psychologist refrains from entering into or promising another personal, scientific, professional, financial, or other relationship with such persons if it appears likely that such a relationship reasonably might impair the psychologist's objectivity or otherwise interfere with the psychologist's effectively performing his or her functions as a psychologist, or might harm or exploit the other party.

(b) Likewise, whenever feasible, a psychologist refrains from taking on professional or scientific obligations when pre-existing relationships would create a risk of such harm.

(c) If a psychologist finds that, due to unforeseen factors, a potentially harmful multiple relationship has arisen, the psychologist attempts to resolve it with due regard for the best interests of the affected person and maximal compliance with the Ethics Code.

1.18. General Standards: Barter (With Patients or Clients). Psychologists ordinarily refrain from accepting goods, services, or other non-monetary remuneration from patients or clients in return for psychological services because such arrangements create inherent potential for conflicts, exploitation, and distortion of the professional relationship. A psychologist may participate in bartering only if (1) it is not clinically contraindicated, and (2) the relationship is not exploitative.

1.19. General Standards: Exploitative Relationships. (a) Psychologists do not exploit persons over whom they have supervisory, evaluative, or other authority such as students, supervisees, employees, research participants, and clients or patients.

(b) Psychologists do not engage in sexual relationships with students or supervisees in training over whom the psychologist has evaluative or direct authority, because such relationships are so likely to impair judgment or be exploitative.

1.21. General Standards: Third-Party Requests for Services. (b) If there is a foreseeable risk of the psychologist's being called upon to perform conflicting roles because of the involvement of a third party, the psychologist clarifies the nature and direction of his or her responsibilities, keeps all parties appropriately informed as matters develop, and resolves the situation in accordance with this Ethics Code.

4.03. Therapy: Couple and Family Relationships. (a) When a psychologist agrees to provide services to several persons who have a relationship (such as husband and wife or parents and children), the psychologist attempts to clarify at the outset (1) which of the individuals are patients or clients and (2) the relationship the psychologist will have with each person. This clarification includes the role of the psychologist and the probable uses of the services provided or the information obtained.

(b) As soon as it becomes apparent that the psychologist may be called on to perform potentially conflicting roles (such as marital counselor to husband and wife, and then witness for one party in a divorce proceeding), the psychologist attempts to clarify and adjust, or withdraw from, roles appropriately.

4.05. Therapy: Sexual Intimacies With Current Patients or Clients. Psychologists do not engage in sexual intimacies with current patients or clients.

4.06. Therapy: Therapy With Former Sexual Partners. Psychologists do not accept as therapy patients or clients persons with whom they have engaged in sexual intimacies.

4.07. Therapy: Sexual Intimacies With Former Therapy Patients. (a) Psychologists do not engage in sexual intimacies with a former therapy patient or client for at least two years after cessation or termination of professional services.

(b) Because sexual intimacies with a former therapy patient or client are so frequently harmful to the patient or client, and because such intimacies undermine public confidence in the psychology profession and thereby deter the public's use of needed services, psychologists do not engage in sexual intimacies with former therapy patients and clients even after a two-year interval except in the most unusual circumstances. The psychologist who engages in such activity after the two years following cessation or termination of treatment bears the burden of demonstrating that there has been no exploitation, in light of all relevant factors, including (1) the amount of time that has passed since therapy terminated, (2) the nature and duration of the therapy, (3) the circumstances of termination, (4) the patient's or client's personal history, (5) the patient's or client's current mental status, (6) the likelihood of adverse impact on the patient or client and others, and (7) any statements or actions made by the therapist during the course of therapy suggesting or inviting the possibility of a post-termination sexual or romantic relationship with the patient or client.

7.03. Forensic Activities: Clarification of Role. In most circumstances, psychologists avoid performing multiple and potentially conflicting roles in forensic matters. When psychologists may be called on to serve in more than one role in a legal proceeding—for example, as consultant or expert for one party or for the court and as a fact witness—they clarify role expectations and the extent of confidentiality in advance to the extent feasible, and thereafter as changes occur, in order to avoid compromising their professional judgment and objectivity and in order to avoid misleading others regarding their role.

7.05. Forensic Activities: Prior Relationships. A prior professional relationship with a party does not preclude psychologists from testifying as fact witnesses or from testifying to their services to the extent permitted by applicable law. Psychologists appropriately take into account ways in which the prior relationship might affect their professional objectivity or opinions and disclose the potential conflict to the relevant parties.

American Medical Association Principles of Medical Ethics with Annotations Especially Applicable to Psychiatry (1996)

Section 1. *Principle.* A physician shall be dedicated to providing competent medical service with compassion and respect for human dignity. *Annotation 1.* The patient may place his/her trust in his/her psychiatrist knowing that the psychiatrist's ethics and professional responsibilities preclude him/her gratifying his/her own needs by exploiting the patient. The psychiatrist shall be ever vigilant about the impact that his/her conduct has upon the boundaries of the doctor/patient relationship, and thus upon the well being of the patient. These requirements become particularly important because of the essentially private, highly personal, and sometimes intensely emotional nature of the relationship established with the psychiatrist.

Section 2. *Principle.* A physician shall deal honestly with patients and colleagues, and strive to expose those physicians deficient in character or competence, or who engage in fraud or deception. *Annotation 1.* The requirement that the physician conduct himself/herself with propriety in his/her profession and in all actions of his/her life is especially important in the case of the psychiatrist because the patient tends to model his/her behavior after that of his/her psychiatrist by identification. Further, the necessary intensity of the treatment relationship may tend to activate sexual and other needs and fantasies on the part of both patient and psychiatrist, while weakening the objectivity necessary for control. Additionally, the inherent inequality in the doctor-patient relationship may lead to exploitation of the patient. Sexual activity with a current or former patient is unethical. *Annotation 2.* The psychiatrist should diligently guard against exploiting information furnished by the patient and should not use the unique position of power afforded him/her by the psychotherapeutic situation to influence the patient in any way not directly relevant to the treatment goals.

Section 4. *Principle.* A physician shall respect the rights of patients, of colleagues, and of other health professionals, and shall safeguard patient confidences within the constraints of the law. *Annotation 14.* Sexual involvement between a faculty member or supervisor and a trainee or student, in those situations in which an abuse of power can occur, often takes advantage of inequalities in the working relationship and may be unethical because: (a) any treatment of a patient being supervised may be deleteriously affected; (b) it may damage the trust relationship between teacher and student; and (c) teachers are important professional role models for their trainees and affect their trainees' future professional behavior.

In addition to consulting relevant codes of ethics, human service professionals facing difficult ethical decisions should carefully consider relevant legal principles, including statutes (laws enacted by state legislatures and Congress), legal regulations (regulations established by public agencies that have the force of law), and case law (legal precedents established by courts of law). Although ethical decisions should not necessarily be dictated by prevailing statutory, regulatory, and case law, practitioners should always take legal guidelines and requirements into account. In some instances, the law may reinforce practitioners' ethical instincts, such as when a state law stipulates that sexual contact with a former client is a felony punishable by imprisonment and/or a monetary fine. In fact, several states have enacted such a law (Madden 1998).

c. *Practice theory and principles from the literature of the human service professions.* Practitioners should also consider the relevance of pertinent practice theory and principles. For example, if a therapist is struggling to decide whether to have post-termination social contact with a client who has been diagnosed with borderline personality disorder, the therapist should pay close attention to practice theory related to this clinical phenomenon. In light of what we know about borderline personality disorder, the therapist may want to avoid adding boundary-related complications to the client's life. Similarly, a counselor who is considering establishing a sexual relationship with a former client who has a history of sexual abuse should pay close attention to practice-based knowledge about post-traumatic stress disorder. And a community mental health administrator who is considering hiring former clients as employees should draw on available knowledge about relapse prevention before making a decision about this boundary issue.

d. *Values (including religious, cultural, and ethnic values and political ideology), particularly those that conflict with one's own.* Human service professionals sometimes face conflicts between their personal values and their professional obligations. A practitioner may have very strong beliefs about clients' right to self-determination—based on the practitioner's personal religious views—that conflict with prevailing ethical standards. This conflict may present a challenge for professionals who make ethical decisions about, for example, attending a client's religious ceremony on a weekend. The professional's agency may have a policy against attending such an event, but the practitioner may believe strongly in the ceremony's religious importance.

A similar challenge may arise when a politically active professional is tempted to organize clients to engage in some form of social protest. Engaging in activity to support one's own political agenda—in the form of recruiting clients to support one's political "cause"—may conflict with the ethical prescription to avoid inappropriate dual relationships. In such instances, human service professionals should consult with colleagues and then make an informed judgment about the most ethical course of action, always keeping in mind the professional's primary duty to clients and prevailing ethical standards in the profession.

5. *Consult with colleagues and appropriate experts (such as agency staff, supervisors, agency administrators, attorneys, and ethics scholars).* Ordinarily, human service professionals should not make ethical decisions alone. This is not to suggest that ethical decisions are always group decisions. Sometimes they are, but in many instances individual practitioners ultimately make the decision once they have had an opportunity to consult with colleagues, supervisors, and appropriate experts.

Typically, practitioners should consider consulting with colleagues who are involved in similar work and who are likely to understand the issues—supervisors, agency administrators, ethics experts, and attorneys. As the NASW *Code of Ethics* (1996) states: "Social workers should seek the advice and counsel of colleagues whenever such consultation is in the best interest of clients" (standard 2.05[a]). Sometimes the consultation may be obtained informally, in the form of casual and spontaneous conversation with colleagues, and sometimes, particularly in agency settings, through more formal means, as with institutional ethics committees (Reamer 1987b, 1995c).

The concept of institutional ethics committees emerged most prominently in 1976, when the New Jersey Supreme Court ruled that Karen Anne Quinlan's family and physicians should consult an ethics committee in deciding whether to remove her from life-support systems (a number of hospitals have had something resembling an ethics committee since at least the 1920s). The court based its ruling in part on an important article that appeared in the *Baylor Law Review* in 1975, in which a pediatrician advocated the use of an ethics committee when health care professionals face difficult ethical choices (Teel 1975).

Ethics committees, which can include representatives from various disciplines, often provide case consultation in addition to education and training (C. Cohen 1988; Cranford and Doudera 1984). Many agency-based ethics committees provide nonbinding ethics consultation and can offer an opportunity for practitioners to think through case-specific issues with colleagues who have knowledge of ethical issues as a result of their experiences, familiarity with relevant ethical concepts and literature, or specialized ethics training. Although ethics committees are not always able to provide definitive opinions about the complex issues that are frequently brought to their attention (nor should they be expected to), they can provide a valuable forum for thorough and critical analyses of difficult ethical dilemmas related to boundaries and dual relationships.

Obtaining consultation is important for two reasons. The first is that experienced and thoughtful consultants may offer useful insights concerning the case and may raise issues the human service professional had not considered. The expression "two heads are better than one" may seem trite, but it is often true.

The second reason is that such consultation may help practitioners protect themselves if they are sued or have complaints filed against them because of the decisions they make. That a practitioner sought consultation demonstrates that the practitioner approached the decision carefully and prudently, and this can help if someone alleges that the practitioner made an inappropriate decision hastily and carelessly.

6. *Make the decision and document the decision-making process.* Once the practitioner has carefully considered the various boundary issues, including

the values and duties that may conflict; identified the individuals, groups, and organizations that are likely to be affected by the decision; tentatively identified all potential courses of action and the participants involved in each, along with any benefits and risks for each; thoroughly examined the reasons in favor of and opposed to each course of action (considering relevant ethical theories, principles, and guidelines; codes of ethics and legal principles; human service practice theory and principles; and personal values); and consulted with colleagues and appropriate experts, it is time to make a decision. In some instances, the decision will seem clear. Going through the decision-making process will have clarified and illuminated the issues so that the practitioner's ethical obligation seems unambiguous.

In other instances, however, practitioners may still feel somewhat uncertain about their ethical obligation. These are the hard cases and are not uncommon in ethical decision making. After all, situations that warrant full-scale ethical decision making, with all the steps that this entails, are, by definition, complicated. If they were not complex, the practitioner could have resolved the situation easily and simply at an earlier stage. Thus it should not be surprising that many ethical dilemmas related to boundaries and dual relationships remain controversial even after practitioners have taken the time to examine them thoroughly and systematically. Such is the nature of ethical dilemmas.

Once the decision is made, human service professionals should always be careful to document the steps involved in the decision-making process. Ethical decisions are just as much a part of practice as clinical, community-based, organizational, and policy interventions, and they should become part of the record (Kagle 1991). This is simply sound professional practice. Both the practitioner involved in the case and other professionals who may become involved in the case may need access to these notes at some time in the future. As the NASW *Code of Ethics* (1996) states, "Social workers should include sufficient and timely documentation in records to facilitate the delivery of services and to ensure continuity of services provided to clients in the future" (standard 3.04[b]).

In addition, preparing notes on the ethical decision making is extremely important in the event that the case results in an ethics complaint or legal proceedings (for example, a lawsuit filed against the practitioner). As mentioned earlier, carefully written notes documenting the professional's diligence can be protection from allegations of malpractice or negligence (Reamer 1994b).

Professionals need to decide how much detail to include in their documentation. Too much detail can be problematic, particularly if the practitioner's records are subpoenaed. Sensitive details about the client's life and circumstances may be exposed against the client's wishes. At the same time, practitioners can encounter problems if their documentation is too brief and skimpy, especially if the lack of detail affects the quality of care provided in the future or by other professionals. In short, practitioners need to include the level of detail that facilitates the delivery of service without exposing clients unnecessarily, consistent with generally accepted standards in the profession (Kagle 1991; Wilson 1980). According to the NASW *Code of Ethics* (1996), "Social workers' documentation should protect clients' privacy to the extent that is possible and appropriate and should include only information that is directly relevant to the delivery of services" (standard 3.04[c]).

7. *Monitor, evaluate, and document the decision.* Whatever ethical decision a practitioner makes is not the end of the process. In some respects, it constitutes the beginning of a new stage. Human service professionals should always pay close attention to and evaluate the consequences of their ethical decisions. This is important in order to be accountable to clients, employers, and funding sources and, if necessary, to provide documentation in the event of an ethics complaint, malpractice claim, or lawsuit. This may take the form of routine case monitoring, recording, or more extensive evaluation using the variety of research tools now available to practitioners (Blythe and Tripodi 1989; Grinnell 1997; Reamer 1998c; Rubin and Babbie 1997; Siegel 1984, 1988).

As I noted in the preceding discussion, it would be a mistake to assume that systematic and ethical decision making will always produce clear and unambiguous results. To expect this would be to misunderstand the nature of ethics. The different theoretical perspectives of human services professionals, their personal and professional experiences, and their biases will inevitably combine to produce differing points of view. This is just fine, particularly if we are confident that sustained dialogue among practitioners about the merits of their respective views is likely to enhance their understanding and insight. As in all other aspects of practice, the process is often what matters most. As Jonsen (1984) notes, ethics guidelines by themselves "are not the modern substitute for the Decalogue. They are, rather, shorthand moral education. They set out the concise definitions and the relevant distinctions that prepare the already well-disposed person to make the shrewd judgment that this or that instance is a typical case of this or that sort, and, then, decide how to act" (4).

The Role of Practitioner Impairment

In some cases involving boundary violations and inappropriate dual relationships, we find evidence of some form of practitioner impairment. In recent years, the subject of impaired professionals has received increased attention. In 1972, for example, the Council on Mental Health of the American Medical Association issued a statement that said that physicians have an ethical responsibility to recognize and report impairment among colleagues. In 1976 a group of attorneys recovering from alcoholism formed Lawyers Concerned for Lawyers to address chemical dependence in the profession, and in 1980 a group of recovering psychologists began a similar group, Psychologists Helping Psychologists (Kilburg, Nathan, and Thoreson 1986; Knutsen 1977; Laliotis and Grayson 1985; McCrady 1989; Reamer 1992).

Social work's first national acknowledgment of the problem of impaired practitioners came in 1979, when NASW issued a public policy statement concerning alcoholism and alcohol-related problems (Commission on Employment 1987). By 1980 a nationwide support group for chemically dependent practitioners, Social Workers Helping Social Workers, had formed. In 1982 NASW formed the Occupational Social Work Task Force, which was to develop a strategy to deal with impaired NASW members. Two years later, the NASW Delegate Assembly issued a resolution on impairment, and in 1987 NASW published the *Impaired Social Worker Program Resource Book* to help members of the profession design programs for impaired social workers. The introduction to the resource book states:

> Social workers, like other professionals, have within their ranks those who, because of substance abuse, chemical dependency, mental illness or stress, are unable to function effectively in their jobs. These are the impaired social workers. . . . The problem of impairment is compounded by the fact that the professionals who suffer from the effect of mental illness, stress or substance abuse are like anyone else; they are often the worst judges of their behavior, the last to recognize their problems and the least motivated to seek help. Not only are they able to hide or avoid confronting their behavior, they are often abetted by colleagues who find it difficult to accept that a professional could let his or her problem get out of hand. (6)

Organized efforts to address impaired employees began in the late 1930s and early 1940s after Alcoholics Anonymous was formed and in response to the need that arose during World War II to sustain a sound workforce. These early occupational alcoholism programs eventually led, in the early 1970s, to the emergence of employee assistance programs (EAPs), designed to address a broad range of problems experienced by employees.

More recently, strategies for dealing with professionals whose work is affected by problems such as substance abuse, mental illness, and emotional stress have become more prevalent. Professional associations and informal groups of practitioners meet periodically to discuss the problem of impaired colleagues and to organize efforts to address the problem (Bissell and Haberman 1984; Prochaska and Norcross 1983).

Both the seriousness of impairment among human service professionals and the forms it takes vary. Impairment may involve failure to provide competent care or violation of the profession's ethical standards, such as serious boundary violations. It may also take such forms as providing flawed or inferior psychotherapy to a client, sexual involvement with a client, or failure to carry out professional duties as a result of substance abuse or mental illness. D. H. Lamb and colleagues (1987) provide a comprehensive definition of impairment among professionals:

Interference in professional functioning that is reflected in one or more of the following ways: (a) an inability and/or unwillingness to acquire and integrate professional standards into one's repertoire of professional behavior; (b) an inability to acquire professional skills in order to reach an acceptable level of competency; and (c) an inability to control personal stress, psychological dysfunction, and/or excessive emotional reactions that interfere with professional functioning. (598)

Although we have no precise estimates of the extent of impairment among human service professionals, speculative data are available. For example, in the foreword to the *Impaired Social Worker Resource Book*, published by the Commission on Employment and Economic Support of the NASW (1987), the commission chair states, "Social workers have the same problems as most working groups. Up to 5 to 7 percent of our membership may have a problem with substance abuse. Another 10 to 15 percent may be going through personal transitions in their relationships, marriage, family, or their work life" (4). The report goes on to conclude, however, that "there is little reliable information on the extent of impairment among social workers" (6).

Prevalence studies among psychologists suggest a significant degree of distress within that profession. In a study of 749 psychologists, Guy, Poelstra, and Stark (1989) found that 74.3 percent reported "personal distress" during the previous three years and 36.7 percent of this group believed that their distress decreased the quality of care they provided to clients. Pope, Tabachnick, and Keith-Spiegel (1988) report that 62.2 percent of the members of Division 29 (Psychotherapy) of the American Psychological Association admitted to "working when too distressed to be effective" (993). In their survey of 167 licensed psychologists, Wood and colleagues (1985) found that nearly one-third (32.3 percent) reported experiencing depression or burnout to an extent that interfered with their work. They also found that a significant portion of their sample reported being aware of colleagues whose work was seriously affected by drug or alcohol use, sexual overtures toward clients, or depression and burnout. In addition, evidence suggests that psychologists and psychiatrists commit suicide at a rate much higher than the general population (Farber 1983, cited in Millon, Millon, and Antoni 1986).

In an interdisciplinary study, Deutsch (1985) found that more than half her sample of social workers, psychologists, and masters-level counselors reported significant problems with depression. Nearly four-fifths (82 percent) reported problems with relationships, 11 percent reported substance abuse problems, and 2 percent reported suicide attempts.

In a comprehensive review of a series of empirical studies focused specifically on sexual contact between therapists and clients, K. Pope (1988) concludes that the aggregate average of reported sexual contact is 8.3 percent by male therapists and 1.7 percent by female therapists. Pope reports that one study (Gechtman and Bouhoutsos 1985) found that 3.8 percent of male social workers admitted to sexual contact with clients.

Impairment among professionals is the result of various causes. Stress related to employment, illness or death of family members, marital or relationship problems, financial problems, midlife crises, physical or mental illness, legal problems, and substance abuse may lead to impairment (Guy, Poelstra, and Stark 1989; Thoreson, Miller, and Krauskopf 1989). Stress induced by professional education and training can also lead to impairment, because of the close clinical supervision and scrutiny students receive, the disruption in students' personal lives caused by the demands of schoolwork and field placements, and the pressures of academic programs (Lamb et al. 1987).

According to Wood and colleagues (1985), psychotherapists encounter special sources of stress that may lead to impairment because their therapeutic role often extends into the nonwork areas of their lives (such as relationships with family members and friends), and because of the lack of reciprocity in relationships with clients (therapists are "always giving"), the slow and erratic nature of therapeutic progress, and personal issues that therapeutic work with clients may stir up. As Kilburg, Kaslow, and VandenBos (1988) observe,

> [The] stresses of daily life—family responsibilities, death of family members and friends, other severe losses, illnesses, financial difficulties, crimes of all kinds—quite naturally place mental health professionals, like other people, under pressure. However, by virtue of their training and place in society, such professionals face unique stresses. And although they have been trained extensively in how to deal with the emotional and behavioral crises of others, few are trained in how to deal with the stresses they themselves will face. . . . Mental health professionals are expected by everyone, including themselves, to be paragons. The fact that they may be unable to fill that role makes them a prime target for disillusionment, distress, and burnout. When this reaction occurs, the individual's ability to function as a professional may become impaired. (723)

Unfortunately, relatively little is known about the extent to which impaired human service professionals, especially those who violate clients' boundaries or engage in unethical dual relationships, voluntarily seek help for their problems. Few ambitious studies have been conducted. Guy, Poelstra, and Stark (1989) found that 70 percent of the "distressed" clinical psychologists they surveyed sought some form of therapeutic assistance. One-fourth (26.6 percent) entered individual psychotherapy, and 10.7 percent entered family therapy. A small portion of this group participated in self-help groups (3.4 percent) or was hospitalized (2.2 percent). Some were placed on medication (4.1 percent). Exactly 10 percent of this group temporarily terminated their professional practice.

These findings contrast with those of Wood and colleagues (1985), who found that only 55 percent of clinicians who reported problems that interfered with their work (substance abuse, sexual overtures toward clients, depression, and burnout) sought help. Two-fifths (42 percent) of all clinicians surveyed by Wood and co-workers, including impaired and unimpaired professionals, reported having offered help to impaired colleagues at some time or having referred them to therapists. Only 7.9 percent of the sample said they had reported an impaired colleague to a local regulatory body. Approximately two-fifths (40 percent) were aware of instances in which they believed no action was taken to help an impaired colleague.

We may draw several hypotheses concerning the reluctance of impaired human service professionals to seek help and the reluctance of their colleagues to confront them about their problems. Until recently, professionals were hesitant to acknowledge impairment within their ranks because they feared how practitioners would react to confrontation and how such confrontation might affect future working relationships among colleagues (Bernard and Jara 1986; McCrady 1989; Wood et al. 1985). As VandenBos and Duthie (1986) have said,

> The fact that more than half of us have not confronted distressed colleagues even when we have recognized and acknowledged (at least to ourselves) the existence of their problems is, in part, a reflection of the difficulty in achieving a balance between concerned intervention and intrusiveness. As professionals, we value our own right to practice without interference, as long as we function within the boundaries of our professional expertise, meet professional standards for the provision of services, and behave in an ethical manner. We generally consider such expectations when we consider approaching a distressed colleague. Deciding when and how our concern about the well-being of a colleague (and our ethical obligation) supersedes his or her right to personal privacy and professional autonomy is a ticklish manner. (212)

Thoreson and colleagues (1983) also argue that impaired professionals sometimes find it difficult to seek help because of their mythical belief in their infinite power and invulnerability. The involvement of an increasing number of psychotherapists in private practice exacerbates the problem because of the reduced opportunity for colleagues to observe their unethical conduct, including boundary violations and inappropriate dual relationships.

In Deutsch's (1985) valuable study, a diverse group of therapists who admitted to personal problems gave a variety of reasons for not seeking professional help, including believing that an acceptable therapist was not available, seeking help from family members or friends, fearing exposure and the disclosure of embarrassing confidential information, concern about the amount of effort required and about the cost, having a spouse who was unwilling to participate in treatment, failing to admit the seriousness of the problem, believing that they should be able to work out their problems themselves, and assuming that therapy would not help.

It is important for professionals to design ways to prevent impairment and respond to impaired colleagues, especially those whose impairment leads to serious boundary violations and inappropriate dual relationships. They must be knowledgeable about the indicators and causes of impairment, so that they can recognize problems that colleagues may be experiencing. Practitioners must also be willing to confront impaired colleagues, offer assistance and consultation, and, if necessary as a last resort, refer the colleague to a supervisor or local regulatory or disciplinary body.

To the social work profession's credit, in 1992 the president of NASW created the Code of Ethics Review Task Force (which I chaired), which proposed adding new principles to the code on the subject of impairment. The approved additions became effective in 1994 and were then modified slightly and incorporated as standards in the 1996 code:

Social workers should not allow their own personal problems, psychosocial distress, legal problems, substance abuse, or mental health difficulties to interfere with their professional judgment and performance or to jeopardize the best interests of people for whom they have a professional responsibility. (standard 4.05[a])

Social workers whose personal problems, psychosocial distress, legal problems, substance abuse, or mental health difficulties interfere with their professional judgment and performance should immediately seek consultation and take appropriate remedial action by seeking professional help, making adjustments in workload, terminating practice, or taking any other steps necessary to protect clients and others. (standard 4.05[b])

Social workers who have direct knowledge of a social work colleague's impairment that is due to personal problems, psychosocial distress, substance abuse, or mental health difficulties and that interferes with practice effectiveness should consult with that colleague when feasible and assist the colleague in taking remedial action. (standard 2.09[a])

Social workers who believe that a social work colleague's impairment interferes with practice effectiveness and that the colleague has not taken adequate steps to address the impairment should take action through appropriate channels established by employers, agencies, NASW, licensing and regulatory bodies, and other professional organizations. (standard 2.09[b])

Other human service professions have established similar ethical standards. For example, the American Counseling Association's *Code of Ethics* (1995) states, "Counselors refrain from offering or accepting professional services when their physical, mental, or emotional problems are likely to harm a client or others. They are alert to the signs of impairment, seek assistance for problems, and, if necessary, limit, suspend, or terminate their professional responsibilities" (standard C.2.g).

Although some cases of impairment must be dealt with through formal adjudication and disciplinary procedures, many cases can be handled primarily by arranging therapeutic or rehabilitative services for distressed practitioners. For example, state chapters of NASW can enter into agreements with local employee assistance programs and use them as referral mechanisms for impaired members (Commission on Employment 1987).

As human service professionals increase the attention they pay to the problem of impairment, they must be careful to avoid assigning all responsibility to the practitioners themselves. Practitioners must also address the environmental stresses and structural factors that can cause impairment. Distress is often the result of the unique challenges in the profession, and remedial resources often are inadequate. Caring professionals who are overwhelmed by the difficulties of their clients—chronic problems of poverty, substance abuse, child abuse and neglect, hunger and homelessness, and mental illness—are prime candidates for high degrees of stress and burnout. Insufficient funding, the stresses of managed care, unpredictable political support, and public skepticism of professionals' efforts often lead to low morale and high stress (Jayaratne and Chess 1984; Johnson and Stone 1986; Koeske and Koeske 1989). Thus, in addition to responding to the individual problems of impaired colleagues, practitioners must confront the environmental and structural problems that can cause the impairment in the first place. This comprehensive effort can also help to reduce unethical behavior and professional misconduct, particularly in the form of boundary violations and inappropriate dual relationships.

There is no question that human service professionals have developed a richer, more nuanced understanding of boundary issues in the profession. To further enhance this understanding, professionals must examine dual relationships that are exploitative and those that are more ambiguous. Practitioners' firm grasp of boundary issues involving their intimate relationships with clients and colleagues, responses to their own emotional and dependency needs, pursuit of personal benefit, altruistic gestures, and responses to unanticipated circumstances will increase their ability to protect clients, colleagues, and themselves. Most important, skillful management of boundary issues will enhance the human services' ethical integrity, one of the hallmarks of a profession. Skillful management of these issues will also reduce the likelihood of ethics complaints and malpractice claims. We will now begin our in-depth exploration of these issues.

2 Intimate Relationships

Many boundary issues involve some form of intimate relationship. Some issues are glaring, such as those involving sexual contact between a therapist and a current client. Other issues, however, are more subtle, such as those involving seemingly innocent affectionate gestures.

I will examine a wide range of boundary issues involving intimacy. They include sexual relationships between professionals and their current or former clients; sexual relationships between professionals and clients' relatives or acquaintances; sexual relationships between professionals who are supervisors or educators and their supervisees, students, trainees, or other colleagues over whom they exercise professional authority; providing professional services to a former lover; and physical contact between professionals and clients.

Sexual Relationships with Clients

Case 2.1. Alfred S. was a counseling psychologist in private practice. For many years, Dr. S. provided clinical services to children and families. He specialized in child behavior management problems and family therapy.

Dr. S. had been providing services to a nine-year-old child, Sam K., and his single mother, Judy K. A school counselor referred Ms. K. and her son to Dr. S.; the faculty had been concerned about Sam's "acting

out" and aggressive behavior in school. Dr. S. met with Sam and his
mother weekly for about eight months.

For several months, Dr. S. felt attracted to Ms. K. He found himself
thinking about Ms. K. outside working hours. Dr. S. went out of his way
to spend extra time with Ms. K. during their counseling sessions; he
scheduled their sessions at the end of the day so that no other client's
appointment would force them to end their session after precisely fifty
minutes. Toward the end of one session, Dr. S. asked Ms. K. if she would
like to spend a little time with him outside the office "so we can get to
know each other a little better." Dr. S. went on to explain to Ms. K. that
he was feeling attracted to her and wanted to know if she was feeling
something toward him. Dr. S. was careful to explain to Ms. K. that
he wouldn't want to do anything to harm her or her son's progress
in treatment. Within four weeks, Dr. S. and Ms. K. were involved sexually.

———

As I noted in chapter 1, a substantial portion of intimate dual relationships
entered into by human service professionals involve sexual contact (Akamatsu 1988; Bouhoutsos 1985; Bouhoutsos et al. 1983; Coleman and Schaefer 1986; Committee on Women 1989; Feldman-Summers and Jones 1984;
Gabbard 1989; Gechtman 1989; Pope and Bouhoutsos 1986; Reamer 1984,
1992, 1994a; Schoener et al. 1989; Sell, Gottlieb, and Schoenfeld 1986). As
Brodsky (1986) notes,

A sexual intimacy between patient and therapist is one example of a
dual relationship. Dual relationships involve more than one purpose
of relating. A therapy relationship is meant to be exclusive and uni-
dimensional. The therapist is the expert, the patient the consumer
of that expertise. Once a patient accepts an individual as a therapist,
that individual cannot, without undue influence, relate to that patient in any other role. Relating to the patient as an employer, business partner, lover, spouse, relative, professor or student would con-
taminate the therapeutic goal. The contamination is much more
intense in a psychotherapy relationship than it would be in the relationship between a client and a professional in any other field—
for example, between a client and an internist, a dentist, a lawyer, or
an accountant. (155)

The Nature of Sexual Misconduct

Inappropriate sexual contact and sexualized behavior with clients can take several forms. These include touching body parts (for example, shoulder, arm, hand, leg, knee, face, hair, neck), hugging, holding hands, holding a client on one's lap, engaging in sexual humor, making suggestive remarks or gestures, kissing, exposing one's genitals, touching breasts, engaging in oral sex, and engaging in sexual intercourse (Stake and Oliver 1991). One useful typology, based on self-reports of sexual contact and behavior by a large sample of licensed psychologists, categorizes these various behaviors into three conceptual groups. The first includes overt sexual behavior, such as sexual intercourse, oral sex, fondling the genital area, touching the breasts, genital exposure, and kissing. The second group of behaviors includes touching behavior, such as touching body parts (for example, shoulders, arm, hand, leg, knee, face, hair, or neck), hugging, holding hands, and holding the client on one's lap. The third group includes suggestive behavior, such as using sexual humor and making suggestive remarks or glances. State laws typically define sexual activity more narrowly as intercourse, rape, the touching of breasts and genitals, cunnilingus, fellatio, sodomy, and inappropriate or unnecessary examinations and procedures performed for sexual gratification (Simon 1999).

Beginning with the Hippocratic oath, all major helping professions have prohibited sexual relationships with current patients and clients. The Hippocratic oath obliges physicians to keep "far from all intentional ill-doing and all seduction, and especially from the pleasures of love with women and men" (*Dorland's Medical Dictionary* 1974:715).

A series of empirical studies demonstrates the seriousness and magnitude of boundary violations and inappropriate dual relationships involving professionals' sexual contact with clients. During a recent twenty-year period, nearly one in five lawsuits (18.5 percent) against social workers insured through the malpractice insurance program sponsored by the NASW Insurance Trust alleged some form of sexual impropriety, and more than two-fifths (41.3 percent) of insurance payments were the result of claims concerning sexual misconduct (Reamer 1995b). Schoener and colleagues (1989) estimate that 15 to 16 percent of male and 2 to 3 percent of female therapists admit erotic contact with clients. Other national data suggest that 8 to 12 percent of male counselors or psychotherapists, and 1.7 to 3 percent of female counselors or psychotherapists, admit having had sexual relationships with a current or former client (Olarte 1997). According to Simon (1999), the reported rate of sexual contact between therapists and clients is generally in the range of 7 percent to 10 percent. Simon cautions that the actual rates are probably higher, because self-report data are known to underestimate actual incidence. Stake and Oliver (1991) provide a general overview of the data:

> In most surveys of therapist sexual misconduct, between 5% and 10% of psychologists (Holroyd & Brodsky, 1977; Pope, Keith-Spiegel & Tabachnick, 1986; Pope, et al., 1979) and psychiatrists (Herman, Gartrell, Olarte, Feldstein & Localio, 1987; Kardener, Fuller and Mensh, 1973) have acknowledged erotic contact with one or more of their clients. The incidence rate was lower in a survey of social workers: Gechtman (1989) found 3.8% of male social workers and no female social workers in her sample reported erotic contact with clients. Rates for male psychologists have generally been in the range of 5% to 12%, in contrast to rates of 1% to 3% for female psychologists (Bouhoutsos, et al., 1983; Gartrell, et al., 1987; Holroyd & Brodsky, 1977; Pope, et al., 1979; Pope, et al., 1986. (297)

K. Pope (1986) reports on the frequency of successful malpractice claims filed against psychologists during a ten-year period. Although the time period covered by Pope is shorter than the period described for social workers (Reamer 1995b), the similarities are clear. As with social workers, the most frequent claims categories for psychologists during the ten-year period were sexual contact (psychologists, 18.5 percent of claims; social workers, 18.5 percent of claims) and treatment error (psychologists, 15.2 percent of claims; social workers, 18.6 percent of claims). Approximately 45 percent of dollars spent in response to claims against psychologists resulted from claims of sexual contact, compared with 41 percent of dollars spent in response to claims against social workers for claims of sexual misconduct.

All the available data suggest that the vast majority of cases involving sexual contact between professionals and clients involve a male practitioner and female client (Brodsky 1986; K. Pope 1988). Gartrell et al. (1986) report in their nationwide survey of psychiatrists that 6.4 percent of respondents acknowledged sexual contact with their own patients; 90 percent of the offenders were male. Simon (1999) cites data that show that 80 percent of sexual contacts involving psychiatrists were between male psychiatrists and female patients, 7.6 percent between male psychiatrists and male patients, 3.5 percent between female psychiatrists and male patients, and 1.4 percent between female psychiatrists and female patients. Of the 38.4 percent who were repeaters, none was a female psychiatrist. G. Pope (1990:193–94) cites a study that found that 93 percent of offending therapists (psychologists, psychiatrists, marriage counselors, clergy, and social workers) who responded to a large-scale survey were men, and 89 percent of the victims were women. The largest group of offenders was psychiatrists (33 percent), followed by psychologists (19 percent), social workers (13 percent), and clergy (11 percent).

Olarte (1997) provides a succinct profile of the offending therapist:

The composite profile that most frequently emerges from the treatment or consultation with offenders is that the therapist is a middle-aged man who is undergoing some type of personal distress, is isolated professionally, and overvalues his healing capacities. His therapeutic methods tend to be unorthodox; he frequently particularizes the therapeutic relationship by disclosing personal information not pertinent to the treatment, which fosters confusion of the therapeutic boundaries. He is generally well trained, having completed at least an approved training program and at times formal psychoanalytic training. (201)

Brodsky's (1986) overview of offending therapists contains a number of strikingly similar attributes:

The following characteristics constitute a prototype of the therapist being sued: The therapist is male, middle aged, involved in unsatisfactory relationships in his own life, perhaps in the process of going through a divorce. His patient caseload is primarily female. He becomes involved with more than one patient sexually, those selected being on the average 16 years younger than he is. He confides his personal life to the patient, implying to her that he needs her, and he spends therapy sessions soliciting her help with his personal problems. The therapist is a lonely man, and even if he works in a group practice, he is somewhat isolated professionally, not sharing in close consultation with his peers. He may have a good reputation in the psychological or psychiatric community, having been in practice for many years.

He tends to take cases through referral only. He is not necessarily physically attractive, but there is an aura of power or charisma about him. His lovemaking often leaves much to be desired, but he is quite convincing to the patient that it is he above all others with whom she needs to be making love. (157–58)

Brodsky (1986) also describes other sexually abusive therapists, including those who tend to be inexperienced and in love with one particular client, and therapists with a personality disorder (typically antisocial personality disorder) who manipulate clients into believing that they—the therapists—should be trusted and they have the clients' best interest at heart.

Reaves (1986:175) cites a case that typifies the sexual abuse of a client by a therapist. According to court records, a Dr. Parzen, a psychiatrist, had sex with a female client over a two-and-a-half year period, during which time he charged her an hourly counseling fee. The plaintiff eventually divorced her husband, lost her rights under California community property law, and lost custody of her two children. Parzen had also prescribed excessive medication for the plaintiff, who claimed that she had tried to commit suicide more than a dozen times using pills obtained from Parzen or his office, according to court records. Parzen ultimately referred the plaintiff to another physician, referring to her as a "borderline psychotic." The jury awarded damages in the amount of $4,631,666.

A small number of therapists named in ethics complaints and lawsuits try to defend their sexual contact with clients (Schutz 1982). One argument they sometimes advance is that the sexual contact was an essential, constructive, and legitimate component of therapy. The therapist typically claims that he was merely trying to be helpful to the client. The defense offered by the lawyer of a Dr. Cooper, who sued the California Board of Medical Examiners in 1972, is illustrative:

Dr. Cooper is a firm believer in the fact that the body has a tremendous significance and influence on our actions; and the awareness of one's body is one of the keys to personal health; mental health; and his techniques may be considered new, revolutionary, and even bizarre perhaps to some people. But none of us knows the potential of the human body in relation to the human mind, and to explore that and make a person whole is Dr. Cooper's dedicated professional goal. (cited in Schutz 1982:34–35)

Another defense is that the sexual relationship was conducted independently of the therapeutic relationship. In these instances, the defendant-therapist usually argues that he and the client were able to separate their sexual involvement from their professional relationship. As Schutz (1982) suggests, however, this argument "has not been a very successful defense, since courts are reluctant to accept such a compartmentalized view of human relationships. A therapist attempting to prove the legitimacy of sexual relations between himself and a patient by establishing that two coterminous-in-time but utterly parallel relations existed has a difficult task" (35).

The list that follows is a mere sample, a diverse cross-section of a large number of court cases and professional disciplinary hearings involving allegations of sexual misconduct:

- A Pennsylvania court upheld the state licensing board's revocation of a psychologist's license to practice because of substantial evidence that he had had sexual relations with a patient before termination of the therapeutic relationship. The psychologist had neither formally terminated nor even discussed termination of the therapeutic relationship before he had sexual relations with the client. He stopped billing the client for therapy sessions around the time they started their sexual relationship, but a psychologist cannot terminate a patient relationship merely by ceasing to bill the patient ("Court Upholds Revocation" 1998:6).

- Two weeks after a social worker took a job at an outpatient mental health program, management observed him socializing with patients while on breaks from therapy sessions. The social worker induced a client—who had been diagnosed with bipolar disorder and alcoholism—to meet him outside the treatment program's facilities. The client testified that the social worker often had recited biblical quotations and she thought he was a good Christian man who could help her by going for long walks and talking. After meeting the social worker off the program's premises, the client entered into a sexual relationship with him. After the second meeting, the client felt tremendous remorse and guilt and had a relapse with alcohol. The jury awarded damages of $123,500 against the social worker and the program ("Social Worker Engages in Sexual Relationship" 1999:2).

- A Florida appeals court upheld the constitutionality of a state statute that was used to convict a psychotherapist for criminal sexual misconduct. In counseling a client with low self-esteem, a licensed psychologist had raised issues involving the client's sexuality, digitally penetrated her, tried to kiss her, and lowered his pants in front of her. The appeals court found ample evidence in the record that the psychologist had committed the misconduct by means of a therapeutic deception, meaning "a representation to the client that sexual contact by the psychotherapist is consistent with or part of the treatment of the client." The client met with the psychologist while wearing a wire, and the police obtained a tape-recording of the psychologist admitting that he had offered to have sex with her as an incentive for her to reach her weight goal and stating that he did not think that what had happened was hurtful but that it helped build her self-esteem. Evidence of similar misconduct with another former client was admitted into evidence ("Court Upholds Law" 1998:2).

- A thirty-seven-year-old woman, who complained of discontent in her life and failure to meet her family's expectations, sought help from a psychiatrist. She claimed that the psychiatrist had committed malpractice during the psychotherapy relationship when, after counseling her for six months, he told her their relationship was going to change and told her to sit on his lap. He then lifted her blouse and kissed her breast. The patient sat there and watched the psychiatrist because she was too stunned to react. He told her that he would kiss her other breast on the next visit. The psychiatrist admitted that the incident had occurred, but contended that it did not constitute malpractice and the patient was not harmed by his actions. The psychiatrist also claimed that the patient had actually seduced him. The jury awarded damages of $142,371 ("Improper Sexual Contact" 1997:4).

- A nineteen-year-old woman received treatment from a psychologist at a mental health center. The therapeutic relationship continued for about ten years. After about one year, the psychologist began having sex with the woman. She had been abused as a child and did not have a father figure in her life. The client alleged that the psychologist had responded to this disclosure by viewing her as a friend, a daughter figure, and a lover. The client claimed that she has poor social skills as a result of the abuse and will never get married or be able to have a normal relationship with a man. She received

$425,000 in a pretrial settlement ("Woman Blames Psychological Problems" 1997:2).

- A woman sought mental health treatment from a counselor, who was a lesbian, to address issues related to a sexual problem she was having with her female roommate and occasional lover. The client believed that the counselor's own sexual orientation would help her deal with the clinical issues. During the course of treatment, the client invited the counselor to have dinner with her and three other women. The counselor and client became sexually involved while the counselor was still providing the woman with counseling services. The California Board of Behavioral Science Examiners ruled the counselor was grossly negligent and revoked her license ("Counselor Begins Sexual Relationship" 1991:1).

- A psychiatrist hospitalized a thirty-year-old housewife and had sexual contact with her in the hospital and subsequently during office visits. The client also accused a psychologist involved in the case of having encouraged her to have sexual relations with the psychiatrist. The psychiatrist did not deny the sexual contact, but claimed that he was in love with the patient. The psychologist argued that she did not encourage their relationship. The client received $275,000 in a pretrial settlement ("Psychologist Encourages Sexual Misconduct" 1989:2).

Causal Factors

A large percentage of clinical practitioners report having felt attracted to their clients—although most do not act on this attraction. In one major survey of practicing psychotherapists, 96 percent of men and 76 percent of women acknowledged attraction to one or more clients. A relatively small percentage of this particular sample—9.4 percent of the men and 2.5 percent of the women—reported having had sexual relations with their clients (Pope, Tabachnick, and Keith-Spiegel 1988). More than half (52.4 percent) of a statewide sample of clinical social workers—two-thirds of whom were women—reported having felt sexually attracted to a client (Jayaratne, Croxton, and Mattison 1997). In a survey of trainees, 86 percent of men and 52 percent of women acknowledged sexual attraction to one or more clients (Gartrell et al. 1988).

The literature offers diverse theories about the causes of, and factors associated with, practitioner sexual misconduct. Simon (1999) argues, for example, that boundary violations are a function of the nature of the client (the client's clinical issues), the type of treatment, the status of the therapeutic alliance (whether it is strong or weak, functional or dysfunctional), and the personality of the therapist, combined with his or her training and experience.

From a psychodynamic perspective, a clinician violates a client's boundaries because of the therapist's difficulty in handling countertransference phenomena—that is, the therapist's transference reaction toward the client (countertransference involves unconsciously feeling toward a client the same feelings the clinician originally had toward someone else). Simon (1999) asserts that one common countertransference trap occurs when

> the therapist subconsciously overidentifies with a patient who he or she then tries to rescue. The therapist is usually struggling with conflicts or has experienced traumatic life events that are also observable in the patient. The patient is treated like a favorite child, with increasing exceptions made to the maintenance of treatment boundaries. As the therapist becomes more deeply immersed in the patient's life, the patient's demands become greater on the therapist. Eventually, the therapist abrogates the role of therapist and enters into a personal, sexual relationship with the patient. Although the therapist becomes aware of increasing boundary violations, he or she feels "powerless" to restore the treatment situation. This scenario is akin to therapists who become sexually involved with patients through "masochistic surrender," one of a variety of countertransference developments in sexual misconduct cases. (38)

Myers (1994) also examines therapist sexual misconduct through a psychodynamic lens as he summarizes a number of countertransference issues that have arisen during supervision he has provided:

> These include the covert encouraging of sexual acting out by the patient with various partners or the provoking of other varieties of "Sturm und Drang" within a patient's life in order to overcome feelings of deprivation or of emptiness within the therapist's life. It is also important to be aware of the wish to protect various patients from the exi-

gencies of life in order to rescue them, as therapists may have wished to rescue various important persons in their lives. (293–94)

Gutheil (cited in Simon 1999) also uses a psychodynamic perspective and focuses on the influence of love in the therapist–client relationship. Gutheil argues that many clients enter treatment with the subconscious wish that a loving, nurturing relationship with the therapist will gratify all needs and repair all hurts. According to Simon (1999),

> The ministrations of the therapist are often perceived by patients as acts of love. For this and a myriad of other conscious and subconscious reasons, patients regularly "fall in love" with their therapists. Some therapists exploit these love feelings for therapist-patient sex. Other therapists mistake these feelings as "true love" and respond to their own needs by establishing a sexual relationship with the patient. Even well-trained therapists may rationalize their behavior by telling themselves that this relationship with the patient is very special and "truly an exception" to the prohibition against sexual involvement with patients. In fact, "love transference" can be extremely capricious, often hiding a destructive hate transference that frighteningly erupts and engulfs the therapist and patient. (37)

Some authors reject this particular psychodynamic interpretation of boundary violations, preferring instead to view violations as manifestations of clinicians' "undue influence" on clients (Gutheil 1989). Gutheil, for example, argues that the concepts of transference and countertransference in relation to boundary violations are demeaning, disrespectful, and unrealistic because of their tendency to characterize the client as a "functional incompetent." Gutheil believes that a client often enters into a sexual relationship with her therapist in a competent manner, although she is misguided and usually unduly influenced by the therapist. Stone (1984) offers yet another perspective, proposing that the therapist breaches the client's fiduciary trust; this theory does not require reference to the client's transference and capacity to consent.

Smith and Fitzpatrick (1995) also highlight the importance of the clinician's training and theoretical orientation. They argue that we must recognize significant differences among different ideological orientations and schools of thought in psychotherapy:

Although all competent clinicians would probably agree that setting appropriate boundaries is a clinical imperative, the wide range of theoretical orientations and techniques pose a major problem when attempting to delineate the proper boundaries of clinical practice. For example, a psychoanalytically oriented clinician may view a colleague's supportive brand of psychotherapy as indulging the patient's transference wishes and as clearly outside the acceptable limits of therapeutic practice. Consider the difference between the clinician who believes that effective psychotherapy can only occur within the four walls of the consulting room versus the therapist who accompanies patients (e.g., those with anxiety disorders) to various locales for in vivo exposure sessions. (500)

Goisman and Gutheil (1992) highlighted the practical consequences of such differences in treatment ideology and theoretical orientation:

We are aware of a case currently in litigation where a number of the charges against an experienced behavior therapist flowed from the testimony of a psychoanalytically trained expert witness, who faulted the behavior therapist for assigning homework tasks to patients, hiring present and former patients for jobs in psychoeducational programs and other benign interventions, and performing a sexological examination and sensate focus instruction in a case of sexual dysfunction. From a psychoanalytic viewpoint all of these would likely constitute boundary violations of a potentially harmful sort, but from a behavioral viewpoint this is not at all the case. (538)

The variation among practitioners' attitudes concerning intimate relationships with clients is noteworthy. In their ambitious survey of forty-eight hundred psychiatrists, psychologists, and social workers, Borys and Pope (1989) found that while virtually no respondents approved of sexual activity with a current client, only 68 percent of the respondents would absolutely prohibit sexual activity with a client after termination. Pope, Tabachnick, and Keith-Spiegel (1995) found that about 7 percent of a group of psychologists (psychotherapists) believed that becoming sexually involved with a former client is ethical under many circumstances or unquestionably ethical, and about 10 percent stated that kissing a client is ethical under many circumstances or unquestionably ethical. Another report provides evidence that fewer female therapists than male therapists believe that sexual contact may be beneficial to the treatment process or that it may be appropriate with former clients (Stake and Oliver 1991). In their survey of more than eight hundred Michigan social workers, Jayaratne, Croxton, and Mattison (1997) found that about 5 percent of respondents said that having sex with a former client is appropriate, 6.4 percent said that going on a date with a former client is appropriate, and 2.6 percent said that kissing a client is appropriate.

Kardener (cited in G. Pope 1990) found differences among therapists with different ideological orientations. For example, 86 percent of psycho-dynamically oriented therapists felt that erotic contact was never of benefit to the client, whereas 71 percent of the "humanistic" and 61 percent of the behavioral therapists embraced that view. Based on his comprehensive review of the data, G. Pope (1990) concludes that psychoanalysts were more conservative in matters regarding sexuality than the nonpsychoan-alytically oriented. Deception of clients and sexual misconduct appear to be more frequent among unlicensed psychotherapists, hypnotists, and mar-riage counselors.

Several authors believe that practitioners who engage in sexual miscon-duct can be categorized conceptually. Twemlow and Gabbard (1989) char-acterize therapists who fall in love with clients—a particular subgroup of clinicians who become sexually involved with clients—as "lovesick" thera-pists. Lovesickness includes several key elements: emotional dependence; intrusive thinking, whereby the therapist thinks about the client almost con-stantly; physical sensations like buoyancy or pounding pulse; a sense of in-completeness, of feeling less than whole when away from the client; an awareness of the social proscription of such love, which seems to intensify the couple's longing for each other; and an altered state of consciousness that fosters impaired judgment on the part of the therapist when in the presence of the loved one.

According to Schoener (1995), he and his colleagues base their widely cited classification scheme—which includes a broader range of offending therapists—on empirical evidence gathered from psychological and psychi-atric examinations of sexually exploitative therapists. These clinical clusters (the italicized terminology is Schoener's) include:

1. *Psychotic and severe borderline disorders.* While few in number, these professionals have difficulties with boundaries because of problems with both impulse control and thinking. They are often aware of current ethical

standards but have difficulty adhering to them because of their poor reality testing and judgment.

a. *Manic disorders*. Most typically, this applies to practitioners diagnosed with mania who go off medication and become quite impulsive.

2. *Sociopaths and severe narcissistic personality disorders*. These are self-centered exploiters who cross various boundaries when it suits them. They tend to be calculating and deliberate in their abuse of their clients (Olarte 1997). They often manipulate the treatment by "blurring the professional boundaries with inappropriate personal disclosure that enhances and idealizes transference, and by manipulating the length or the time of the sessions to facilitate the development of a sexual relationship with the client. . . . If caught, they might express remorse and agree to rehabilitation to protect themselves or their professional standing, but they will show minimal or no character change through treatment" (Olarte 1997:205).

3. *Impulse control disorders*. This includes practitioners with a wide range of paraphilias (sexual disorders in which unusual fantasies or bizarre acts are necessary for sexual arousal) and other impulse control disorders. These professionals often have impulse control problems in other areas of their lives. They are typically aware of current ethical standards, but these do not serve as a deterrent. These practitioners often fail to acknowledge the harm that their behavior does to their victims and show little remorse.

4. *Chronic neurotic and isolated*. These practitioners are emotionally needy on a chronic basis and meet many needs through their relationships with clients. They may suffer from long-standing problems with depression, low self-esteem, social isolation, and lack of confidence. At times, these practitioners disclose personal information to clients inappropriately. Typically, they deny engaging in misconduct or justify the unethical behavior as their "therapeutic" technique designed to enhance their suffering client's self-esteem. They may also blame the client's claims on the client's pathology. Such practitioners are often repeat offenders.

5. *Situational offenders*. These therapists are generally healthy with a good practice history and free of boundary problems, but a situational breakdown in judgment or control has occurred in response to some life crisis or loss. These practitioners are generally aware of current ethical standards. According to Olarte (1997), "Their sexual contact with a client is usually an isolated or limited incident. Frequently at the time of the boundary violation, these therapists are suffering from personal or situational stresses that foster a slow erosion of their professional boundaries. They most often show remorse for

their unethical behavior, frequently stop such violations on their own, or seek consultation with peers" (204).

6. *Naïve.* In the absence of pathology, these therapists have difficulty understanding and operating within professional boundaries because they suffer from deficits in social judgment. Their difficulties stem in part from their lack of knowledge of current ethical standards and their confusion about the need to separate personal and professional relationships.

In contrast to this framework Simon (1999) offers a typology that includes somewhat different clinical dimensions. Simon places vulnerable therapists in five categories:

- *Character disordered.* Therapists diagnosed with symptoms of borderline, narcissistic, or antisocial personality disorder.
- *Sexually disordered.* Therapists diagnosed with frotteurism (recurrent intense sexual urges and sexually arousing fantasies in regard to a nonconsenting person), pedophilia, or sexual sadism.
- *Incompetent.* Therapists who are poorly trained or have persistent boundary blind spots.
- *Impaired.* Therapists who have serious problems with alcohol, drugs, or mental illness.
- *Situational reactors.* Therapists who are experiencing marital discord, loss of important relationships, or a professional crisis.

Drawing on the concept of transference, Simon (1999) highlights several themes in therapist–client sexual relationships—for example, clients who idealize their therapist or regard the therapist as a savior or as omniscient. Simon classifies these themes, reflecting clients' perceptions of their therapists, as follows:

- *Dr. Perfect.* The client idealizes the therapist's attributes.
- *Dr. Prince.* The client idolizes the therapist romantically, hoping the therapist will "rescue" him or her.
- *Dr. Good Parent.* The client experiences the therapist as a nurturing parent and may use therapy for "reparenting" purposes.
- *Dr. Magical Healer.* The client regards the therapist as his or her savior.
- *Dr. Beneficent.* The client regards the therapist as the devoted caretaker, akin to a nanny or first doctor.

- *Dr. Indispensable*. The client believes that only this therapist is able to cure.
- *Dr. Omniscient*. The client believes that the therapist knows and understands all.

Based on his extensive experience with vulnerable and offending therapists, Simon (1999) argues that boundary violations are often progressive and follow a sequence, or "natural history," that leads ultimately to a therapist–client sexual relationship. The sequence includes:

- Gradual erosion of the therapist's neutrality. The therapist begins to take special interest in the client's issues and life circumstances.
- Boundary violations begin "between the chair and the door." As the client is leaving the office and both client and worker are standing, the therapist and client may discuss personal issues that are not part of the more formal therapeutic conversation.
- Socialization of therapy. More time is spent discussing "nontherapy" issues.
- Disclosure of confidential information about other clients. The therapist begins to confide in the client, communicating to the client that she is special.
- Therapist self-disclosure begins. The therapist shares information about his own life, perhaps concerning marital or relationship problems.
- Physical contact begins (for example, touching, hugs, kisses). Casual physical gestures convey to the client that the therapist has very warm and affectionate feelings toward her.
- Therapist gains control over client. The client begins to feel more and more dependent on the therapist, and the therapist exerts more and more influence in the client's life.
- Extratherapeutic contacts occur. The therapist and client may meet for lunch or for a drink.
- Therapy sessions are longer. The customary fifty-minute session is extended because of the special relationship.
- Therapy sessions rescheduled for end of day. To avoid conflict with other clients' appointments, the therapist arranges to see the client as the day's final appointment.

- Therapist stops billing client. The emerging intimacy makes it difficult for the therapist to charge the client for the time they spend together.
- Dating begins. The therapist and client begin to schedule times when they can be together socially.
- Therapist–client sex occurs.

Simon (1995) presents the following clinical vignette to illustrate this progression or natural history:

Ms. G, a 34-year-old single woman with previously diagnosed Borderline Personality Disorder and drug abuse, seeks treatment for severe depression following a spontaneous abortion. The psychiatrist is 49 years old and recently divorced. His ex-wife was a very attractive, talented artist who ran off with a concert pianist. The psychiatrist increasingly relies on alcohol to tranquilize his grief.

Ms. G is very bright and attractive. She comes to treatment to find relief from feelings of depression, isolation, and emptiness. Clear vegetative signs of depression are present. Ms. G had hoped for a child as a cure for her loneliness and despondency.

The psychiatrist is vaguely aware of Ms. G's resemblance to his ex-wife. He quickly becomes enamored of Ms. G, overlooking and minimizing her major depression. His clinical judgment is further distorted by the appearance of improvement in Ms. G's depression as the psychiatrist shows a personal interest in her. The psychiatrist looks forward to seeing Ms. G for her twice-a-week appointments, finding solace and relief from his own loss. For the first 2 months, the treatment boundary remains reasonably intact. But then, gradually, the sessions take on a conversational, social tone.

The psychiatrist and Ms. G begin to address each other by their first names. The psychiatrist discloses the facts surrounding his divorce, talking at length about his wife's infidelity and his feelings of betrayal. He also confides in Ms. G intimate details about his other patients, thus treating her as a confidant. Ms. G is distressed at hearing the psychiatrist's unhappiness and feels guilty that she cannot be of more assistance.

In the beginning, the psychiatrist sits a comfortable distance from Ms. G, but gradually moves his chair closer. Eventually, the psychia-

trist and Ms. G sit together on the sofa. Occasionally, the psychiatrist
puts his arm around Ms. G when she tearfully describes her childhood
physical and sexual abuse. Treatment sessions become extended in
time, some lasting as long as 3 hours. Ms. G feels grateful that she is
receiving so much special treatment.

Because the extended sessions disrupt the psychiatrist's schedule,
Ms. G is seen at the end of the day. Occasionally, the psychiatrist and
Ms. G also meet at a nearby park or at a bar for a drink. Because Ms.
G complains of sleeping problems, the psychiatrist prescribes barbiturates. He has not kept up with developments in psychopharmacol-
ogy, having used medications very sparingly in his practice over the
years. The psychiatrist is unaware of Ms. G's previous addiction to
narcotics. He does not explain to her the risks of taking barbiturate
medications. Over time, Ms. G requires increasingly higher doses of
barbiturates that eventually interfere with her ability to function independently. The psychiatrist begins to make day-to-day decisions for
Ms. G, including balancing her checkbook.

During sessions, the psychiatrist and Ms. G begin to embrace and
kiss. The psychiatrist finds Ms. G. more compliant to his advances
when she has had a few drinks. During one session when Ms. G becomes intoxicated, sexual intercourse takes place. The psychiatrist
stops billing Ms. G as their sexual relationship continues.

A few months later, the psychiatrist takes an extended vacation.
While he is away, Ms. G learns from another patient that the psychiatrist revealed details of her childhood sexual abuse. Ms. G becomes
extremely depressed and takes a near-lethal overdose of barbiturates.
While hospitalized, she is weaned from barbiturates. She discloses the
fact of her sexual involvement with her outpatient psychiatrist. Ms. G
is successfully treated for major depression with antidepressants and
supportive therapy. The diagnosis of Borderline Personality Disorder
is also made by her treating psychiatrist. This disorder is severely ag-
gravated due to the sexual exploitation by her therapist. The exploiting
psychiatrist attempts to contact Ms. G on his return. She refuses. One
year later, Ms. G brings a $1 million malpractice suit against the psy-
chiatrist for sexual misconduct and psychological damages. (90–91)

Gutheil and Gabbard (1993) agree with Simon that sexual misconduct
usually begins with relatively minor boundary violations "which often show

a crescendo pattern of increasing intrusion into the patient's space that cul-minates in sexual contact" (188). They caution, however, that not all bound-ary crossings or even boundary violations lead to or represent evidence of sexual misconduct:

> A clear boundary violation from one ideological perspective may be standard professional practice from another. For example, the so-called "Christian psychiatry movement" might condone the therapist's atten-dance at a church service with one or more patients, and various group therapeutic approaches or therapeutic communities may involve in-herent boundary violations, as when some behaviorist schools permit hiring patients in therapy to do work in the treatment setting. Bad training, sloppy practice, lapses of judgment, idiosyncratic treatment philosophies, regional variations, and social and cultural conditioning may all be reflected in behavior that violates boundaries but that may not necessarily lead to sexual misconduct, be harmful, or deviate from the relevant standard of care. (188–89)

One common theme in the literature on sexual misconduct is the in-adequacy of professional education and training. Comprehensive surveys of practicing clinicians and trainees (Gartrell et al. 1987; Olarte 1997; Pope, Keith-Spiegel, and Tabachnick 1986) have found that most cite in-adequate training to help them deal constructively with their sexual at-traction to their clients. According to Olarte (1997), "The majority reported insufficient training on the recognition and resolution of erotic transfer-ence phenomena and minimal discussion during supervision of counter-transference feelings pertaining to the development of clients' erotic trans-ference onto therapists" (197).

Clinical and Professional Consequences

Sexual misconduct typically has devastating consequences. For victim-ized clients, common consequences include destroyed self-esteem, destruc-tive dependency, mistrust of the opposite sex, distrust of therapists, difficulty in subsequent intimate relationships, impaired sexual relationships, guilt, self-blame, suicidal ideation, substance abuse, loss of confidence, cognitive dysfunction, increased anxiety, identity disturbances, sexual confusion, mood lability, suppressed rage, depression, psychosomatic disorders, and feelings of anger, rejection, isolation, and abandonment (Elliott, Wolber, and Ferriss 1997; Olarte 1997; Smith and Fitzpatrick 1995; Stake and Oliver 1991). Bouhoutsos and colleagues (1983) had psychologists describe the effects of therapist–client sex on clients (current and former) who had reported sexual involvement with therapists. Nearly all the respondents (90 percent) reported adverse effects, ranging from negative feelings about the experience to suicide. According to G. Pope (1990),

> The effects of sexual exploitation on patients may vary, depending on individual personality and situational factors. Questionnaires in previously mentioned studies dealt also with the issue of patient's reactions. From 80 to 98% of the therapist responders felt that such contact was "usually or always harmful" to the patient. Others considered it "as a serious public health problem" and many courts labeled it as deceit, assault, coercion and abuse of trust, perpetrated upon the patient. The victim's emotional-psychological reactions may be akin to psychopathology occurring in rape and/or incest. . . . Common reactions may include: guilt and shame, grief, anger/rage, loss of self-esteem and depression, ambivalence and confusion, fear and generalized distrust.
>
> Some authors describe the damage done to the patient as multi-faceted: (1) delay of competent therapy; (2) psychopathology exacerbated when the "love affair" is terminated; (3) mistrust and ambivalence may grossly interfere with a new therapeutic relationship; (4) if a therapeutic relationship is established, the patient's expectations may be exaggerated and inappropriate; (5) the patient's ability to relate to spouse, etc., may be severely damaged. (195)

Although we must be concerned primarily with the detrimental consequences of sexual misconduct for victimized clients, we should not ignore the effect on the therapists who are involved in these relationships. Both practicing therapists and trainees report that being attracted to their clients evoked guilt, confusion, and anxiety (Gartrell et al. 1987; Olarte 1997; Pope, Keith-Spiegel, and Tabachnick 1986). In addition, in a growing number of states, practitioners who sexually exploit clients may face criminal charges. In 1983 Wisconsin became the first state to enact a statute making psychotherapist–client sexual exploitation a criminal offense. Minnesota,

North Dakota, California, Maine, Florida, and Colorado soon followed. According to Strasburger, Jorgenson, and Randles (1995),

> Deterrence is the primary argument in favor of criminalization of psychotherapist-patient sexual activity. A criminal law articulates to everyone the wrongfulness of such behavior. Proponents believe that sexual contact would be restrained by an unmistakable legal message that such behavior is severely damaging and totally unconscionable backed by the threat of a felony conviction and a prison sentence. Controversy exists over the probable effectiveness of this deterrence, but among the categories of exploitative therapists, those who are naive, uninformed, or undergoing the effects of midlife crisis may well respond to the prospect of punishment. (229)

Risk Management Strategy

Practitioners can take various steps to protect clients and to minimize the likelihood of ethics complaints and lawsuits associated with sexual misconduct. Simon (1999) highlights five useful basic principles underlying constructive boundary guidelines:

1. Rule of abstinence: Practitioners should strive, above all else, to avoid sexual involvement with clients and to resist acting on sexual attraction toward clients.
2. Duty of neutrality: Practitioners should seek to relate to clients as neutrally as possible. Neutrality entails the absence of favoritism, preferential consideration, and special treatment.
3. Patient autonomy and self-determination: Practitioners should respect clients' right to self-determination, which means avoiding any manipulative behaviors or behaviors that might promote clients' dependence or constitute "undue influence."
4. Fiduciary relationship: Fiduciary relationships are based on trust. Clients must be able to trust their therapists and to assume that their therapists would not engage in manipulative, exploitative, or seductive behaviors for self-interested purposes.
5. Respect for human dignity: Practitioners must maintain deep-seated respect for their clients, act only in a caring and compassionate manner, and avoid engaging in destructive behaviors. (32)

More concretely, practitioners should adhere to a number of guidelines to protect clients and minimize risks associated with sexual attraction (Calfee 1997; Simon 1999):

- Maintain relative therapist neutrality (the absence of favoritism)
- Foster psychological separateness of the client
- Protect client confidentiality
- Obtain informed consent for treatments and procedures
- Interact with clients verbally
- Ensure no previous, current, or future personal relationship with the client
- Minimize physical contact
- Preserve relative anonymity of the therapist
- Establish a stable fee policy
- Provide a consistent, private, and professional setting for treatment
- Define the time and length of the treatment session

Beyond these broad guidelines, therapists should pay special attention to clients' unique clinical issues that may complicate boundary phenomena. For example, if a therapist senses that a client is feeling attracted to him or her, the therapist might avoid scheduling the client at times when no one else is in the office suite. As Gutheil and Gabbard (1993) observe, "From a risk-management standpoint, a patient in the midst of an intense erotic transference to the therapist might best be seen, when possible, during high-traffic times when other people (e.g., secretaries, receptionists, and even other patients) are around" (191). Therapists in solo private practice must be especially careful because of professional isolation and the absence of institutional or collegial oversight and restraints (Simon 1995).

Further, therapists who sense potential boundary issues involving sexual attraction should avoid out-of-the-office contact with clients. A common example includes counseling sessions conducted during lunch in a restaurant: "This event appears to be a common way station along the path of increasing boundary crossings culminating in sexual misconduct. Although clinicians often advance the claim that therapy is going on, so, inevitably, is much purely social behavior; it does not *look* like therapy, at least to a jury. Lunch sessions are not uncommonly followed by sessions during dinner, then just dinners, then other dating behavior, eventually including intercourse" (Gutheil and Gabbard 1993:192).

Boundary violations can also arise from seemingly innocent gestures, such as offering a stranded client a ride home after a counseling session. Clinically relevant discussion may continue during the ride and while the therapist and client are parked in front of the client's home. Conducting sensitive discussion in the context of the therapist's personal space can lead to boundary ambiguity, confusion, and, ultimately, violation: "From a fact finder's viewpoint, many exciting things happen in cars, but therapy is usually not one of them" (Gutheil and Gabbard 1993:192).

As always, one must consider these guidelines in relation to different treatment approaches and ideologies. Some treatment techniques assume that therapists will spend time with clients outside the office. As Gutheil and Gabbard (1993) note,

It would not be a boundary violation for a behaviorist, under certain circumstances, to accompany a patient in a car, to an elevator, to an airplane, or even to a public restroom (in the treatment of paruresis, the fear of urinating in a public restroom) as part of the treatment plan for a particular phobia. The existence of a body of professional literature, a clinical rationale, and risk-benefit documentation will be useful in protecting the clinician in such a situation from misconstruction of the therapeutic efforts. (192)

Simon (1995) urges practitioners to conduct an "instant spot check" to identify whether the therapist has committed or is at risk of committing a boundary violation. Using this approach, the first question to ask is whether the treatment is for the benefit of the therapist or for the sake of the client's therapy. Second, is the treatment part of a series of progressive steps in the direction of boundary violations (for example, inviting the client to have lunch after a counseling session in order to continue discussion of "compelling" clinical issues)? Simon argues that a yes answer to either question should put the therapist on notice to desist immediately and take correction action.

Simon (1995) cautions that early boundary violations in psychotherapy usually first appear in the transition zone between the chair and the door: "Attention to emerging boundary issues in this therapy space can help identify and prevent progressive boundary violations" (93). In this vein, Epstein and Simon (1990) have devised the "Exploitation Index," which provides therapists with early warnings of treatment boundary violations. A survey of 532 psychiatrists who were administered the Exploitation Index showed that

43 percent found that one or more questions alerted them to boundary violations. Another 29 percent said that the questionnaire stimulated them to make specific changes in their treatment approaches and techniques.

Practitioners should also be alert to certain gender-specific issues. That most cases of sexual misconduct involve male clinicians and female clients is compelling. This pattern reflects long-standing, enduring cultural patterns involving male dominance in heterosexual relationships. As Gabbard (1990) and Olarte (1997) observe, therapists of both genders need to be aware of the effect of their deep-seated sex-related interaction styles and patterns. For instance, a male clinician who has little insight into his tendency to act in a somewhat controlling and authoritative manner may encourage his female client's dependency, passivity, and compliance, which may serve as precursors to boundary violations involving sexual misconduct.

Moreover, sexual misconduct ultimately entails the exploitation of clients—that is, the inappropriate use of the power that therapists can exercise in their authoritative role. This, too, raises gender issues. As Blackshaw and Miller (1994) note,

> Boundaries are necessary to prevent exploitation when a power differential is present. Power differentials exist between therapists and patients and also between men and women. The situation of male therapist and female patient presents a large power difference; this may be one reason why male therapists are more likely than female therapists to cross boundaries and to sexually exploit patients. One approach to safeguarding patients is to strengthen boundaries. Another parallel approach is to reduce the power differential. Some inequality of power will always remain since the patient comes to the therapist for help. However, in addition to maintaining appropriate boundaries, and with a clear focus on the patient's needs and problems, more mutual relationships in therapy are possible. . . . This results in a "power-with" rather than a "power-over" dynamic. (293)

The overarching concept to keep in mind is prevention. Practitioners must anticipate the possibility of boundary complications and take assertive steps to prevent problems. As Simon (1995) concludes,

> The identification of inchoate treatment boundary violations can be a powerful prevention tool in the hands of competent therapists. Al-

though it may sound like one is preaching to the choir, the significant number of cases of otherwise competent therapists who gradually cross treatment boundaries to become sexually involved with their patients is very sobering. Marginally competent or poorly trained therapists also may benefit from identification of early boundary violations. Many of these therapists naively attempt to re-parent their patients, crossing treatment boundaries as they become overly involved in their patients' lives. Other therapists masochistically surrender to the demands of certain patients. They become unable to extricate themselves over the course of progressive boundary violations. (91)

Rehabilitation Efforts

Relatively little research has been conducted on the effectiveness of efforts to rehabilitate impaired professionals who engage in ethical misconduct (Sonnenstuhl 1989; Trice and Beyer 1984). Many investigations have serious methodological limitations; few studies control adequately for extraneous factors that may account for changes over time in practitioners' attitudes and behavior.

In recent years, several organized efforts have tried to identify and address the problems of impaired professionals and ethical misconduct. The consensus is growing that a model strategy for addressing impairment among professionals should include several components (Reamer 1994a; Schoener and Gonsiorek 1990; Sonnenstuhl 1989; VandenBos and Duthie 1986). First, we need adequate means for identifying impaired professionals. Professionals must be willing to assume responsibility for acknowledging impairment among colleagues. And as Lamb and colleagues (1987) note, it certainly would help to develop reasonably objective measures of what constitutes failure to live up to professional standards, incompetent skills, and impaired professional functioning.

Second, a professional who spots a colleague who may be impaired should first speculate about the causes and then proceed with what Sonnenstuhl (1989) describes as "constructive confrontation." Third, once a practitioner decides who (typically, a professional colleague) shall confront the exploitative colleague, the practitioner must decide whether to help the impaired colleague identify ways to seek help voluntarily or to refer the colleague to a supervisor or local regulatory body (such as a licensing board or professional association's ethics adjudication committee).

Assuming the data are sufficient to support a rehabilitation plan, the impaired practitioner's colleague, supervisor, or local regulatory body should make specific recommendations. The possibilities include close supervision, personal psychotherapy, or other appropriate treatment (for example, substance abuse treatment). In some cases, a local regulatory body or professional association may need to impose some type of sanction such as censure, limitations on the practitioner's practice (for example, concerning type of clientele served or practice setting), termination of employment, suspension or expulsion from a professional association, or license revocation.

With specific regard to treatment that follows the filing and processing of a formal complaint, Schoener (1995) argues that, ideally, a comprehensive assessment of the practitioner would be conducted by a licensing or regulatory body and would involve several steps, including

- Gathering data about the practitioner's professional training, professional work history, and personal history (including noteworthy "ups" and "downs"), and the nature of the practice-related complaint (boundary violation)
- Generating hypotheses about causal factors that may be involved in the boundary violation
- Formulating a rehabilitation plan, when feasible
- Coordinating the rehabilitation plan with the licensing board, professional association, and practitioner's employer
- Implementing the corrective action (for example, psychotherapy, supervision, consultation, continuing education) and, when necessary, appropriate sanctions (for example, license suspension or revocation, expulsion from professional association)
- Evaluating the practitioner's progress in regard to the possibility of allowing him to reenter practice and the profession

This comprehensive assessment approach includes a key feature: interviewing the original victim or complainant. According to Schoener (1995), "This often proves invaluable. Beyond helping us avoid being taken in by intentional distortions on the part of the practitioner being evaluated, it provides a much more complete picture of the events in question. Even a completely honest, nondefensive professional who is being cooperative does not know all that happened. Each party experienced the events differently" (98).

Schoener (1995) believes that a formal assessment of an exploitative practitioner should not be conducted, or a rehabilitation plan developed, unless (1) the practitioner admits wrongdoing and understands that the client suffered harm; (2) the practitioner believes that he or she has a problem that requires rehabilitation; (3) the practitioner is willing to agree to the assessment and realizes that its outcome may not be favorable; and (4) the essential facts of the case are not in dispute. Once the practitioner has completed the rehabilitation plan, those responsible for overseeing it must be able to answer yes to two questions: "To a reasonable degree of psychiatric or psychological certainty, have the problems you were treating been fixed or resolved?" and "Would you have any qualms whatsoever if your spouse or child went to see this person for individual therapy?"

We do have evidence that ambitious, skilled treatment of offending practitioners can be effective (Simon 1999). However, prospects are not encouraging for practitioners who have been diagnosed with serious personality disorders or paraphilias, or who are deemed incompetent (Schoener 1995; Simon 1999).

Sexual Relationships with Former Clients

Case 2.2. George M. was a licensed counselor at a community mental health center. He provided individual counseling to a thirty-eight-year-old woman, Carolyn L., who was having difficulty coping with the death of her twelve-year-old child. Ms. L.'s daughter had died after a long struggle with bone cancer. Mr. M. and Ms. L. met for counseling for six sessions. The two agreed to terminate the therapy after Ms. L. reported that she felt much better able to move on with her life and handle her loss.

A little more than six years after they terminated their professional–client relationship, Mr. M. and Ms. L. encountered each other unexpectedly at a mutual acquaintance's Fourth of July party. The host, a distant cousin, invited Mr. M. to the party. Ms. L. was the host's neighbor and acquaintance.

Mr. M. and Ms. L. recognized each other at the party and chatted briefly. Mr. M. asked Ms. L. how she was doing, and Ms. L. brought him up to date. During their brief encounter, Mr. M., who was divorced, found himself feeling attracted to Ms. L. He began thinking about asking Ms. L. out for a dinner date. Mr. M. knew that some colleagues might not approve of his dating a former client, but he felt in his heart that enough time had passed since the termination of the professional–client relationship; he believed that Ms. L. was quite mature emotionally and would be able to handle a personal relationship with her former therapist. Being rather cautious, however, Mr. M. decided to bring up the issue at the next meeting of his peer consultation group.

Although the human service professions agree that sexual relationships with current clients are inappropriate, they are not unanimous regarding sexual relationships of practitioners with *former* clients. The NASW *Code of Ethics* and the American Medical Association's *Principles of Medical Ethics with Annotations Especially Applicable to Psychiatry* assert that sexual relationships with former clients are unethical. However, the NASW code also states that exceptions may be warranted under "extraordinary circumstances," such as when the social worker was involved in a nonclinical relationship with the client (for example, a social worker employed as a community organizer who became involved with a neighborhood resident): "If social workers engage in conduct contrary to this prohibition or claim that an exception to this prohibition is warranted because of extraordinary circumstances, it is social workers—not their clients—who assume the full burden of demonstrating that the former client has not been exploited, coerced, or manipulated, intentionally or unintentionally" (1996:standard 1.09[c]). In contrast, ethical standards promulgated by the American Psychological Association, the American Counseling Association, and the American Association for Marriage and Family Therapy prohibit sexual relationships with former clients for only the two-year period immediately following termination of treatment. Although these codes discourage sexual relationships with former clients, they offer practitioners more latitude once the two-year period is reached.

Survey results demonstrate impressive diversity of opinion among professionals concerning the ethics of sexual relationships with former clients. Akamatsu (1988) found that about 45 percent of a sample of 395 members of American Psychological Association Division 29 (Psychotherapy) said that intimate relationships with former clients were highly unethical. Slightly less than a third of this group (about 31 percent) felt that such relationships were neither ethical nor unethical, or even felt them to be ethical to some degree; 23.9 percent felt that such relationships were only somewhat unethical. About 14 percent of the men in this sample and about 5 percent of the women admitted to intimate relationships with former clients. The average interval between termination and the commencement of the relationships was 15.6 months. In contrast, Jayaratne, Croxton, and Mattison (1997) found that about 5 percent of their sample of clinical social workers believed that having sex with a former client is appropriate and about 6 percent believed that going on a date with a former client is appropriate. About 1 percent of this sample reported having dated a former client, and about the same percentage reported having had sex with a former client.

One major practical consideration for practitioners to keep in mind is that a growing number of state legislatures have enacted laws making sexual contact with a former client a criminal offense, punishable by imprisonment and/or a fine (Calfee 1997; Strasburger, Jorgenson, and Randles 1997). Beyond this practical consideration, however, it is most important that practitioners consider the potentially devastating emotional effect that a sexual relationship may have on the former client. For example, former clients often face challenging issues in their lives after the formal termination of the professional–client relationship. New emotional issues, relationship problems, or developmental crises, for instance, may emerge, and former clients may wish to contact the practitioner for assistance. The practitioner's familiarity with the client's circumstances and the established relationship between the parties may be especially helpful in such cases; starting over with a new provider may be both inefficient and intimidating. Clearly, however, a practitioner and a former client who have entered into a sexual relationship could have difficulty resuming an effective professional–client relationship. Practitioners and former clients who enter into sexual relationships after termination of their professional–client relationship essentially forfeit any resumption of that relationship, and this may not be in the client's best interest.

In addition, former clients may encounter less challenging yet important new issues or problems in their lives and still may find it helpful to speculate about what their former therapist would have said about the matter. The former client may not feel the need to resume a formal relationship with the practitioner; however, the client might find it helpful merely to reflect on the therapist's perspective. A sexual relationship between the practitioner and the former client presumably would interfere with the former client's ability to draw on what he or she has learned from the practitioner's professional expertise, given the shift from a professional to an intimate relationship. Thus practitioners should consider their clients as "clients in perpetuity": once a client, always a client.

Practitioners must also realize that courts of law may regard sexual contact with former clients as evidence of professional negligence. In one case ("Woman Claims Improper Sexual Conduct" 1996), for example, a married couple claimed that the psychologist who had treated their two sons over a fifteen-month period for emotional problems was negligent when he had sexual relations with the wife after the treatment ended. The wife presented evidence of her resulting depression, panic disorder, anxiety, and adjustment disorder. A jury found that the psychologist was negligent and that the wife was contributorily negligent (negligence was apportioned 40 percent to the wife and 60 percent to the psychologist). The jury found that the wife was entitled to punitive damages in the amount of $75,000.

Recognizing that several professions have not entirely prohibited practitioners' sexual relationships with former clients—a position I do not endorse—practitioners who believe that an exception is warranted should ask themselves several key questions (Reamer 1998a):

- How much time has passed since termination of the professional–client relationship? Clearly, a sexual relationship that begins shortly after termination is more suspect than one that begins long after the practitioner's services to the client have ended. This question is difficult to address in part because there is no magical length of time that must elapse so that a sexual relationship can be "appropriate."
- To what extent is the client mentally competent and emotionally stable? A sexual relationship with a former client who has a lengthy history of emotional instability and vulnerability is a greater cause for concern than a relationship with a former client who is clearly competent and emotionally stable.
- What issues were addressed in the professional–client relationship? A sexual relationship after a professional–client relationship that involved discussion or examination of emotionally sensitive and intimate issues—for example, related to the client's history of childhood sexual abuse—is more problematic than a relationship limited to behavior management techniques the client might use with her children.

- How long did the professional–client relationship last? Should a sexual relationship develop, a professional–client relationship that lasted for many months is a greater cause for concern than a relationship that lasted for two brief meetings.
- What circumstances surrounded the termination of the professional–client relationship? Was it terminated so that the practitioner and client could begin a sexual relationship, or did it come to a natural conclusion because the compelling therapeutic work was done? The practitioner must carefully examine the motives and circumstances surrounding the termination of the professional–client relationship.
- To what extent is there foreseeable harm to the client or others as a result of the sexual relationship? How likely is it that a sexual relationship, especially if that relationship ends unpleasantly, could harm the client? Could those who are close to the client—such as a spouse or partner—be harmed by the practitioner's sexual relationship with the former client? To what extent could the client's ability to trust therapists be harmed by the relationship? Could rumors about the relationship undermine practitioners' integrity in general?

Counseling Former Sexual Partners

Case 2.3. Dennis G. was a psychiatrist in private practice. His practice focused primarily on adults with mood and anxiety disorders. Dr. G. has been in practice for twelve years.

Toward the end of his residency, Dr. G. began dating Dr. B., who was a resident in internal medicine at the same hospital where Dr. G. trained. Dr. G. and Dr. B. lived together for about ten months before deciding, quite amicably, to end their intimate relationship. The two remained friendly for about two years and then lost touch when Dr. B. moved to another city to pursue a fellowship.

Dr. B. recently moved back to the city where Dr. G. lived, having accepted a position at a local health center. After about six months in her new job, Dr. B. found herself struggling with symptoms of depression, which had affected her off and on since her college years. Dr. B. had not been in touch with Dr. G. but decided to call him for a consultation about her depression. Dr. G. and Dr. B. met for lunch, got reacquainted, and talked about Dr. B.'s symptoms. Dr. B. felt very comfortable with Dr. G. and trusted his advice and the treatment approach he suggested. Dr. B. asked Dr. G. whether he would be willing to oversee her treatment, which would include a combination of psychotherapy and psychotropic medication.

Practitioners have personal lives that may involve sexual relationships. Ideally, such relationships involve mutually intimate sharing of information and feelings. In its purest form, an intimate relationship between two people is not hierarchical in nature, with one person assuming more authority, power, or control than the other.

Moving from an intimate sexual relationship to a professional–client relationship can be detrimental to the client. Former lovers who become clients—no matter how much time has elapsed—may find it difficult to shift from the role of an egalitarian partner in a relationship to a party who, to some degree, is in a dependent or subordinate position. No matter how much a therapist believes in empowering clients and engaging clients as equal partners in the helping relationship, clients are, by definition, in the position of asking for or being required to receive assistance (a form of dependency), and the practitioner is in the position of authority charged with providing assistance. This inescapable dynamic places clients in a vulnerable position that reflects the power imbalance in the relationship. This view is supported in the views of a sample of clinical social workers who were surveyed about boundary issues: less than 2 percent stated that accepting a former romantic partner as a client is appropriate (Jayaratne, Croxton, and Mattison 1997).

Confusion about the nature of the relationship could cause a client who was sexually involved with a therapist before the onset of the professional–client relationship to be unable to benefit fully from the therapist's expertise. The client may have difficulty distinguishing between the therapist's professional and personal roles in her or his life. The couple's interpersonal history and dynamics may interfere with the client's ability to receive help and the therapist's ability to provide help. The therapist's influence and credibility might be undermined because of the client's intimate familiarity with the therapist's personal life and issues.

In psychodynamic terms, the transference and countertransference involved in such a relationship are likely to limit the therapist's effectiveness and the ability of both client and practitioner to maintain appropriate professional boundaries. Transference is a frequent phenomenon in psychotherapy. Former experiences, relationships, or developmental conflicts in the client's life may stimulate or trigger the client's emotional reactions in the current relationship with the therapist. Given the possibility of transference, emotional experiences in the sexual relationship with the therapist that preceded the professional–client relationship may complicate the client's feelings about and reactions to the therapist. In countertransference, a therapist's emotional reactions to a client may have originated in the therapist's own previous experiences, relationships, or developmental conflicts (Barker 1999). In this context, the once-intimate relationship with the client that predates the professional–client relationship may affect the practitioner's feelings about and reactions to the client.

Sexual Relationships with Clients' Relatives or Acquaintances

Current ethical standards also prohibit human service professionals from engaging in sexual activities or sexual contact with a client's relative, or another individual with whom the client maintains a close personal relationship, when the relationship carries a risk of exploitation or potential harm to the client. For example, the NASW *Code of Ethics* (1996) asserts:

> Sexual activity or sexual contact with clients' relatives or other individuals with whom clients maintain a personal relationship has the potential to be harmful to the client and may make it difficult for the social worker and client to maintain appropriate professional boundaries. Social workers—not their clients, their clients' relatives, or other individuals with whom the client maintains a personal relationship— assume the full burden for setting clear, appropriate, and culturally sensitive boundaries. (standard 1.09[b])

A practitioner's sexual relationship with a client's relative or another person to whom the client is close may cause the client to feel betrayed and can undermine confidence in the practitioner and the practitioner's profession. Human service professionals are obligated to protect clients' interests and must avoid conflicts of interest that may be harmful to clients.

In some cases, a practitioner's relationship with a client's relative or another individual with whom the client has a close personal relationship is clearly inappropriate, as in the following examples:

Case 2.4. A counselor at a child guidance clinic provided counseling to a nine-year-old child who was referred by the principal at the child's grade school. The student, who was in foster care, was having difficulty managing his behavior in the classroom and was engaging in some physically risky activities (for example, jumping from high places).

The counselor met with the child and with the child's foster mother for an initial assessment and intake interview. The counselor then met with the child individually and, sporadically, with the child's foster mother. During the course of the counselor's professional relationship with the child, the counselor began to date the child's foster mother. On several occasions, the counselor spent time socially with the child and his foster mother at their home, including several overnight stays.

Case 2.5. A social worker at a major teaching hospital provided counseling services to an elderly patient, a seventy-two-year-old man who had fallen and fractured his hip. During the patient's hospital stay, the social worker became acquainted with the patient's son, who visited his father regularly. The patient's son was attracted to the social worker—with whom he had spent considerable time planning his father's transfer to a rehabilitation facility—and asked her out on a date. The social worker accepted the invitation, and the two began an intimate relationship.

Serious medical complications that required the patient to stay in the hospital delayed his transfer to a nursing home. The patient had developed a life-threatening infection and eventually had to be placed on a ventilator. When the patient's prognosis became grim, the social worker and the patient's son discussed the decision the son might need to make about terminating the ventilator. The social worker found that her intimate relationship with the patient's son complicated her role as a professional who was attempting to help a patient's adult child make a difficult decision about termination of life support.

——————

——————

Case 2.6. A clinical psychologist at a center that provides services to people with physical disabilities facilitated a support group for caregivers. The group's primary purpose was to provide emotional support and mutual aid to relatives and acquaintances of the center's primary clients.

One group member was the sister of a center resident, a forty-two-year-old woman who was paralyzed as a result of a skiing accident. The client was living with the sister, who was having difficulty juggling the various demands in her life.

After one support group meeting, the client's sister stayed to chat with the psychologist. The sister said she wanted some advice about how to handle a difficult family issue involving the client's care.

Following their brief discussion, the client's sister told the psychologist that she had something else she wanted to discuss. She told the psychologist she felt a bit foolish, but she wondered whether he would be interested in accompanying her to her employer's annual golf outing. The psychologist found the client's sister appealing and eagerly accepted the invitation. The two began to date and quickly developed an intimate relationship.

——————

In each of these examples, it is easy to imagine how the client might feel betrayed by the practitioner's intimate relationship with the relative or acquaintance and how this relationship could interfere with the practitioner's professional effectiveness. In other cases, however, practitioners may disagree about whether a sexual relationship with a client's relative or another individual to whom a client is close is inappropriate. Here are examples that may generate disagreement among practitioners:

——————

Case 2.7. A counselor employed in the forensic unit of a state psychiatric hospital provided counseling to a patient who had been charged with the crime of arson and in criminal court had been found not guilty by reason of insanity. The counselor happened to meet the distant cousin of the patient at a friend's dinner party, and the two started dating. At the time, neither knew of the other's connection to the patient.

About two months after their intimate relationship began, the counselor learned of his sexual partner's relationship to the counselor's current patient. The counselor was unsure whether professional duty required him to terminate the relationship.

―――

―――

Case 2.8. A social worker in a residential program for children with serious emotional and behavioral problems provided counseling to a fifteen-year-old resident. The social worker also met occasionally with the client's parents. At a neighborhood block party, the social worker met a man who was a "good friend" of the client's father. The social worker and the man began to date.

―――

In such cases, where practitioners may disagree about the appropriateness of a sexual relationship with a client's relative or acquaintance, the practitioner should seek consultation with colleagues and carefully examine the potential risks to the client. In the end, practitioners must assume the full burden and the associated risks if they decide to enter into an intimate relationship.

Sexual Relationships with Supervisees, Trainees, Students, and Colleagues

Human service practitioners also must avoid sexual relationships with staff members whom they supervise and students, trainees, and other colleagues over whom they exercise some form of authority. Supervisees, for example, are typically dependent on their supervisors and could feel pressured to accede to a supervisor's initiation of a sexual relationship out of fear of jeopardizing the supervisory relationship (Congress 1996). Such a relationship is likely to be exploitative and probably illegal, as it would constitute sexual harassment.

Case 2.9. A psychiatric resident was receiving clinical supervision from an experienced psychiatrist at a private mental health facility. The supervision was a requirement of the resident's training. For several months, the supervising psychiatrist and the resident met weekly in the supervisor's office to discuss clinical issues that arose in cases that the resident was handling. The supervisor, who was married, found that he was becoming attracted to the resident. He suggested that they begin to socialize together at the end of their supervision sessions, first by going out for a drink. Eventually, the two had dinner together following one late-night supervision session. Before long, the supervisor suggested that the two begin a sexual affair.

The resident felt overwhelmed by the supervisor's sexual overtures. She was afraid to resist his advances, in part because she found him attractive and in part because she did not want to jeopardize her professional future, which could be affected by the supervisor's evaluations and recommendations. The resident agreed to have a sexual relationship with her supervisor, although she felt somewhat exploited by him.

In this case, the supervisor was unethical because he took advantage of his position of authority to enter into a sexual relationship with his supervisee. The supervisee was emotionally troubled by the situation and worried that her sexual involvement with her supervisor eventually could injure her reputation and harm her career.

Students and other trainees are similarly vulnerable to exploitation. Practitioners who function as practicum or field supervisors for students, for example, maintain control over their students' lives and careers in much the same way that work-setting supervisors have control over their supervisees' lives and careers. Field instructors have considerable influence on the grades that students receive for the internships, and students may feel that their educational and professional careers would be jeopardized if they were to resist field instructors' attempts to become involved with them sexually. Trainees may feel similarly vulnerable when practitioners have authority over them in the context of continuing education or professional development programs. Instructors who engage in sexual relationships with students or trainees expose themselves to the risk of formal ethics complaints and sexual harassment allegations.

Practitioners are obligated to avoid engaging in sexual relationships not only with colleagues over whom they exercise professional authority, but also with any colleague with whom a potential conflict of interest exists. The following illustrates how this can be done:

Case 2.10. A social worker employed by a state human services agency was responsible for overseeing a contract between the department and a large community mental health center that was providing clinical services to teenage parents. As part of her duties, the social worker met periodically with the agency's director to discuss the program's services, goal attainment, and budget. Over time, the two individuals became attracted to each other and began dating. When it appeared that the two were embarking on a sexual relationship, the social worker notified her supervisor, informed her of the evolving relationship, and suggested that the supervisor assign another staff person in the office to assume responsibility for oversight of this contract.

Physical Contact

Not all physical contact is explicitly sexual, although sometimes it carries sexual overtones. Practitioners must be careful to distinguish between appropriate and inappropriate physical contact with clients. Most professions' codes of ethics do not comment on this phenomenon directly. An exception is the NASW *Code of Ethics* (1996): "Social workers should not engage in physical contact with clients when there is a possibility of psychological harm to the client as a result of the contact (such as cradling or caressing clients). Social workers who engage in appropriate physical contact with clients are responsible for setting clear, appropriate, and culturally sensitive boundaries that govern such physical contact" (standard 1.10).

Appropriate physical contact may take various forms; its essential feature is that it is not likely to cause the client psychological harm, as in the following examples:

Case 2.11. A psychologist worked in a residential program for children who had been adjudicated delinquent. The psychologist learned from his supervisor that the court had just terminated the parental rights of the single mother of a resident, following the mother's third conviction for drug use and possession; eventually, the child, who was twelve, would be placed with a foster family and, ideally, would be adopted.

Upon learning this news, the child started to sob hysterically and cried out for his birth mother, whom he loved deeply. The psychologist put his arm around the boy and held him briefly in an effort to comfort him.

_____

_____

Case 2.12. A couple sought counseling from a social worker following the sudden death of their infant. The social worker met with the couple weekly during a five-month period. During that time, the social worker helped the couple explore their grief and cope with their tragic loss.

At the end of their last session together, the couple hugged the social worker and thanked him for his invaluable help.

_____

_____

Case 2.13. A hospital-based counselor worked in the facility's hospice unit. Patients in the unit had been diagnosed with a terminal illness and were in the final stages of dying.

One of the counselor's patients was a sixty-one-year-old woman who had been diagnosed with ovarian cancer. As she spoke with the counselor, the patient reminisced about important moments in her life, mainly related to her marriage and children. The patient cried as she spoke; the counselor reached over and held the patient's hand during their conversation.

_____

In these situations, the practitioner had brief and limited physical contact that is generally considered acceptable. None of these clients would likely be psychologically harmed by the contact. To the contrary, they probably would find the physical contact emotionally comforting, as a form of consolation or "therapeutic touch." A Georgia court ruled that physical touch is not necessarily evidence of negligence ("Patient's Claims" 1998). The state appeals court affirmed the dismissal of claims brought by a patient who had been treated by a psychiatrist for nine years. The patient, who was diagnosed with anorexia nervosa and borderline personality disorder, had met with the psychiatrist for therapy once per week. On approximately six occasions, the psychiatrist permitted the patient to hold his hand during therapy, and they would hug at the end of the session. The patient acknowledged that none of the contact was of a sexual nature. The court ruled that the contact between the patient and the psychiatrist did not constitute a battery and that the patient had consented to the limited physical contact as part of her treatment.

Clearly, many professionals believe that limited forms of physical contact can be appropriate. More than four-fifths (83.1 percent) of a sample of clinical social workers stated that hugging or embracing a client can be appropriate, and two-fifths (39.9 percent) stated that touching a client as a regular part of the therapy process can be appropriate. In contrast, relatively few stated that it is appropriate to use massage with a client (13.7 percent) or kiss a client (2.6 percent); only about 2 percent of this sample reported having engaged in either of these activities (Jayaratne, Croxton, and Mattison 1997). Similarly, nearly all respondents in a survey of a national sample of psychologists (psychotherapists) stated that under some circumstances hugging a client is ethical, and the vast majority (nearly 87 percent) reported having hugged a client (Pope, Tabachnick, and Keith-Spiegel 1995).

In general, inappropriate physical touch occurs when the nature of the touch might exacerbate the client's transference in harmful ways, thus confusing or troubling the client. In other instances, the touch is inappropriate because it might suggest that the relationship between the practitioner and client extends beyond the formal professional–client relationship, as in the following examples:

Case 2.14. A counselor in private practice specialized in providing group therapy to women who had been physically and sexually abused. As a routine part of therapy, the counselor asked group members to sit in a circle on the floor ("to get down low, on the same level, and as a way to get in touch with the small child within themselves," the counselor said), and then she lowered the office lights and turned on soothing music. In the course of this part of the therapy, each client had an opportunity to experience being nurtured by the counselor: the counselor sat on the floor with her legs spread open, and the client sat with her back against the counselor's chest and the counselor's arms wrapped around her. The counselor rocked the client and spoke softly to the client's "inner hurt child." At times, the counselor would wipe away the client's tears and gently stroke her hair. The counselor said this provided clients with a "corrective emotional experience" and "constructive reparenting."

Case 2.15. A psychologist had a long-standing interest in the therapeutic value of massage. She had not received formal training as a massage therapist but had learned a number of massage techniques from a close friend. The psychologist was providing counseling to a thirty-two-year-old woman who was dealing with her recent realization that she had been sexually abused as a child by her mother's boyfriend. During one session, the client commented that for weeks she had felt as if her body were tied up in knots and that she was "filled with painful tension." The psychologist suggested that some massage might be helpful and offered to rub the client's shoulders, neck, head, face, arms, and back during their therapy session.

Case 2.16. A marriage and family therapist provided counseling to a young couple who were having marital difficulties. The couple disagreed about whether to have children, and this disagreement was the source of considerable tension in their relationship. On several occasions, the therapist met alone with the wife. Toward the end of one such session, the wife began to cry intensely; the therapist got up from his chair and sat next to the client on the sofa to comfort her; he put his arms around the client, and she leaned against the therapist as she cried. The therapist stroked her head softly while the client continued to talk about her distress.

These situations can be problematic because the therapists' conduct has the potential to confuse clients about the nature of the professional–client relationship and introduce complex boundary issues into the relationship. Some forms of touch—especially cradling and caressing, which typically have a sexual connotation—are likely to distract both practitioner and client from their therapeutic agenda and thus jeopardize the client's well-being. Other than brief contact for exclusively therapeutic purposes—such as a quick hug to say good-bye or to console a terribly distraught client—physical touch has the potential to cause psychological harm and interfere with the professional–client relationship. Gutheil and Gabbard (1993) offer the following practical advice:

> From the viewpoint of current risk-management principles, a handshake is about the limit of social physical contact at this time. Of course, a patient who attempts a hug in the last session after 7 years of intense, intensive, and successful therapy should probably not be hurled across the room. However, most hugs from patients should be discouraged in tactful, gentle ways by words, body language, positioning, and so forth. Patients who deliberately or provocatively throw their arms around the therapist despite repeated efforts at discouragement should be stopped. An appropriate response is to step back, catch both wrists in your hands, cross the patient's wrists in front of you, so that the crossed arms form a barrier between bodies, and say firmly, "Therapy is a talking relationship; please sit down so we can discuss your not doing this any more." If the work degenerates into grabbing, consider seriously termination and referral, perhaps to a therapist of a different gender. (195)

There is legitimate debate about whether some forms of therapy should be allowed to incorporate physical touch as a component of the therapeutic approach. This debate is not easily settled. However, practitioners who incorporate physical touch should consider the following vignette (Gutheil and Gabbard 1993):

> A therapist—who claimed that her school of practice involved hugging her female patient at the beginning and end of every session, without apparent harm—eventually had to terminate therapy with the patient for noncompliance with the therapeutic plan. The enraged patient filed a sexual misconduct claim against the therapist. Despite the evidence showing that this claim was probably false (a specious suit trig-

gered by rage at the therapist), the insurer settled because of the likelihood that a jury would not accept the principle of "hug at the start
and hug at the end but no hugs in between." If the claim was indeed
false, this is a settlement based on boundary violations alone. (195)

Practitioners should also be sensitive to cultural and ethnic norms pertaining to physical touch. For example, it would be inappropriate for a practitioner to shake the hand of an Orthodox Jewish woman because Orthodox
rules proscribe physical contact between unmarried members of the opposite
sex. Similarly, a practitioner should not touch the head of a Cambodian
(Khmer) client, because some believe that the soul resides in the head and
should not be disturbed. Such gestures would violate sacred religious and
ethnic norms. As Smith and Fitzpatrick (1995) note,

> Like the issue of dual relationships, the issue of physical contact (ex-
> clusive of overtly sexual contact) with clients in therapy is not easily
> resolved. On one side, a gentle, reassuring touch or hug can be the
> most appropriate response at certain times or with certain clients
> (Holub & Lee, 1990; Simon, 1992). On the other hand, clinicians
> practicing such behavior can run the risk of having it interpreted as a
> sexual advance, leading to undesired consequences for both the cli-
> nician and the client (see Gutheil, 1989, pp. 600–601, for a descrip-
> tion of such a case). There are also cultural factors to be considered.
> For example, in Montreal where the dominant culture is French-
> Canadian, kissing on both cheeks is a widely practiced greeting
> among friends and even casual acquaintances. When it occurs be-
> tween a therapist and client (as it sometimes does on special occa-
> sions), it does not carry the erotically charged meaning it might else-
> where in North America. (502–3)

Physical touch can also be an issue in nonpsychotherapeutic contexts.
For example, in many circumstances human service professionals instinc-
tively initiate or respond to a handshake upon meeting someone in a professional setting, such as a meeting of community residents or an administrators' meeting. However, a child-abuse-and-neglect investigator may decide
not to shake the hand of a parent whom the professional is in the process of
investigating following child abuse or neglect allegations. The investigator
may believe that the handshake conveys a sense of familiarity, alliance, and

comfort that is inconsistent with the potentially adversarial nature of the encounter—an encounter that could lead to the involuntary termination of parental rights. Whether to shake another party's hand in this kind of situation depends on the practitioner's judgment about its connotation and the potential for boundary confusion and emotional harm.

Many boundary issues involve intimate relationships with clients, former clients, clients' relatives or acquaintances, practitioners' former sexual partners, and individuals with whom practitioners have professional relationships (such as supervisees and students). Boundary issues that do not explicitly involve sexual relationships also arise frequently, often as a result of the practitioner's unique emotional and dependency needs. I will now turn to these issues.

3 Emotional and Dependency Needs

Boundary problems arising from a practitioner's personal issues can take many other forms in addition to inappropriate intimate relationships. Some manifestations amount to boundary violations, by which clients and others are exploited or harmed. Others constitute boundary crossings, introducing complex issues that do not rise to the level of actual violations but must be managed carefully nonetheless.

What many of these phenomena have in common is that they are rooted in the practitioner's emotional and dependency needs, such as those stemming from childhood experiences, marital issues, aging, career frustrations, or financial and legal problems. Research on impaired professionals provides ample evidence that troubled practitioners sometimes find themselves enmeshed in boundary-related complications (Guy, Poelstra, and Stark 1989; Kilburg, Kaslow, and VandenBos 1988; Reamer 1992; Thoreson, Miller, and Krauskopf 1989). Emotional distress among professionals generally falls into two categories: environmental stress, which is a function of employment conditions (actual working conditions and the broader culture's lack of support or appreciation of the human service mission), and professional training and personal stress, caused by problems with marriage, relationships, emotional and physical health, and finances (Reamer 1992). Of course, these two types of stress are often interrelated, as suggested by Freudenberger's (1986) overview of impaired professionals:

I have worked with at least 60 impaired professionals, psychologists, social workers, dentists, physicians, and attorneys during the past ten years and have found certain personality characteristics to be common. For the most part, impaired professionals are between 30 and 55 years of age. This is in essential agreement with Farber and Heifitz (1981) who suggested that "suicides of physicians, when they happen, are most likely to occur in the 35–54 age group" (p. 296). Early childhood impoverishment is another common characteristic. This is in agreement with Vaillant, Brighton, and McArthur (1970), who pointed to the "lack of consistent support and concern from their parents" in his study of drug-using physicians.

Most, if not all, of the patients I worked with led consistently unhealthy lifestyles. They tended to be masochistic, to have low self-images, and to be self-destructive in their personal and professional lives. Eighteen of the 60 had been married more than one time, 10 were bachelors, and the remainder were separated or divorced. Those who were married had frequent extramarital affairs. They all worked excessively long hours and, as Pearson and Strecker (1960) suggested, "had poor organizational habits . . . seldom took vacations, lunch hours and had few outside interests" (p. 916).

Their masochism made them prone to their patients beyond their own personal limits. All tended to be perfectionists and were usually never pleased with their work. "I know I can be better, I'm not good enough, I could have done more" are frequently heard refrains. They tended to conduct their lives, both at home and in the office, in such a way that they found little, if any, relief from their chores. They had a desperate need to be needed and rationalized, denied and overcompensated to an excessive degree. While expressing a sense of dedication and commitment, they denied that abusing drugs or alcohol or sexually abusing clients might eventually lead to their destruction. As a group they were risk takers with their own as well as their patients' lives. (137–38)

Of course, practitioners' emotional needs are not always this extreme. As we shall see shortly, sometimes the issues are much more subtle with respect to both their causes and their manifestation.

Boundary issues arising from a practitioner's emotional and dependency needs assume a variety of forms, including forming friendships with clients or former clients, engaging in personal self-disclosure to clients, communicating with clients affectionately, and deliberately interacting with clients in the context of community-based groups or activities.

Friendships with Clients

Occasionally, human service professionals establish such special rapport with clients that they enter into friendships with them. Sometimes these friendships meet practitioners' deep-seated emotional needs; they may be lonely or in the midst of a personal crisis, and the friendship with a "special" client may provide solace and important support, as in the following case:

Case 3.1. Mark L. was a social worker at an outpatient clinic that provides clinical services to armed forces veterans. One of Mr. L.'s clients was Sam T., fifty-seven, who was being treated for anxiety symptoms associated with post-traumatic stress disorder.

Mr. L. was also a veteran, and he had grown disillusioned with his career. He had been turned down for promotions several times and was feeling alienated from his colleagues. Also, Mr. L.'s twenty-three-year marriage had recently ended, and he was estranged from his two children. Mr. L. was very lonely and isolated and started drinking heavily (he was a recovering alcoholic). In general, Mr. L. was feeling burned out.

During their work together, Mr. L. and Mr. T. learned they had a number of interests in common. They were both divorced and felt jaded about their jobs. Both felt eager for a fresh start in life—new relationships, new jobs, and a change of scenery.

As their professional work together began to wind down, Mr. L. mentioned to Mr. T. that they might enjoy spending some time together socially. Mr. T. responded enthusiastically, and the two first arranged to go to a local football game together. Before long, Mr. L. and Mr. T. were spending considerable social time together, having dinner, going to movies, fishing, and taking day trips to local attractions.

All friendships between practitioners and former clients do not necessarily arise from a practitioner's personal struggles, crises, or deep-seated pathology; rather, they may develop because of the practitioner's wish to maintain the close emotional connection established during the professional–client relationship, as in the following example:

Case 3.2. Mary Anne V. was a counselor at a group psychotherapy practice. One of her clients was a forty-two-year-old woman, Alberta D., who sought counseling to help her decide whether to abandon her long-term career to pursue new interests. Ms. V. identified with Ms. D.'s dilemma, because she had gone through a similar process when she had left her career in business to pursue graduate-level education in the counseling field.

Ms. V. and Ms. D. often commented about how they were "on the same wavelength." Ms. D. once told Ms. V., "Gee, I feel like we've known each other for years. Have you noticed how often we're able to finish each other's sentences, as if we're reading each other's mind?" Ms. V. responded by saying how she agreed that they seemed to have very similar perspectives on life.

At the conclusion of their counseling, Ms. D. asked whether they might be able to stay in touch as friends. In fact, Ms. V. was quite interested in maintaining contact with Ms. D. Although Ms. V. recognized that it was typically unwise for counselors to maintain friendships with former clients, she believed that this particular situation was unique. Ms. V. regarded Ms. D. as an unusually mature client who would not have difficulty handling a shift in their relationship from professional–client to friendship.

Attitudes vary among practitioners about entering into friendships with clients. In their survey of a large sample of randomly selected members of the American Psychological Association Division 29 (Psychotherapy), Pope, Tabachnick, and Keith-Spiegel (1995) found that only 6.4 percent believed that developing a social friendship with a former client was "unquestionably not ethical." Nearly half (51.1 percent) stated that such relationships could be ethical "under rare circumstances," and nearly 30 percent stated that such relationships could be ethical "under many circumstances" or were "unquestionably ethical." More than half the sample reported having begun a social friendship with a former client. In contrast, Jayaratne, Croxton, and Mattison (1997) found in their survey of clinical social workers that about one-fifth (21 percent) believed that it is appropriate to develop a friendship with a client; approximately the same percentage (21.2 percent) reported having actually developed such a friendship.

As with sexual relationships between practitioners and clients, friendships between professionals and clients can be harmful. Former clients who become a practitioner's friend may wish to resume counseling to address new or reemerging issues in their lives. The friendship between the parties likely would interfere with the practitioner's ability to provide truly professional, unbiased, and impartial service. Having to locate and initiate counseling with a new practitioner — starting all over again — could be costly to the client both financially and emotionally. In addition, practitioners who develop friendships with clients or former clients expose themselves to significant legal risks. In one case ("Counselor, Counseling Center" 1997), for example, a client and her twin daughters went to a mental health clinic for counseling and family therapy. The client developed a close personal relationship with the counselor, which included family trips together. The client eventually sued the counselor and the clinic for harm, alleging that "the defendants had mismanaged her transference phenomenon and that the plaintiff would require future treatment and hospitalization due to the defendants' negligence" (6). The parties settled the case for $315,000.

Even practitioners with the best of intentions, and whose motives are beyond reproach, risk harming clients by confusing the boundaries with a friendship. As Bograd (1993, cited in Corey and Herlihy 1997:185) observes,

> The basic argument against dual relationships goes something like this: the hierarchical nature of the therapist-client or teacher-student relationship, which seems a necessary aspect of the professional encounter, undermines the truly equal consent to the nonprofessional connection. Even an ethical practitioner may unconsciously exploit or damage clients or students, who are inherently vulnerable in the relationship. Once the clarity of professional boundaries has been muddied, there is a good chance for confusion, disappointment and disillusionment on both sides.

Unconventional Interventions

A significant number of ethics complaints and lawsuits filed against human service professionals allege boundary violations arising from a practitioner's use of intervention approaches that are variously described as unconventional, nontraditional, and unorthodox (Austin, Moline, and Williams 1990; Barker and Branson 2000; Reamer 1994b, 1998a). In substantiated cases, evidence often shows that the practitioner introduced the unethical or negligent intervention in part to meet her or his own emotional needs. The following diverse cases illustrate this phenomenon:

Case 3.3. The *Daily News-Herald* of Harrisonburg, Virginia reported that a former client sued a clinical social worker, claiming that the social worker had violated the client's boundaries (Barr 1997). The lawsuit, which sought $400,000 in compensatory damages and $350,000 in punitive damages, alleged that the social worker had used "past life regression" and what the social worker called spiritual "guides and masters" as treatment techniques. The claim also asserted that the client often had been under the influence of medication during clinical sessions, at the social worker's request, and that the social worker had involved the client in nontherapeutic discussion groups in which the social worker was personally involved. The client further claimed that the social worker had taken the client flying in a plane he rented. The state Board of Social Work found that the social worker had not kept "appropriate therapeutic boundaries" with the client because he had invited her to join a nontherapeutic discussion group in which he was involved, visited her in the hospital where she was being treated for an unspecified illness, and lent her money.

Case 3.4. The *New York Times* reported that a child psychiatrist who was a third-year resident disclosed in a therapy session with his own treating psychiatrist that he was a pedophile and had gone to South America to "find a nice child" (Bruni 1998). Four months later, according to the news report, the psychiatric resident molested a ten-year-old boy at a Connecticut hospital. According to court records, the offending psychiatrist would turn out the lights to play hide-and-seek; upon finding the child, the psychiatrist would rub his groin against the boy's buttocks while holding the boy's hands behind his back. The boy testified, "I felt really disgusting. I felt nasty. It changed me so much. I still don't feel like me. I don't know who the hell I am sometimes."

Case 3.5. A thirty-seven-year-old woman sought counseling from a counseling psychologist. During their first clinical session, the woman reported that she had a history of unsuccessful relationships with men and wanted to explore whether an underlying personality issue might account for this distressing pattern. The client ultimately sued the psychologist, alleging that he had encouraged her to watch pornographic videos as part of her "treatment." The former client said that the psychologist had attempted to convince her that one of her underlying clinical issues stemmed from her discomfort with her own sexuality and that viewing pornographic videos with her therapist would help her address that chronic issue. She claimed that she and the psychologist had watched pornographic videos together on six occasions; the two did not have sexual contact with each other, however.

The psychologist initially claimed that his treatment approach, while admittedly unconventional, was defensible as a legitimate therapeutic intervention designed to enhance his client's comfort with her sexuality. The psychologist's testimony during his trial revealed that in fact he had been treated in the past for paraphilia (engaging in bizarre acts to achieve sexual arousal).

Case 3.6. A forty-two-year-old woman sought counseling from a social worker to address issues stemming from sexual molestation she had experienced as a child. The client reported that recently she had been in counseling with a licensed counselor in the community but felt she had not been making progress.

About two months into their professional–client relationship, the client disclosed to the social worker that she had terminated her therapy with the counselor for other major reasons. She explained that although the therapy with the counselor began normally, over time the counselor had engaged in a series of behaviors that the client eventually found deeply disturbing. According to the client, the counselor seemed to become more and more attached to her emotionally and wanted to become more and more involved in her daily life. The client disclosed pertinent details, including allegations that during a six-month period the counselor had several candle-light dinners with the client in the counselor's home, exchanged expensive gifts with the client, traveled with the client to attend a professional meeting, shared a hotel room with the client while attending the meeting, went camping with the client and shared a pup tent with her, and watched movies with the client in the counselor's home.

After exploring with the social worker the clinical ramifications of these boundary violations, the client decided to file an ethics complaint against the counselor with the state licensing board and to sue her for professional negligence. The counselor responded to the formal complaints by acknowledging that these various activities had occurred and by stating that they were thoughtfully designed components of a legitimate therapeutic approach that she dubbed "reparenting therapy." In her testimony during the trial, the counselor said that in her professional opinion the client—who had not had the benefit of nurturing parents during her childhood—would benefit from the counselor's assumption of a "parental role," in which she could provide the client with "sustained, supportive, and loving care in the way that a parent should." The counselor acknowledged that she felt emotionally attached to the client but denied that her "therapeutic actions" departed significantly from acceptable standards of care. The court ultimately ruled that the counselor had violated the client's boundaries and was negligent and awarded damages. The counselor's license was revoked by the state licensing board.

———

———

Case 3.7. A forty-seven-year-old psychologist provided counseling to a forty-nine-year-old client who sought help with his recent onset of dysthymia symptoms (a mood disorder characterized by feelings of pessimism, sadness, fatigue, irritability, low self-esteem, and indecisiveness). During their work together, the psychologist and client occasionally reminisced about similar life-altering experiences they had had during the tumultuous 1960s. The two learned that they had a number of similar experiences related to rock music, sexual experimentation, and drug use.

During one clinical session, the client told the psychologist that he still enjoyed smoking marijuana as much as he had during the 1960s. The psychologist responded by telling the client that he understood because he, too, continued to enjoy smoking marijuana and found that "it's a great way to relieve stress and relax. In fact, both of us might find that a little grass would enhance the quality of the time we spend together in therapy, you know what I mean?" The client said he liked the idea: "I'd really like to join you for a joint!" Subsequently, on several occasions before the therapy ended the psychologist and client smoked marijuana together during clinical sessions.

These cases illustrate the diverse circumstances under which a human service professional's emotional issues can lead to boundary violations and crossings that arise from unconventional, unorthodox, and nontraditional interventions. In some situations—as illustrated by the cases involving pedophilia and a clinician's use of pornography—practitioners may use these novel treatment approaches to exploit clients. Their actions have a manipulative and coercive quality. In other situations, the evidence suggests practitioner impairment that leads to boundary problems, although little or no evidence of intentional exploitation may exist. In the latter circumstances, practitioners may believe, typically in a delusional and self-deceptive way, that the nontraditional and unorthodox intervention may be in the client's best interest. The practitioners' lack of insight concerning the likely harmful consequences—both for clients and themselves—is often a clear sign of the depth of their impairment.

We must acknowledge differences of opinion among professionals about the use of nontraditional and unorthodox treatment approaches. For example, Jayaratne, Croxton, and Mattison (1997) found that more than two-fifths of their sample of clinical social workers believed that praying with a client is appropriate; nearly one-fifth of the group reporting having done so. Three-fifths of the sample stated that using techniques such as tai chi chuan and yoga is appropriate, although only 15 percent reported having used these

.niques with clients. In contrast, only 4 percent of the sample said that using psychic readings or astrology as a treatment approach is appropriate; virtually none (0.5 percent) reported having used such techniques. Pope, Tabachnick, and Keith-Spiegel (1995) found that about three-fifths of their sample of psychologists believed that leading nude group therapy or "growth" groups is never ethical; only 7 percent said that such activity is ethical under many circumstances or unquestionably ethical.

Self-disclosure

When I conduct workshops related to boundary and other ethical issues, I often ask the audience of human service professionals how many of them have disclosed to clients personal information about themselves or their families. Typically, the majority raise their hands. What the subsequent discussion reveals, inevitably, is that despite this common practice, professionals have widely varying opinions about the circumstances under which self-disclosure is appropriate, the extent to which personal details should be shared with clients, the content of appropriate self-disclosures, and the clinical ramifications.

This diversity of opinion is reflected in research data as well. Pope, Tabachnick, and Keith-Spiegel (1995) found that more than two-thirds (69 percent) of their sample of clinical psychologists reported that using self-disclosure as a therapy technique is ethical under many circumstances or unquestionably ethical. Only 2 percent stated that such self-disclosure is never ethical. Further, nearly three-fourths of the sample reported having used self-disclosure at least sometimes; about one-third stated that they used self-disclosure fairly or very often. Senger (1994) argues that self-disclosure by therapists can sometimes be used deliberately in effective ways:

> My 30 years in full-time office practice have led me to some modification of my originally conservative view of self-disclosure. Often I've found that patients have benefited from, more than been burdened by, appropriate discussion of my human response to them including answering some of their questions. To do so models openness, usually facilitating rather than hampering exploration of patients' fantasies. The traditional reply, "Why do you ask?" often provokes sullen or guilty withdrawal.

To say that we therapists have successfully analyzed our idiosyncrasies away is utopian. To believe we can hide our values from observant patients is naive. To think that we can prevent our biases from influencing therapy is, at best, a hope. To claim that patients cannot process these data often underrates them. If we discuss relevant personal information, then patients can make a more informed decision about whether and how to continue their treatment. (294)

In principle, self-disclosure may occur for a variety of reasons. In some cases—which I will discuss in chapter 5—practitioners may self-disclose in an effort to be helpful—for example, when a clinician attempts to empathize with a grieving client whose parent has just died by making a reference to his own experience when his parent died. A clinician may believe sincerely that the client would benefit from the clinician's carefully constructed and handled disclosure. As Senger (1994) asserts,

> Obviously there can be too much therapist openness: disclosure is not for therapist aggrandizement nor to begin the well-known slide down the "slippery-slope." Like all tools, disclosure can be abuse. Yet I wonder how often we therapists are protecting primarily ourselves when we try so hard to conceal all because that is supposedly "best for the patient." Perhaps we could discuss with (nonanalytic) patients what might be helpful for them to know about us, as well as why they are curious. I do not believe risk management should put the burden of proof on therapists who disclose relevant personal information more than on therapists who conceal it and who thereby limit informed consent.
>
> A second (and more important reason) for exploring countertransference with selected patients is its therapeutic value. To limit patient discussion to an intrapsychic focus sacrifices the rich enlightenment obtained through a mutual interpersonal exploration of the therapeutic relationship. We often wait too long—until provoked to desperation by a borderline patient. Not wanting to "burden" the patient with our countertransference, we use self-disclosure as a last resort—to learn with relief that the patient, too, is relieved and responds. Countertransference disclosures can be of great benefit (if less dramatic) with nonborderline patients as well. Let us not exclude "high-level" patients from interpersonal enlightenment as a price they must pay for being healthier. (294)

Gutheil and Gabbard (1993) express a similar sentiment: "Few clinicians would argue that the therapist's self-disclosure is always a boundary crossing. Psychoanalysis and intensive psychotherapy involve intense personal relationships. A useful therapeutic alliance may be forged by the therapist's willingness to acknowledge that a painful experience of the patient is familiar to himself" (194).

In other circumstances, however, self-disclosure may occur inappropriately because of the practitioner's own deep-seated emotional or dependency needs. This may happen because of the clinician's (perhaps unconscious) wish to establish a personal relationship with the client; sharing personal details may be a way to set this process in motion. As Gutheil and Gabbard (1993) observe,

> When a therapist begins to indulge in even mild forms of self-disclosure, it is an indication for careful self-scrutiny regarding the motivations for departure from the usual therapeutic stance. Gorkin observed that many therapists harbor a wish to be known by their patients as a "real person," especially as the termination of the therapy approaches. While it may be technically correct for a therapist to become more spontaneous at the end of the therapeutic process, therapists who become more self-disclosing as the therapy ends must be sure that their reasons for doing so are not related to their own unfulfilled needs in their private lives but, rather, are based on an objective assessment that increased focus on the real relationship is useful for the patient in the termination process. (194)

In some instances, then, a clinician may be so absorbed or overwhelmed by his or her own personal issues, perhaps as a result of problematic countertransference, that the clinician leaks personal information and details without recognizing that the leak is occurring or without a sense of its inappropriateness. The following case illustrates inappropriate self-disclosure that occurs because of a practitioner's unmet needs:

Case 3.8. Jim L. was a school social worker who provided counseling services to students enrolled in three urban high schools. Mr. L. worked primarily with students with learning disabilities and significant behavioral problems. He provided one-on-one counseling to students, led sev-

eral treatment groups, and worked with a number of the students' parents
to address home-based issues that might be contributing to the youths'
difficulties.

One of Mr. L.'s clients was a sixteen-year-old named Mark, who had
been suspended by the school on two occasions for fighting. Mark had
also been arrested when a teacher found Mark threatening another student with a knife.

In addition to meeting weekly with Mark, Mr. L. met with Mark's
mother, who had divorced Mark's father shortly after Mark's birth. Mark's
mother, Ms. M., shared considerable detail with Mr. L. about the family's
struggles, including Mark's abandonment by his father, Mark's premature
birth (which contributed to his learning disabilities), and Ms. M.'s isolation after recently moving to this community.

Over the course of several months, Mr. L., who was single, became
attached to Mark and his mother. Mr. L. sensed accurately that he was
having a major positive influence on Mark and that Ms. M. was also
finding Mr. L.'s advice helpful. Mr. L. was beginning to feel as if he was
assuming the role of a father figure in Mark's life; on occasion, he fan-
tasized about developing a relationship with Mark's mother and assuming
the father role more formally.

Mr. L. was unaware that he spent increasing amounts of time with
Ms. M. in sharing personal information, such as his single status and that
he enjoyed some of the same kinds of activities that Ms. M. had said she
enjoyed (such as ballroom dancing and bird-watching). Unconsciously,
Mr. L. was offering Ms. M. personal tidbits somewhat flirtatiously and in
an effort to pique Ms. M.'s interest in a more intimate relationship. His
self-disclosure reflected his own emotional needs more than his client's.

———————

Practitioner self-disclosure is clearly inappropriate in some instances and,
handled judiciously and circumspectly, may be appropriate in others. Realistically, some circumstances will always fall in a middle range that is
difficult to assess; these are the cases in which thoughtful and reasonable
practitioners may disagree, in part because of their different training and
ideological orientations. Smith and Fitzpatrick (1995) capture this reality:

> In certain circumstances . . . self-disclosure by the therapist can be a
> powerful intervention, and many contemporary schools of psycho-

therapy encourage its practice (see Stricker & Fisher, 1990, for a comprehensive review). The hallmark of appropriate self-disclosure is that it is done for the client's benefit within the context of the therapeutic process. Used as a tool to instruct or illustrate, the therapist's disclosure of some past event or problem can help the client overcome barriers to therapeutic progress (Dryden, 1990; Lane & Hull, 1990). Informing the client about personal conditions that might cause interruptions, such as illness or pregnancy, may also be necessary (Land & Hull, 1990; Simon, 1991). Disclosures by the clinician that are generally not considered suitable include details of current problems or stressors, personal fantasies or dreams, and social, sexual, or financial circumstances (Gutheil & Gabbard, 1993; Simon, 1991).

These distinctions, which seem clear-cut on paper, can become murky in practice. Consider the case of a young graduate student in therapy for 18 months who becomes pregnant by her new boyfriend. She comes to her session trying to resolve the question of whether to have an abortion, which she considers the rational choice given her life circumstances, or to keep the baby, which she wants. Her therapist, a married woman in her early 40's who recently miscarried after trying to conceive for many years, is aware of being too emotionally invested in the decision. In the course of the session, the client says to the therapist, "I feel as if you want me to have this baby." Does the therapist disclose the fact that her professional objectivity has been compromised? Would disclosure help the client by allowing her to weigh the therapist's bias into her decision or would it hinder her by adding another consideration to an already complex problem? Judging what is of benefit to the client is an ideal that can be very difficult to practice. (503)

Affectionate Communications

I have encountered a number of instances when a human service professional decides to send a client or former client a warm, affectionate note. Typically these messages are sent on personal stationery, not on professional letterhead. In addition, the notes are usually handwritten rather than typed. The practitioner's choice of this informal style of communication in itself often sends a signal that the message is more personal than professional.

Affectionate communications can occur for a variety of reasons, some of which seem quite appropriate and ethical and some of which do not. Sending a client (or former client) a condolence note following the death of someone close to the client is an example of a warm, informal message that most practitioners would consider appropriate. Sending such a message on agency letterhead may be unnecessarily and insensitively cold and stiff.

In other situations, however, warmly and affectionately worded notes on personal stationery may communicate to a client that the practitioner is interested in something other than a professional–client relationship.

Case 3.9. Mildred D. was a counselor in a family service agency. Most of her clients were referred by the personnel office of the local city government in conjunction with its employee assistance program. City employees who were having job-related problems that might be addressed through counseling—for example, declining job performance associated with an employee's alcohol abuse or marital difficulties—were referred to Mildred D. and one of her colleagues.

One of Ms. D.'s clients was a midlevel administrator in the city's parks and recreation department. The client, Barbara S., was referred by her supervisor because of the supervisor's concerns about Ms. S.'s frequent absences and deterioration in the quality of her work. Ms. S. acknowledged to Ms. D. that indeed she was having some serious problems in her life, associated primarily with her recent divorce and child custody dispute with her former husband. Ms. S. also reported an ongoing and troubling conflict she was having with one of her co-workers, Melanie N. It happens that Melanie N. was also a client of Ms. D., having been referred to the employee assistance program by her supervisor because of her problem with alcoholism.

Ms. D. helped Ms. S. identify counseling goals that might help her function more productively in her personal and professional life. They met weekly for about three months and accomplished a great deal. Ms. S. and Ms. D. then terminated their working relationship; Ms. D. wrote a favorable report to Ms. S.'s supervisor.

By the end of their work together, Ms. S. and Ms. D. had developed a close relationship. In fact, Ms. D. told Ms. S. during their last session that she would truly miss their meetings, that Ms. S. had become one of Ms. D.'s "special" clients.

For months after the termination of their professional–client relationship, Ms. D. found herself thinking about Ms. S. and fantasizing about having a friendship with her. About six months after their working relationship terminated, Ms. D. decided to write Ms. S. a casual note on informal stationery, mainly to say hello and to wish Ms. S. well. At the end of the note, Ms. D. wrote: "So, I hope this note finds you well and that you're as content as you were when we last saw each other. I have great faith in your ability to manage life's challenges. You really are very special to me; I hope, somehow, we will be able to share time together in the future. P.S. Last week I saw Melanie. I guess you know she's having big problems again. I gather she may have relapsed. I hope this doesn't affect you."

Ms. S. felt honored by Ms. D.'s note and Ms. D.'s willingness to confide in her about one of her other clients; however, she also felt somewhat confused about Ms. D.'s intentions. She was not sure whether Ms. D. was reaching out to her in an effort to begin a friendship.

This case illustrates how a practitioner can lose sight of appropriate boundaries with a client to whom she feels emotionally attached. The clinician's informal written communication not only suggested a dual relationship that her former client found confusing (albeit flattering) but also breached the confidentiality of another of the clinician's clients, an additional indicator of the inappropriate breach of boundaries in this case.

A gesture as seemingly innocuous as sending a client a holiday card can also be problematic. On the surface, it may appear that the card is sent as a reflection of social custom. However, some clients may interpret from this message—particularly if the return address reveals that the card was sent from the practitioner's home—that the practitioner is treating the client as special and is interested in more than a professional relationship. In fact, in some cases this is an accurate conclusion on the client's part. The holiday card may be an indirect and relatively subtle—and not always conscious— way for the clinician to address his or her emotional needs and wish to connect with a particular client on more than a professional level.

Not surprisingly, practitioners differ in their views of the appropriateness of sending holiday cards to clients. Pope, Tabachnick, and Keith-Spiegel (1995) found considerable variation among clinical psychologists' opinions. About one-fourth of their sample (23.4 percent) stated that sending holiday greeting cards to clients is unethical (although to varying degrees); however, nearly half the group said that sending holiday greeting cards is ethical under many circumstances or is unquestionably ethical. About two-fifths (37 percent) of the sample said that they had sent clients holiday greeting cards.

Community-based Contact with Clients

Human service professionals often encounter clients in the community. This may occur by happenstance—for example, when a practitioner and a client encounter each other unexpectedly in the supermarket aisle or at an athletic event—or, more predictably, for example, when practitioners and clients learn that they are members of the same community-based group or organization and can expect to run into each other at social events. In the remainder of this chapter, I will focus on community-based contact that is predictable and that may trigger issues related to a practitioner's emotional and dependency needs (for discussion of unanticipated community-based encounters, see chapter 6).

Certainly, it is reasonable for practitioners to want to pursue their personal community activities without being constrained by their relationships with clients. Ideally, practitioners' and clients' personal worlds would not intersect. Realistically, however, we know that for most practitioners community-based encounters with clients are inevitable. Although such encounters may not occur frequently, they can be laden with meaning and potential repercussions.

Case 3.10. Marsha R. was a therapist who had been in private practice for fourteen years. Ms. R. is a lesbian and is visible and active in the local lesbian community.

A number of Ms. R.'s clients are lesbians who seek her professional services because of Ms. R.'s strong reputation in the lesbian community. Many of her referrals come by word of mouth within the lesbian community.

Over time, Ms. R. has grown increasingly uncomfortable with the expanding overlap between her professional and personal worlds. It is not unusual for Ms. R. to attend a party, social gathering, or political event related to gay and lesbian issues and encounter several current clients. Ms. R. has become much more self-conscious at these events and has had difficulty just being herself. Ms. R. often feels on display, as if her clients are observing her actions and behaviors to see what their therapist is really like.

This sort of dilemma has no simple solution. In principle, Ms. R. would not knowingly put herself in a social situation that may generate complicated boundary crossings. Ms. R. understands that such boundary crossings may ultimately be confusing to clients, which could harm them emotionally. Such crossings may also be confusing to Ms. R., which could affect the quality of her work and her ability to be helpful to clients.

At the same time, Ms. R. has her own legitimate emotional and social needs. Is it realistic and fair to expect that Ms. R. would avoid all social gatherings where she has reason to believe she may encounter one or more clients? To do so would mean that Ms. R. would have to abstain from virtually all of her meaningful social activity.

How can a practitioner handle this predicament in a way that protects clients and does not require the complete forfeiture of her personal and social life? This set of circumstances contains the core ingredients of an ethical dilemma, where two or more rights and duties conflict. To use the language of the philosopher W. D. Ross (1930), this situation entails conflicts between prima facie duties. Prima facie duties entail obligations that people are inclined to meet simultaneously. When prima facie duties clash, people must attempt to determine whether rank-ordering the conflicting obligations, or some other mechanism, will lead to a way to reconcile the conflict.

Such ethical decision making has no simple formula. In such a situation, practitioners may find it useful to consult with thoughtful colleagues and supervisors, consult relevant literature and ethical standards, and so on. In some cases, a solution will be clear-cut; in other cases, practitioners and consultants are likely to disagree about what is ethical. For example, Jayaratne, Croxton, and Mattison (1997) found that about 30 percent of their sample of clinical social workers believed that participating in recreational or social activities with clients is appropriate; one-fourth of this group had engaged in such activity. Nearly three-fifths (58.7 percent) of this sample stated that serving on community boards or committees with clients is appropriate; nearly one-fourth of the sample reported having actually served on community boards or committees with clients.

The overriding concern in a situation of this sort is for the practitioner to minimize potential harm to the clients. The language in two standards contained in the NASW *Code of Ethics* (1996) is instructive:

> Social workers should be alert to and avoid conflicts of interest that interfere with the exercise of professional discretion and impartial judgment. Social workers should inform clients when a real or potential conflict of interest arises and take reasonable steps to resolve the issue in a manner that makes the clients' interests primary and protects clients' interests to the greatest extent possible. In some cases, protecting clients' interests may require termination of the professional relationship with proper referral of the client. (standard 1.06[a])

> Social workers should not engage in dual or multiple relationships with clients or former clients in which there is a risk of exploitation or potential harm to the client. In instances when dual or multiple relationships are unavoidable, social workers should take steps to protect clients and are responsible for setting clear, appropriate, and culturally sensitive boundaries. (Dual or multiple relationships occur when social workers relate to clients in more than one relationship, whether professional, social, or business. Dual or multiple relationships can occur simultaneously or consecutively.) (standard 1.06[c])

Two standards in the American Psychological Association's *Ethical Principles of Psychologists and Code of Conduct* (1992) are similarly pertinent:

> In many communities and situations, it may not be feasible or reasonable for psychologists to avoid social or other nonprofessional contacts with persons such as patients, clients, students, supervisees, or research participants. Psychologists must always be sensitive to the potential harmful effects of other contacts on their work and on those persons with whom they deal. A psychologist refrains from entering into or promising another personal, scientific, professional, financial, or other relationship with such persons if it appears likely that such a relationship reasonably might impair the psychologist's effectively performing his or her function as a psychologist, or might harm or exploit the other party. (standard 1.17[a])

If a psychologist finds that, due to unforeseen factors, a potentially harmful multiple relationship has arisen, the psychologist attempts to resolve it with due regard for the best interests of the affected person and maximal compliance with the Ethics Code. (standard 1.17[c])

The ethics standards for social work and psychology that pertain to dual and multiple relationships suggest that practitioners should approach these circumstances incrementally. Thus in case 3.10, Ms. R., the therapist, should be alert to the possibility that her simultaneous involvement with clients professionally and socially may affect her judgment and pose a risk of harm to clients. Once she becomes aware of potential harm, Ms. R. should take reasonable steps to protect clients to the greatest extent possible. Practically speaking, Ms. R. could take several measures. First, she can prevent problems by referring certain potential clients to other providers, particularly if Ms. R. has already had significant social contact with these individuals. This step would be consistent with the widely held belief that it is unethical for a practitioner to accept as a client an individual who has been a friend or close acquaintance (Jayaratne, Croxton, and Mattison 1997; Pope, Tabachnick, and Keith-Spiegel 1995). Ms. R. can explain to friends or social acquaintances who approach her for psychotherapy services that ethical standards in her profession discourage such arrangements and explain the rationale (the ways in which providing counseling services to a friend or acquaintance could prove to be harmful and not in the client's best interests).

Second, Ms. R. can take preventative steps at the beginning of her professional relationship with clients who are neither friends nor social acquaintances but who, Ms. R. anticipates, she might encounter in the community in various settings or at social events. As a matter of routine, early in the professional–client relationship Ms. R. can broach the subject of how the two can handle foreseen and unforeseen encounters they might have in the community in a way that minimizes the risk of misunderstandings, inappropriate dual relationships, and hurt feelings. Ms. R. might pose several hypothetical but plausible scenarios or encounters and discuss with the client appropriate ways of handling them. For example, if Ms. R. and her client should encounter each other at a party, in order to avoid a dual relationship and complicated boundaries they might agree that they will not spend time socializing. If Ms. R. and a client find themselves involved in some ongoing community-based activity—for example, as members of a committee sponsored by a social action group—they can agree to discuss the situation to decide whether one of them should withdraw from the activity. Third, Ms. R. can take steps to deal constructively with dual relationships that emerge after the professional–client relationship has begun. For example, Ms. R. might be surprised to learn some time after therapy has commenced that her client is part of the local lesbian community. If Ms. R. then anticipates that this could lead to a complicated dual relationship, she can bring up the subject—and reasonable ways of handling the boundary issues—in the context of a counseling session. Although these steps do not provide a simple, guaranteed solution to all challenging circumstances, the process can help minimize harm and help practitioners comply with prevailing ethical standards.

Similar complications can arise for practitioners who are active members of cultural, ethnic, or religious communities. This can occur, for example, if a Cambodian practitioner is actively involved in his community's relatively small and visible Cambodian mutual aid society, or if a therapist who is very active on her synagogue's board of directors learns that one of her clients has just been appointed to the board and to the subcommittee that the therapist chairs. These complicated possibilities are illustrated by the following case:

Case 3.11. Dianne S. was a therapist in a medium-size city. In her thriving practice, Ms. S. specializes in the treatment of children with behavioral and emotional difficulties. Ms. S. also works extensively with adoptive families, especially in relation to clinical issues pertaining to adoptees' and adoptive parents' relationships with birth parents. Ms. S.'s clinical interests and expertise in adoption-related issues stem in part from her experiences as an adoptive parent. Ms. S. has been active in an adoptive families support group and in an advocacy group that focuses on adoption-related bills introduced in the state legislature.

Because of her clinical expertise, community groups often ask Ms. S. to speak about adoption issues, particularly the emotional issues that can arise among members of adoptive families throughout the life cycle. Members of her various audiences often approach Ms. S. afterward to inquire about the possibility of arranging to see her for clinical services.

Ms. S. knows from experience that some of her clients who seek counseling for adoption-related issues may encounter her in other contexts—for example, at meetings of the adoptive parents' support group or at meetings of the legislative advocacy group in which Ms. S. is active. As a result, Ms. S. has been careful to broach the possibility of such dual relationships when embarking on counseling with clients whom she anticipates she will encounter in the community. When she begins working with clients with whom she has had no prior relationship—such as those who approach Ms. S. following her talks to community groups— Ms. S. speaks with them about how they will handle community-based encounters, should they occur; Ms. S. especially emphasizes this issue with clients who apparently travel in similar social and community circles as Ms. S.

Occasionally, Ms. S. receives a request for counseling services from adoptive parents she has come to know well through her community-based activities. In these situations, Ms. S. typically explains that it would be difficult for her to begin relating to these individuals professionally, in light of their shared social history, and why. Ms. S. then helps these individuals locate an appropriate counselor who may be helpful.

————

These examples illustrate various steps that practitioners can take to minimize any harm that might arise from a dual relationship that develops because of a practitioner's encounters with clients in social, cultural, ethnic, or religious contexts that are meaningful emotionally to client and practitioner. This risk-management strategy enhances the protection of clients and practitioners alike.

Human service practitioners embark on dual and multiple relationships for a variety of reasons. Some boundary problems reflect clear exploitation and manipulation to satisfy the practitioner's self-centered and prurient interests. Others reflect a practitioner's more subtle emotional and dependency needs, which produce dual relationships characterized by, for example, forming friendships with clients or former clients, interacting inappropriately with clients in the context of community-based groups or activities, engaging in excessive personal self-disclosure to clients, and sending clients affectionate written communications.

Preventing boundary problems associated with a practitioner's emotional and dependency needs requires diligent and sustained efforts by the practitioner to constantly examine her or his motives and intentions when behaving in ways that are not consistent with prevailing clinical and ethical standards. Practitioners must be able and willing to examine their actions in a constructively critical way and be open to feedback from colleagues and supervisors. To use the language of the trade, practitioners must be exceedingly skilled in their "use of self."

4   Personal Benefit

Some boundary and dual relationship issues emerge because of pragmatic concerns, specifically, the possibility that the practitioner's relationship with the client could produce tangible, material benefits or favors for the practitioner beyond simple monetary payment for services rendered. Some such dual relationships arise from relatively benign motives—for example, when a client with specialized knowledge or expertise offers to help a practitioner with a personal challenge—and some arise from more sinister motives—for example, when a practitioner attempts to exploit a client for material gain.

This chapter explores this wide range of circumstances, focusing on issues related to bartering for professional services, entering into business and financial relationships with clients, seeking advice or services from clients, accepting favors or gifts from a client (including client bequests), and engaging in self-interested conflicts of interest (for example, paying for referrals and soliciting clients).

Barter for Services

The majority of clients (or their insurance providers) pay fees for social services, but in a relatively small number of cases a practitioner participates in a barter arrangement when a client is unable to pay for services and offers goods or services as a substitute. Bartering also occurs in some communities that have established norms involving such nonmonetary exchange of goods and services (Reamer 1998a).

On the surface, barter may not seem to pose ethical problems if the parties participate willingly. In actuality, though, barter may lead to troubling ethical questions (not to mention complicated issues when practitioners file their tax returns).

Case 4.1. A psychologist in private practice provided counseling services to a forty-six-year-old man who had been diagnosed with symptoms of an anxiety disorder. In general, the client functioned well; he was married and actively involved in the parenting of his two teenage children. He was concerned, however, about the family's finances; the client's income was derived primarily from his work on construction sites, and construction had been slow in the local area because of a recent economic downturn. During the winter, the family sometimes struggled to pay the bills, although the client occasionally earned extra income by plowing snow. With the counselor's help, the client embarked on a constructive strategy to manage his anxiety symptoms.

The client's insurer authorized seven counseling sessions. The company was not willing to authorize additional sessions, despite the counselor's detailed explanation of the client's emerging progress and wish for additional assistance. In an effort to be helpful to the client, the counselor offered to work out an arrangement by which the client would perform some badly needed repairs in the practitioner's office (putting up drywall in an unfinished area of the office, putting down ceramic tile, painting and plastering) in exchange for counseling services. The client agreed to the proposal, and, after some discussion about the fair market value of the client's services, the two determined the number of counseling sessions that would be bartered for them (the fair market value for the construction services divided by the counselor's customary hourly fee).

About six weeks after the client finished his work, and while the client was still in counseling, the counselor noticed a major defect in the tile floor that the client had laid. The floor was uneven, and several tiles had cracked or were loose. Apparently the surface had not been prepared properly before the tile was laid.

The counselor, assuming that the client would willingly repair the defect, shared his concerns with the client. The client acknowledged the problem but denied that he was responsible. The client claimed that the subflooring must have had a latent defect that neither party knew about. The client agreed to try to fix the problem but said that he might not be able to do the work for several months because he had recently started work on a new construction site. The counselor grew increasingly frustrated with the client's handling of the situation. In his peer consultation group, the counselor acknowledged that his feelings about the client's behavior were affecting the professional relationship.

———

This case illustrates what can be ethically problematic in barter arrangements. Negotiations about the fair market value of the goods or services to be exchanged and, in particular, about the handling of defects in a product or service can interfere with the professional–client relationship in a way that is harmful to the client. In addition, the services the practitioner provides may be determined in whole or in part by the market value of the goods or services provided by the client rather than by the client's clinical needs. Especially because the client may be dependent on the practitioner, and because of the unequal power in their relationship, the client may be vulnerable to exploitation, conflicts of interest, and coercion. As Peterson (1996, cited in Woody 1998:174) notes, "Bartering exposes the psychologist to all of the potential problems of any nonsexual dual relationship. Psychologists who barter with clients risk exploitation of the client by accepting goods and services that may be worth an undetermined amount or much more than the market value of therapy."

Practitioners are in some disagreement about the extent to which barter arrangements in the human services should be permitted. Some practitioners are clearly opposed to barter. Woody (1998), for example, asserts, "Although bartering is not prohibited by ethics or law, I argue against the use of bartering for psychological services. In point of fact, bartering seems so fraught with risks for both parties that it seems illogical even to consider it as an option" (176).

Other practitioners, however, argue that barter is ethical, particularly in communities where it is an accepted practice (for example, where farmers in rural areas exchange produce for plumbing or electrician services). Nearly two-fifths (38.3 percent) of a sample of clinical social workers stated that it is appropriate for clinicians to accept goods or services from clients instead of money; almost 10 percent of this sample (9.5 percent) reported that they had actually accepted goods or services from clients in exchange for professional services (Jayaratne, Croxton, and Mattison 1997). Only one-fifth (22.6 percent) of a sample of psychologists who are psychotherapists stated that accepting services from a client in lieu of a fee is unquestionably unethical, and about one-third (31.1 percent) reported having accepted such services (Pope, Tabachnick, and Keith-Spiegel 1995). An even smaller percentage of this group believed that accepting goods, rather than money, for payment is unquestionably unethical, and about one-third (31.8 percent) reported having accepted such goods.

Professional ethics codes provide some guidance on this issue. For example, after much discussion the NASW Code of Ethics Revision Committee concluded that categorically prohibiting barter arrangements between social workers and clients would be inappropriate. Rather, the committee took the position that social workers should avoid bartering and that they should accept goods or services from clients as payment for professional services only in limited circumstances (Reamer 1998a):

> Social workers should avoid accepting goods or services from clients as payment for professional services. Bartering arrangements, particularly involving services, create the potential for conflicts of interest, exploitation, and inappropriate boundaries in social workers' relationships with clients. Social workers should explore and may participate in bartering only in very limited circumstances when it can be demonstrated that such arrangements are an accepted practice among professionals in the local community, considered to be essential for the provision of services, negotiated without coercion, and entered into at the client's initiative and with the client's informed consent. Social workers who accept goods or services from clients as payment for professional services assume the full burden of demonstrating that this arrangement will not be detrimental to the client or the professional relationship. (standard 1.13[b])

The American Psychological Association's *Ethical Principles of Psychologists and Code of Conduct* (1992) conveys a similar sentiment: "Psychologists ordinarily refrain from accepting goods, services, or other nonmonetary remuneration from patients or clients in return for psychological services because such arrangements create inherent potential for conflicts, exploitation, and distortion of the professional relationship. A psychologist may participate in bartering only if (1) it is not clinically contraindicated, and (2) the relationship is not exploitative" (standard 1.18). Further, the American Counseling Association's *Codes of Ethics and Standards of Practice* (1995) states,

> Counselors ordinarily refrain from accepting goods or services from clients in return for counseling services because such arrangements create inherent potential for conflicts, exploitation, and distortion of the professional relationship. Counselors may participate in bartering only if the relationship is not exploitive, if the client requests it, if a clear written contract is established, and if such arrangements are an accepted practice among professionals in the community. (standard A.10.c)

Practitioners who are considering barter arrangements should carefully address several questions (Reamer 1998a). First, to what extent are such arrangements an accepted practice among professionals in the local community? The widespread local use of barter can strengthen a practitioner's contention that this was an appropriate practice in a particular case. Second, to what extent is barter essential for the provision of services? Is it used merely because it is the most expedient and convenient form of payment available, or is it the only reasonable way for the client to obtain needed services? As a general rule, barter should be a last resort, used only when more conventional forms of payment have been ruled out and only when it is essential for the provision of services. As Woody (1998) observes, "The psychologist often believes, at least consciously, that accepting a bartering arrangement is for the benefit of the client. As one psychologist said, 'The client desperately needed treatment but could not afford to pay for it—besides, I needed another car for my teenager'" (174).

Third, is the barter arrangement negotiated without coercion? Human service professionals should not pressure clients to agree to barter. For example, a client may agree reluctantly to give a practitioner a valuable jewelry item that the client's business manufactures primarily because the practitioner has commented on how much he or she would like to own such an item; in this situation, the client may feel pressured. Clients who agree to participate in a barter arrangement must do so freely and willingly, without any direct or indirect coercion from the practitioner. Fourth, was the barter arrangement entered into at the client's initiative and with the client's truly informed consent (Reamer 1987c)? To avoid coercing clients or the appearance of impropriety, practitioners typically should not take the initiative to suggest barter as an option. Such suggestions should come from clients. Practitioners who decide to barter should explain the nature and terms of the arrangement in clear and understandable language and discuss potential risks associated with barter (for example, how the professional–client relationship could be adversely affected, particularly if the goods or services provided by the client in exchange for the professional's services prove to be defective), reasonable alternatives for payment (for example, a reduced monthly payment rather than a single payment in full), the client's right to refuse or withdraw consent, and the time frame covered by the consent.

In addition to these broad questions, practitioners should heed Woody's (1998) specific risk-management guidelines:

1. Unique financial arrangements should be minimized: that is, terms and conditions for any compensation, including the use of bartering, should be as close to established practices as possible and be consonant with the prevailing standards of the profession.
2. The rationale for any compensation decision, including the use of bartering, should be documented in the case records.
3. Discussions about any financial matters should be detailed in writing, giving equal emphasis to what is said by the practitioner and the client.
4. If bartering is used, there should be a preference for goods instead of services; this will minimize (but not eliminate) the possibility of inappropriate personal interactions.
5. The value of the goods (or services) should be verified by an objective source; this may, however, involve additional cost.
6. To guard against any semblance of undue influence, both parties should reach a written agreement for the compensation by bartering.
7. Any new, potentially relevant observations or comments about compensation by bartering should be entered into the client's records, even though a previous agreement exists.
8. The agreement should contain a provision for how valuations were determined and how any subsequent conflicts will be resolved (e.g., a mediator); this may, however, involve additional cost (and a concern about confidentiality), which will have to be accom-

modated by the practitioner (i.e., the added expense should not elevate the cost to the client beyond the established fee for service).

9. If a misunderstanding or disagreement begins to develop, the matter should be dealt with by the designated conflict resolution source (e.g., a mediator), not the practitioner and client; again, recall the issues of added cost and concern for confidentiality stated in the preceding guideline.

10. If monitoring by the individualized treatment plan reveals a possible negative effect potentially attributable to the compensation arrangement, it should be remedied or appropriate termination of the treatment relationship should occur. (177)

Woody is quick to caution, however, that even if the practitioner "adheres strictly to these guidelines, bartering still imposes a high risk of allegation of misconduct" (178).

Human service professionals must recognize that even when all these conditions have been met, the practitioner assumes the full burden of demonstrating that bartering will not be detrimental to the client or the professional relationship (Gutheil and Gabbard 1993). Their principal responsibility is to protect the client: practitioners must exercise sound judgment when considering the risks associated with barter.

Business and Financial Relationships

In a relatively small percentage of cases, human service professionals are accused of entering into inappropriate business and financial relationships with clients. This can occur in several ways. First, clients sometimes raise issues in counseling about their own financial conditions and futures. Some clients are in financial distress and send out signals that they are eager for assistance. For a practitioner to respond instantaneously with the offer of a loan would be highly unusual, but practitioners who have crossed boundaries with a client for other reasons or in other ways—for example, to pursue a friendship or romantic relationship—may end up lending a client money as part of the broader dual relationship.

Case 4.2. Sam G. was a psychiatrist who provided medication, advice, and counseling to Anna C., a woman who sought his help because of her symptoms of depression. Over a period of months, the relationship between Dr. G. and Ms. C. moved gradually from a purely professional–client relationship to a sexual affair.

During the course of their affair, Ms. C. received a notice of foreclosure on her home. Because of her depression, Ms. C. had missed a considerable amount of work. As a result, she was fired from the insurance company where she had been employed and fell behind on her mortgage payments. Ms. C. owed her bank approximately $4,800. After Ms. C. disclosed the foreclosure to Dr. G., he wrote Ms. C. a check for the amount she owed the bank, plus late fees.

After their intimate relationship fell apart, Ms. C. filed an ethics complaint and lawsuit against Dr. G. One piece of evidence introduced in court by Ms. C.'s attorney, in her effort to demonstrate the psychiatrist's negligent handling of boundary issues, was a photocopy of the canceled check that Dr. G. had made out to Ms. C.

———

In other situations, a practitioner may encounter a client who is in counseling to think through a midlife career change that involves establishing a new business that requires venture capital. From this conversation may come a client's invitation for the counselor, for whom the client feels great appreciation, to invest in this new opportunity.

———

Case 4.3. Diane P. was a counselor in a small group practice. One of Ms. P.'s clients was a fifty-two-year-old man, Allen F., who was coping with what he described as "your all-purpose, predictable midlife crisis." Mr. F. explained to Ms. P. that he was "just plain tired of getting up in the morning and repeating the rhythm of yesterday, and the day before, and the day before, and . . . oh, you get the idea. I really need a fresh challenge, something that would make me want to jump out of bed in the morning." During counseling sessions, Mr. F. and Ms. P. spent time talking about what was holding Mr. F. back from pursuing his dream of a major change.

After several months of exploration, Mr. F. reported to Ms. P. that he had finally settled on a new and exciting venture: Mr. F. was planning to work with a local consultant he had met to design and inaugurate an Internet-based business that makes books available to college students electronically. Mr. F. described how excited he was and the terrific financial returns he expected from this cutting-edge venture. Mr. F. explained that he would need to spend several months recruiting a handful of investors who would likely enjoy a remarkable return on their initial minimum investment of $25,000.

Mr. F. then paused and asked whether Ms. P. might be interested in "getting in on this wonderful opportunity at the front end." Ms. P. said that she would like to take some time to think about the offer. In fact, Ms. P. had become quite interested recently in investing some of her money outside the traditional stock market.

———

Finally, on occasion practitioners who are experiencing their own personal financial problems have disclosed this fact (inappropriately) to clients of means, hoping—perhaps unconsciously—that the client would offer to help the practitioner out financially.

———

Case 4.4. Malcolm A. was a marriage and family therapist. Dr. A. also sponsored monthly "marriage encounter" groups for local couples who were interested in spending "intensive weekends" designed to nurture and strengthen their marriages.

Sarah and John H. signed up for one of Dr. A.'s marriage encounter sessions. During the weekend, Dr. A and the couple found that they both had children attending the same college about 150 miles away. Shortly after the marriage encounter weekend, the couple called Dr. A. to ask whether they could see him "for several sessions to talk about some issues that emerged during their marriage encounter experience." They saw Dr. A. for six sessions to discuss some issues concerning their communication styles and patterns.

After the fourth session, the couple called Dr. A. and asked him whether he might want to travel with them when they drove to the parents' weekend at the college their respective children attended. Dr. A., who enjoyed their company, agreed, and the trio spent a lovely weekend traveling to and from the college campus.

During the long drive, Dr. A. told the couple how much he enjoyed his work as a marriage and family therapist. He mentioned that the only drawback was that with current managed care reimbursement policies, he was having considerable difficulty making ends meet. To make matters worse, Dr. A. said, he was in considerable debt because of extraordinary expenses he had incurred during the past year when his recently deceased wife was ill and he took considerable time off from work. Dr. A. said that he was actually considering abandoning his career as a therapist, which he loves, in order to pursue more lucrative employment.

One week after their trip, the affluent couple called Dr. A. to tell him that they had decided to lend him money interest-free to help him out of his financial bind and to enable him to continue the work he loves. They explained how much they admired Dr. A.'s work and that they found his expertise helpful; they wanted to do whatever they could to help him out. Dr. A. thanked them for their generous offer and said he wanted to take some time to think about it.

———

Professionals disagree about engaging in financial transactions with clients, although most practitioners appear to oppose the practice as a matter of principle. Pope, Tabachnick, and Keith-Spiegel (1995) report that two-fifths (40.6 percent) of psychologists in their sample believed that lending money to a client is unquestionably unethical; a similar proportion (38.8 percent) believed that such a practice is ethical only under rare circumstances. An overwhelming majority of psychologists (86.2 percent) believed that borrowing money from a client is unquestionably unethical; 11 percent stated that borrowing money from clients was permissible under rare circumstances. Virtually none of these respondents said that they had ever lent clients money or borrowed money from them. This pattern is reflected as well in the views of the clinical social workers surveyed by Jayaratne, Croxton, and Mattison (1997) — only 4.4 percent said that lending or borrowing money from clients is appropriate; 6.7 percent acknowledged having engaged in such a practice. (To be fair, we do not know from these responses whether the professionals who reported having engaged in this practice included loans of modest sums — say, $3 to take public transportation home from an agency — as opposed to lending or borrowing much larger amounts of money. This distinction may be meaningful when assessing the ethics of financial transactions between practitioners and clients.)

The psychologists surveyed by Pope, Tabachnick, and Keith-Spiegel (1995) were somewhat more willing to consider entering into a business relationship with clients, although with former clients. More than one-fourth (28.9 percent) of the psychologists surveyed by Pope, Tabachnick, and Keith-Spiegel stated that going into business with a former client would be ethical under rare circumstances; about 15 percent of the group stated that such a business relationship with a former client would be ethical under many circumstances or unquestionably ethical. Approximately 13 percent of this sample reported having actually gone into business with a former client. In contrast, nearly four-fifths (78.5 percent) of these psychologists stated that going into business with a current client is unethical under all circumstances; only 2 percent of the sample reported having actually gone into business with a current client.

What these various scenarios have in common is the inappropriate blurring of boundaries and the possibility of client exploitation. Introducing financial transactions into the professional–client relationship has great potential to distract both practitioners and clients from the social service agenda with which they began their work, compromise clients' interests, and introduce conflicts of interest (where the practitioner's judgment and behavior are affected by the business and financial concerns). Such transactions can also expose practitioners to legal risk—for example, when a client files an ethics complaint against the clinician with a disciplinary board or sues the practitioner, alleging that the professional unduly influenced or manipulated the client for self-interested purposes. In a Massachusetts case ("Psychiatrist Censured," 1996), for example, a court affirmed a disciplinary board's decision to sanction a licensed psychiatrist for having engaged in multiple commercial transactions with a patient in a manner that "demonstrated deplorable clinical judgment and deviated from acceptable standards of care" (6).

In another case ("Therapist Marries Patient" 1996), the former patient married her psychiatrist and sued him six years after the marriage began; the plaintiff, who had been diagnosed with multiple personality disorder, alleged that the psychiatrist had exploited her condition for his personal benefit, staging public lectures where he charged admission and showcased her as a subject (the plaintiff was awarded $350,000 plus interest). In yet another case (Woody 1998:175), a psychologist invested a substantial sum of money in a client's new business. When the business was successful, the attorney for the client demanded that the psychologist accept a refund of the initial investment only (that is, no interest or gain), saying, "Your control of my client's mind was the only thing that got you into the deal." Whether such an allegation is true is almost irrelevant. A panel of peers on an ethics review committee or a jury could very well be influenced by the obvious appearance of impropriety.

Advice and Services

Human service professionals sometimes provide services to clients who have expertise from which the professionals themselves might benefit. This can happen under two sets of circumstances. The first occurs when a practitioner faces personal problems and challenges that might be addressed by using a client's expertise.

Case 4.5. Judy C. was a social worker who provided counseling to Miriam R., a nurse who worked at a local hospital in the maternity unit. Ms. R. sought counseling to address issues related to her recent decision to separate from her husband.

Sometimes Ms. R. would begin counseling sessions by talking about work-related stress. On several occasions, she mentioned how hard it was for her to see teenagers deliver babies, yet how gratifying it was when she was able to help a teenager make an informed decision to place her baby with an adoptive couple eager to parent.

Ms. C. and her husband had been struggling with infertility for many years. They were eager to adopt but had several private prospective adoptions fall through after pregnant women with whom they had developed a relationship changed their mind about making an adoption plan for their baby. Ms. C. was thinking seriously about asking Ms. R. whether she might be able to help her and her husband pursue the private adoption of a baby delivered at Ms. R.'s hospital.

Case 4.6. Sandy M. worked for the state child welfare agency. Her job included screening and licensing foster parents. In addition, Ms. M. was responsible for supervising several children placed in foster care.

Ms. M. interviewed and ultimately approved a license for Mr. and Mrs. J., who owned a large farm. For years, the couple had been eager to provide foster care.

Soon after the license was approved, the state agency placed a thirteen-year-old runaway girl, who was having serious conflict with her parents, with Mr. and Mrs. J. Ms. M. was responsible for supervising the placement.

Shortly after they met, the couple and Ms. M. became good friends. Mr. and Mrs. J. invited Ms. M., a single parent who was experiencing chronic financial and child care problems, to join them at their church and invited her to a number of social functions. On one occasion, they provided child care for Ms. M.'s three-year-old daughter when Ms. M. traveled out of town. In addition, they invited Ms. M. and her daughter to move into a small cottage on their vast property; Ms. M. accepted their offer. During this period, Ms. M. was still supervising the foster placement in the couple's home.

Two months after the runaway was placed in the home, she was examined by a doctor appointed by the state child welfare agency. The doctor found that the girl was pregnant. The girl then disclosed that Mr. J., the foster father, had had sexual intercourse with her on five occasions. A state-appointed lawyer for the girl sued the child welfare agency and the social worker, Ms. M., for negligence. A principal allegation was that Ms. M. had engaged in an inappropriate dual relationship with Mr. and Mrs. J.—as evidenced by her pursuing a social relationship with them, her allowing the couple to take care of her daughter while they were also functioning as foster parents for a child whose foster care Ms. M. was supervising, and her moving her residence onto their property. The plaintiff's lawyer argued that the dual relationship and boundary violations were a "proximate cause" of the injury sustained by the foster child as a result of the foster father's sexual abuse—that is, that the dual relationship impaired the social worker's professional judgment and that her failure to supervise the placement properly was a cause of the sexual abuse. The case was ultimately settled for $750,000.

The second circumstance occurs when a practitioner is eager to draw on a client's expertise, not so much to address a problem but to enhance the quality of the practitioner's life.

Case 4.7. Henry A. was a counselor with a regional program that provides services to families coping with a severely disabled relative. His primary duties entailed coordinating respite services for these families and providing crisis intervention when necessary.

One family receiving services from Mr. A. was caring for an adult child with severe autism. For years, the parents had provided loving care for their child, who was now forty-seven, but were having difficulties with some of their own health problems.

The mother, Ms. D., was a successful stockbroker. She told Mr. A. one day that she was eager to offer Mr. A. occasional stock tips, as a token of her and her husband's appreciation for the valuable services that Mr. A. had provided to their family. She invited Mr. A. to come to their home one evening to talk about his financial goals and investments he might make.

Accepting advice or services from clients has the potential to create boundary confusion. Over time, human service professionals may begin to feel indebted to their clients or eager for specialized treatment from them; this may cloud the practitioner's judgment and, ultimately, lead to the perception of compromised care, actual compromised care, conflicts of interest, exploitation, and other forms of ethical misconduct and negligence.

Favors and Gifts

Unique boundary issues sometimes emerge when clients offer gifts or special favors to human service professionals. A client's presentation of a gift to a practitioner is a particularly complex issue. Clearly, some clients offer practitioners gifts—often modest in value—as genuine expressions of appreciation, with no ulterior motive or hidden agenda. Examples include clients who give the practitioner a plate of home-baked cookies at holiday time, an infant's outfit when the counselor has had a baby, or a handmade coffee mug at the conclusion of treatment. Typically, these gifts represent tokens of appreciation—nothing more and nothing less. The client would likely feel wounded or insulted if the professional rejected such a gift on ethical grounds. In fact, only 5 percent of the sample of psychologists surveyed by Pope, Tabachnick, and Keith-Spiegel (1995) stated that accepting a gift worth less than $5 is unquestionably unethical; more than half the sample (56.6 percent) said that accepting such a gift is appropriate under many

circumstances or unquestionably appropriate. Moreover, only a small minority of the respondents (8.6 percent) stated that they had never accepted
this kind of modest gift.

In contrast, however, are more complicated situations, involving clients
who offer practitioners gifts of considerable value or gifts that represent a
more complex practitioner–client relationship (sometimes from the client's
view, sometimes from the practitioner's, and sometimes from both). Consider, for example, the following cases:

Case 4.8. Aaron C. was a psychologist in a residential program that provides services to people with substance abuse problems. One of his clients,
Marie Y., was being treated for her cocaine addiction. Ms. Y. and Dr. C.
met weekly to address a variety of pertinent issues, including her sexual
abuse history. Dr. C. helped Ms. Y. understand more clearly how her
early-life trauma contributed to her initial drug abuse.

Toward the end of their work together, Ms. Y. was having fantasies of
dating Dr. C.; she had been attracted to him for months. During their
last session, Ms. Y. gave Dr. C. an expensive watch, told him how much
he meant to her, and said she hoped that they would be able to spend
some time together once she returned to the "free world."

Case 4.9. Rosemary G. was a social worker in a nonresidential program
for people with developmental disabilities. One patient was a thirty-five-
year-old man, Al K., who had serious brain impairment. Ms. G. provided
case management services and supportive counseling to Mr. K. She also
met with Mr. K.'s parents sporadically to provide them with information
about their son's status and care.

Mr. K.'s parents were eager to have their son placed in a residential
program. His condition was deteriorating, and the parents were finding
it more and more difficult to care for him. Ms. G. explained that it would
be very difficult for her to recommend that Mr. K. be placed in the
agency's residential program, given the current criteria for admission. Ms.
G. told his parents that she would have to really exaggerate the signifi-

cance of his symptoms in order to justify admission, and she was not comfortable doing that.

One week later, Ms. G. received a note from the parents letting her know how much they appreciated her efforts. The note also said that they hoped "you can find it in your heart to do what you can to help Al get into that program." Also inside the envelope were three $100 bills.

In both cases, the gift givers had ulterior motives in mind. One party hoped the gift might lead to an intimate relationship, and the other party hoped their gift—essentially a bribe—might influence the practitioner to provide special assistance or favoritism. Clearly, in both cases the practitioner would have to find a tactful way to return the gift, explaining why it would be inappropriate to accept it.

On occasion, a client will give a practitioner an expensive gift with no strings or ulterior motive. Clients of means—and sometimes clients with modest assets—will feel moved to give a practitioner a gift as a gesture of pure, unadulterated generosity.

Case 4.10. Don S. was a counselor in a day program for senior citizens. One of his clients, Mildred P., was a spry eighty-seven-year-old who had attended the program daily for six years. Ms. P. often told her children how special and helpful Mr. S. was to her. Mr. S. and Ms. P. often talked about their shared love of art; Ms. P. was known locally for her large and valuable art collection.

Ms. P.'s health deteriorated badly, and it became clear to her and her two adult children that she would need a nursing home placement. Mr. S. helped Ms. P.'s children locate and assess the suitability of several local facilities. He went above and beyond the call of duty to spend time with Ms. P. and her children as they made their decision.

Several days after Ms. P. entered a nursing home, Mr. S. received a large special-delivery package. He was surprised to find that the P. family had sent him a small sculpture by an internationally famous artist, as a token of their heartfelt appreciation. The art had been in Ms. P.'s personal collection. Mr. S. estimated that the market value of the sculpture was about $7,500.

Most practitioners agree that in many instances—when there is no evidence of ulterior motives that might lead to egregious boundary violations—human service professionals may keep gifts of modest value. Some social service agencies permit staff to do so, although they may stipulate that staff members must thank the clients on behalf of the agency. That is, making it clear that the gift will be shared with the agency's staff at large can defuse the interpersonal dynamic and potential boundary confusion between the client and practitioner; this depersonalization of the transaction may help staff members to avoid complicated boundary issues.

In contrast, the psychologists surveyed by Pope, Tabachnick, and Keith-Spiegel (1995) were generally inclined to believe that accepting expensive gifts was unethical. About one-third of the group (34.2 percent) stated that accepting a client's gift worth at least $50 was unquestionably unethical, and a similar portion (36.2 percent) stated that doing so was ethical only under rare circumstances. Only about 12 percent of the sample stated that accepting a gift of this sort was ethical under many circumstances or unquestionably ethical; nearly three-fourths of the sample (72.1 percent) stated that they had never accepted this kind of gift. Similarly, only a small fraction (2.3 percent) of the clinical social workers surveyed by Jayaratne, Croxton, and Mattison (1997) stated that accepting expensive gifts from clients was appropriate, and few (1.9 percent) reported having ever accepted such gifts.

Practitioners face unique challenges when they receive gifts that appear to have no ulterior motive but could introduce complex boundary issues. Sometimes clients may not be consciously aware of the emotional meaning and significance—and the mixed messages and complications—that may be attached to a gift. Practitioners sometimes face double-edged swords in these situations: a decision to reject a gift can have significant clinical repercussions—because the client may feel hurt, wounded, humiliated, or guilty—and a decision to accept a gift may trigger boundary issues that complicate and reverberate throughout the clinical relationship. In such circumstances, practitioners are wise to obtain sound consultation and supervision to think through how best to handle the client's gesture, including assessing the apparent (and perhaps not so apparent) meaning behind the gift, the ethical and clinical implications, the potential responses and related consequences, and any risk-management issues (related to potential ethics complaints and lawsuits).

Similar issues can arise when clients offer meals to practitioners who provide in-home services. Typical examples include practitioners employed by home health care agencies and programs that provide in-home services for high-risk families (for example, family preservation programs that provide intensive in-home services for families following allegations of child abuse or neglect). It is not unusual in these situations for practitioners to visit a home at mealtime and to be invited to join the family at the table. In many cultures, however, sharing a meal—breaking bread—is a social and somewhat intimate event. Some family members may view the sharing of a meal as a signal that their relationship with the practitioner has moved to a new plane, one that entails social as well as professional purposes. The dynamics can be especially complicated when the family belongs to a particular ethnic or cultural group that attaches great meaning and symbolic significance to such invitations. Members of some cultural groups may be hesitant to trust a practitioner who is unwilling to break bread with the family; the practitioner's willingness to eat with family members may be an important signal that the practitioner accepts them. A practitioner who (presumably politely and diplomatically) rejects the family's meal invitation risks insulting the family, hurting its members' feelings, and so on. Here, too, discussion with colleagues and staff in advance and in anticipation of such invitations can provide critically important preventative maintenance. Role playing such scenarios as part of agency in-service training can be valuable. In one family preservation program, for example, staff members concluded that in some instances they could finesse the situation by saying they were not particularly hungry but would be happy to have a cup of tea or coffee, a gesture that tends to be far less culturally significant but that may help establish and preserve comfortable relationships with clients. With families that are more insistent, practitioners may need to explain that their employer or their profession's ethical standards prohibit this kind of activity.

In some contexts, sharing a meal with a client may be entirely acceptable. This would occur in programs where staff are expected, as part of their intervention approach, to provide services to people outside a formal office setting, perhaps at a residential facility or home. In these instances, widely accepted standards and practices in the human services would permit sharing meals with clients.

Case 4.11. Connie T. was an outreach worker in a program in a southern state that provided social services to homeless youths. Because of its warm climate, the area attracts many teenagers who have run away from home.

Many of these youths get involved in drug-related activity and prostitution once they arrive in the area.

Ms. T. spent much of her time walking the streets where these teenagers tend to congregate in an effort to develop relationships with them. In fact, Ms. T. was provided with money so she could offer meals to these youths in local fast-food restaurants. Ms. T. and her staff understood that they were much more likely to reach and connect with these youths by sitting down with them in a fast-food restaurant than by inviting the youths to come to the agency's offices for more formal meetings. That is, having meals with these youths was part of the program design.

Case 4.12. Wayne D. was a psychologist at a community mental health center. He specialized in the treatment of anxiety disorders. One of his clients was Ms. L., forty-seven, who had been diagnosed with agoraphobia. Ms. L. lived with a sister and rarely left her home. Her symptoms had become more severe after the sisters' parents died in an automobile accident.

Ms. L. was being treated with a combination of psychotropic medication, prescribed by the mental health center's psychiatrist, and psychotherapy. One technique Mr. D. was using with Ms. L. involved systematic desensitization, where Mr. D. gradually helped Ms. L. leave the house—first by opening the front door, then by moving onto the sidewalk, then out to the street, then into the car, and so on—working closely with Ms. L. at each step to help her manage her anxiety symptoms. Ms. L. had made considerable progress. As part of the treatment, Ms. L. and Mr. D. agreed that they would try to visit a nearby restaurant together for lunch.

Sometimes clients offer practitioners intangible favors, as opposed to tangible gifts. Examples include an invitation for the practitioner to attend the client's holiday party or to contact the client's relative who specializes in repairing the kind of automobile transmission trouble that the practitioner mentioned when he or she was late for a scheduled appointment. The clinical and ethical issues are similar, with one significant exception: tangible gifts that the practitioner and her or his colleagues are inclined to accept—

because of the negative clinical ramifications their refusal might entail—can be accepted by the agency instead, to minimize boundary complications between the client and the individual practitioner. This is not possible with offers that involve intangible benefits.

Case 4.13. Sally N. was a counselor with an early intervention program that provides services for children younger than three who show some signs of failure to thrive or other developmental delays. Ms. N.'s job required her to visit clients' homes, consult with them about their parenting techniques, provide crisis intervention, and offer other supportive services.

Ms. N. was scheduled to visit a client, Amy C., at 2:00 P.M. However, on her way to Ms. C.'s home, Ms. N.'s car would not shift gears. Ms. N. used her car phone to call for roadside assistance. She also called Ms. C., told her about her car problems, and said she would get to her home as soon as possible.

It turned out that she had major transmission trouble. Ms. N. had her car towed to the garage and took a taxi to Ms. C.'s home, arriving about an hour late. When she arrived, Ms. C. told Ms. N. that her sister owns a small shop that specializes in transmission repair. Ms. C. told Ms. N. that she had already asked her sister whether she could help Ms. N. and give her a "special deal" since Ms. N. had been so helpful to Ms. C. Ms. C. was very excited that she was able to arrange this kind of assistance for her counselor.

Case 4.14. Paul G. was a caseworker in a vocational training program that provides services to people who have major disabilities. Mr. G. coordinates and facilitates a variety of social services—such as counseling, food stamp and housing benefits, and health care—for the program's clients.

One of his clients was Daniel M., a forty-two-year-old who was recovering from a major stroke. Mr. G. had spent many hours helping Mr. M.'s parents identify and coordinate benefits for their son. The parents deeply appreciated Mr. G.'s efforts. As a token of their appreciation, they told Mr. G. that they would like Mr. G. and his family to use a guest apartment at their oceanfront vacation home during the upcoming July Fourth weekend.

As in any case in which a client offers a practitioner a gift or favor, human service professionals must carefully examine the potential for significant boundary problems, in the form of either boundary violations or boundary crossings. Most practitioners are likely to agree that if a client offers to get his cousin to provide the practitioner with a "special deal" on his automobile repair, the practitioner should thank the client and explain that he or she has a regular mechanic who will address the problem (assuming that is true). If the client persists, the practitioner might consider explaining why his or her profession discourages practitioners from doing business with clients' relatives or close acquaintances. As with barter arrangements, practitioners who conduct business transactions with clients' relatives or close acquaintances open the door for boundary problems, particularly if any dispute arises in regard to the goods or services involved in the transaction. Most clients will accept these responses and explanations.

Similarly, practitioners expose themselves to considerable risk if they accept a client's invitation to attend a social event or to use a client's personal property for vacation or other social purposes. Although in rare instances a practitioner's attendance at a social event (an issue I will address more fully in chapter 5) may offer therapeutic benefits for the client, in general practitioners are likely to introduce significant boundary complications if they accept. A client can easily misconstrue the practitioner's attendance. Most psychologists surveyed on the issue agreed that generally it is a mistake to accept a client's invitation to a party, although professionals disagree about where to draw the line. Pope, Tabachnick, and Keith-Spiegel (1995) found that about one-fourth of their sample (25.7 percent) believed that it is never appropriate to accept such an invitation. Slightly less than half (46.1 percent) believed that it is ethical to accept a client's invitation to a party only under rare circumstances. Three-fifths of the sample (59.6 percent) said that they have never accepted such an invitation.

Whenever a practitioner seriously considers accepting a gift or favor from a client—of whatever value or tangibility—the practitioner should consult with thoughtful colleagues and supervisors and critically examine the clinical and ethical implications (including current ethical standards and agency policy), the client's and practitioner's motives, any alternatives, and so on. The practitioner should carefully document in the case record the client's offers, the process the practitioner used to make the decision (for example, relevant consultation), the nature of the decision, and the rationale. This documentation can prove to be enormously helpful if the client or some other party raises questions about the appropriateness of the practitioner's decision.

Conflicts of Interest

One principal risk associated with dual and multiple relationships concerns conflicts of interest from which practitioners may benefit. Conflicts of interest occur when a professional's services to or relationship with a client (or former client, or other pertinent party) are compromised, or might be compromised, because of decisions or actions in relation to another client, a colleague, the professional, or some other third party. Using more formal language, a conflict of interest involves "a situation in which regard for one duty leads to disregard of another . . . or might reasonably be expected to do so" (Gifis 1991:88).

Conflicts of interest in the human services can take several forms. They may occur in the context of practitioners' relationships with clients or in their roles as community organizers, supervisors, consultants, administrators, policy officials, educators, researchers, or program evaluators. Practitioners must be careful to avoid conflicts of interest that might harm clients because of their decisions or actions involving other clients, colleagues, themselves, or third parties. Examples—illustrated in the cases that follow—include practitioners who are named in a client's will, have a financial interest in other service providers to which they refer clients, pay referral fees to colleagues, accept a referral fee, sell goods to clients, and solicit clients.

Case 4.15. A social worker employed in a hospice program, Allan S., counseled an elderly man, Sam V., who had been diagnosed with liver cancer. Mr. V., a widower, looked forward to Mr. S.'s weekly visits and over time grew close to him. Mr. V. told Mr. S. on several occasions how important their conversations were, especially because so few of Mr. V.'s friends and relatives felt comfortable talking about death and dying.

Shortly after Mr. V. died, Mr. S. received a notice from Mr. V.'s lawyer. The notice said that Mr. V. had named Mr. S. in his will, specifying that Mr. S. should receive $25,000 from Mr. V.'s estate.

Case 4.16. A counselor employed by a state department of corrections, Alma L., also administered the prison system's substance abuse treatment program as a private contractor. Ms. L. conducted treatment groups for inmates who were serving sentences for drug-related offenses, such as sale or possession of narcotics or other illegal drugs. When inmates were eligible for parole, Ms. L. made recommendations to the parole board concerning each inmate's readiness for release and, for those deemed ready, follow-up substance abuse treatment services that the board should mandate as a condition of release.

In addition to her duties with the state department of corrections, Ms. L. was a partner in a community-based substance abuse treatment program. In her job with the department of corrections, she recommended to the state parole board that parolees be referred to the community-based substance abuse treatment program with which she was affiliated; however, Ms. L. did not disclose her own affiliation with, and financial stake in, the program.

Case 4.17. Sandra T. was a psychologist in private practice. She had worked for years on the staff of a health maintenance organization that recently declared bankruptcy. Rather than look for a position with another organization, Dr. T. had decided to start a solo private practice.

To generate clients for her fledgling practice, Dr. T. sent a letter to physicians, clergy, and other agencies in the area likely to provide referrals to inform them of her new endeavor and her areas of expertise. The letter encouraged recipients to consider referring appropriate prospective clients to Dr. T. The letter also said that during the next six months she would be sending the source of each new referral a $25 gift certificate to a popular local restaurant.

Case 4.18. Pam K. was a counselor in a group practice. After obtaining her master's degree and working in the field for several years, Ms. K. became interested in the use of herbal remedies to alleviate stress and promote mental health. Ms. K. eventually became affiliated with a national herb distributor; in her spare time, Ms. K. recruited and supervised local sales representatives. Ms. K. provided her clients with literature on various herbal products and sold them to clients who wished to purchase them. Ms. K. earned commissions on the products she sold clients.

Case 4.19. Harris F., a psychologist, recently left his job at a community mental health center in order to join a group practice. Shortly before he left, he obtained a copy of the center's client mailing list. Dr. F. soon sent a letter to all the center's clients, informing them of his new practice and inviting them to contact him if they were interested in his services.

These cases broach a diverse set of issues pertaining to actual or potential conflicts of interest. As with most ethical issues, no single standard provides clear-cut guidance. In some instances, conflicts of interest are so blatant that they leave little or no room for discussion — for example, when practitioners refer clients to colleagues based on financial incentives offered by these colleagues, encourage clients to purchase profitable products from them, or extend treatment beyond what is clinically necessary in order to enhance their income from clients or third-party payers. Other instances leave room for legitimate debate — for example, whether practitioners employed in an agency should be permitted to establish a part-time private practice within the same city or county, and to what extent it is appropriate for practitioners to rely on clients for research that is not likely to benefit the clients themselves.

Several professions' codes of ethics comment on phenomena germane to conflicts of interest. For example, with regard to the issue of referrals and fees, the code of the American Psychological Association (1992) states that "when a psychologist pays, receives payment from, or divides fees with another professional other than in an employer-employee relationship, the payment to each is based on the services (clinical, consultative, administrative, or other) provided and is not based on the referral itself" (standard 1.27). Similarly, the NASW (1996) code states that "social workers are prohibited from giving or receiving payment for a referral when no professional service is provided by the referring social worker" (standard 2.06[c]). The code of the American Association for Marriage and Family Therapy (1998) states, "Marriage and family therapists do not offer or accept payment for referrals" (standard 7.1), and the American Counseling Association (1995) code states, "Counselors do not accept a referral fee from other professionals" (standard D.3.b).

Professional codes also comment on conflict-of-interest issues involving solicitation of clients. The American Psychological Association (1992) code states that "psychologists do not engage, directly or through agents, in un-invited in-person solicitation of business from actual or potential psycho-therapy patients or clients or other persons who because of their particular circumstances are vulnerable to undue influence" (standard 3.06). The American Counseling Association (1995) code states, "Counselors do not use their places of employment or institutional affiliation to recruit or gain clients, supervisees, or consultees for their private practices" (standard C.3.d). The NASW (1996) code states that "social workers should not engage in uninvited solicitation of potential clients who, because of their circum-stances, are vulnerable to undue influence, manipulation, or coercion" (standard 4.07[a]).

Another conflict-of-interest issue on which several codes comment con-cerns the use of confidential client information for practitioners' own pur-poses (such as for research, public presentations, media interviews). Accord-ing to the code of the American Psychological Association (1992),

> Psychologists do not disclose in their writings, lectures, or other public media, confidential, personally identifiable information concerning their patients, individual or organizational clients, students, research participants, or other recipients of their services that they obtained during the course of their work, unless the person or organization has consented in writing or unless there is other ethical or legal authori-zation for doing so. (standard 5.08)

The American Counseling Association (1995) code states, "Identification of a client in a presentation or publication is permissible only when the client has reviewed the material and has agreed to its presentation or publication" (standard B.5.b). Similarly, the NASW (1996) code states that "social workers who report evaluation and research results should protect participants' confidentiality by omitting identifying information unless proper consent has been obtained authorizing disclosure" (standard 5.02[m]).

Clearly, the spirit of the ethical standards concerning conflicts of interest is similar in the codes of the various human service professions, as are practitioners' opinions about how to handle various conflicts of interest. For example, only about 15 percent of the psychologists surveyed by Pope, Tabachnick, and Keith-Spiegel (1995) believed that it is ethical to ask favors (for example, a ride home) from clients or give gifts to those who refer clients; about 18 percent believed it is ethical to accept a client's invitation to a party, less than 1 percent believed that it is ethical to get paid to refer clients to someone, about 5 percent believed that it is ethical to sell goods to clients, and only about 3 percent believed that it is ethical to directly solicit a person to be a client.

In summary, when potential conflicts of interest arise, professionals have an obligation to be alert to and avoid actual or potential conflicts of interest that might interfere with the exercise of their professional judgment. Practitioners should resolve the conflict in a manner that makes the client's (or potential client's) interests primary and protects the client's interests to the greatest extent possible.

5   Altruism

A number of boundary issues arise because of practitioners' genuinely altruistic instincts and gestures. The vast majority of human service professionals are caring, dedicated, and honorable people who would never knowingly take advantage of clients. Ironically, practitioners who are remarkably generous and giving may unwittingly foster dual and multiple relationships that are counterproductive and harmful to the parties involved.

Boundary issues related to altruism fall into several conceptual categories: giving gifts to clients; meeting clients in social or community settings; offering clients favors; accommodating clients' unique needs and circumstances; and disclosing personal information to clients.

Giving Gifts to Clients

At first blush, it may appear that human service professionals should not give clients gifts under any circumstances, even with the most altruistic of motives. After all, clients may easily misinterpret even a modest gift as a message that they are in some special, perhaps exalted, relationship with the practitioner that entails some nonprofessional dimension. Gifts often imply friendship and, at times, intimacy. Gifts can lead to confusion about the nature of the client–professional relationship. As I noted earlier, in some instances a practitioner may give a client a gift as a way to communicate the practitioner's interest in developing an intimate relationship. In other instances, gifts from a practitioner to a client may reflect the practitioner's inappropriate emotional dependency on the client. Survey data clearly show that few mental health professionals (in this case, psychologists) believe that giving clients valuable gifts is ethical or have engaged in this practice (Pope, Tabachnick, and Keith-Spiegel 1995).

A practitioner may, however, encounter occasional circumstances where a modest gift seems appropriate, perhaps as a humane gesture in response to a client's illness or a major life-altering event that was addressed in treatment. In such situations, especially when the client may be relatively alone in the world, a modest get-well card or socially appropriate gift may seem innocuous. Gutheil and Gabbard (1993) offer the following illustration and comment:

> A patient in long-term therapy had struggled for years with apparent infertility and eventually, with great difficulty, arranged for adoption of a child. Two years later she unexpectedly conceived and finally gave birth. Her therapist, appreciating the power and meaning of this event, sent congratulatory flowers to the hospital.
>
> In this case, the therapist followed social convention in a way that— though technically a boundary crossing—represented a response appropriate to the real relationship. Offering a tissue to a crying patient and expressing condolences to a bereaved one are similar examples of appropriate responses outside the classic boundaries of the therapeutic relationship. (193)

Even though many altruistic gestures in the form of a modest gift are completely benign on the surface, practitioners should always consider potential negative ramifications, particularly with respect to the possibility that the client will misinterpret the gift's meaning. When practitioners' sense confusion could arise, they should seek collegial consultation and supervision and consider constructive risk-management strategies designed to protect both client and practitioner. Here is an example of a sound risk-management approach to a seemingly problem-free situation:

Case 5.1. Allison P., seventeen, was a client in a residential program for youths and in the custody of the county child welfare department. Allison was placed in the program after her single mother was sentenced to a long prison term for selling drugs. Allison did not have other relatives with whom she could live. The program was designed to provide youths in similar circumstances with a variety of educational and social services, including preparation for independent living.

After ten months in the program, Allison was ready to move into her own subsidized apartment. Staff members had worked diligently with her so that she would have the knowledge and skills to live on her own. Allison was proud of her accomplishments; she invited her primary counselor at the program, Melanie N., to come to her new apartment during the open house Allison had scheduled for the following weekend. Ms. N. very much wanted to go to Allison's new home but was unsure whether such a visit would be appropriate. In addition, Ms. N. was unsure whether she should give Allison a modest housewarming gift (for example, a scented candle or kitchen utensil) if she did decide to attend.

In this case—which in a variety of ways is typical of situations in which practitioners are tempted to give a client a modest gift—the counselor was torn between her instinct to accept the invitation and bring a small gift and her awareness that the client might misinterpret such a gesture. It happens that this client, who did not have an ongoing, constructive relationship with her parents, found the counselor's nurturing support appealing. In some respects, the counselor functioned as the client's surrogate parent. The counselor worried that visiting the client's new home—which would be remarkably unusual—might reinforce whatever fantasies the client might have about an ongoing, post-termination relationship or friendship she might have with the counselor. At the same time, the counselor wanted to be supportive and understood fully how meaningful it would be to the client to show the counselor her new home, particularly in light of all the hard therapeutic work they had done together. Also the counselor understood how devastated and hurt Allison was likely to feel if Ms. N. turned down the invitation.

Wisely, the counselor shared her dilemma with her immediate supervisor, who suggested that Ms. N. present the scenario at the next day's weekly group supervision meeting. As a result of this consultation, which entailed thorough examination and discussion of the clinical and ethical aspects of the situation, the counselor devised a risk-management strategy designed to enhance protection of the client (the central priority), the counselor's program, and the counselor herself. The plan included three key elements.

First, both Ms. N. and several colleagues concluded that sound clinical reasons to accept Allison's invitation existed, primarily those related to bolstering her self-esteem, reinforcing her sustained and diligent efforts to achieve independence, and avoiding hurting her emotionally. To minimize any confusion or misunderstanding, Ms. N. planned to talk to Allison explicitly about why she accepted the invitation and what her visit would represent (that is, helping the client celebrate this remarkable achievement) and about how important it was that Allison understand the need for appropriate boundaries in their relationship. Second, to protect the program and herself, Ms. N. decided to briefly document in Allison's case record the invitation to the open house, Ms. N.'s consultation with her supervisor and colleagues, and the rationale for her decision to accept the invitation. This documentation makes it clear, in the event that any party should ever raise questions about what happened, that the counselor's actions were the product of careful deliberation, sound decision making, and professional judgment. That is, the record provides ample evidence that the counselor did not visit the client's new home in an effort to pursue a friendship or some other type of inappropriate relationship.

The final element of this risk-management strategy specifically concerned the gift. The counselor and her colleagues agreed that a modest gift, consistent with social custom, would be appropriate. The case record also would document the gift. However, rather than sign a card saying that the gift was from Ms. N., the card would make it clear that the gift was from the *agency and its staff.* Ms. N. and her colleagues agreed that this apparently subtle adjustment could have profound meaning; instead of suggesting that Ms. N. was giving the gift—which could be misinterpreted—the card's message would defuse and depersonalize the situation by making it clear that the entire staff and the program itself were giving the gift. This thoughtful, comprehensive approach increases the likelihood that the client's legitimate and understandable needs and wishes will be met *and* that the gift will not trigger boundary-related complications and confusion.

Meeting Clients in Social or Community Settings

Earlier I discussed how human service professionals might become involved in dual relationships with clients in community settings and social circumstances as a result of their emotional and dependency needs. These situations involve boundary issues that arise when practitioners have difficulty separating their professional duties from their personal relationship needs and wishes (for example, when practitioners accept a client's invitation to a social event because the event fills a void in the practitioner's personal life or provides the practitioner with an opportunity to pursue a personal relationship with the client).

In contrast, practitioners are sometimes inclined to have contact with clients in social or community settings for more genuinely altruistic reasons. In these situations, the practitioner's motivation is a sincere wish to be helpful and supportive to the client. Yet this admirable altruism may trigger complicated boundary issues. Skillful handling of these circumstances is necessary to avoid harming the client and exposing the practitioner to ethical and liability risks.

Case 5.2. Ivy E. was a psychologist at a community mental health center. Her client, Karen R., was in recovery following years of cocaine abuse. Ms. R. had lost custody of her two children after the county child welfare agency investigated her for child neglect. In her earnest effort to turn her life around, Ms. R. sought counseling from Dr. E. and enrolled in an ambitious outpatient drug treatment program. Ms. R. also resumed her studies at a local community college, from which she had dropped out after her drug use escalated.

One day Ms. R. handed Dr. E. an envelope and asked her to open it. "I've been looking forward to this day for months," she said. Dr. E. opened the envelope and found an invitation from Ms. R. to attend her community college graduation and a reception at her home that evening. "You're one of the only people in my life who stuck with me. You've believed in me. I never could have done this without you," Karen R. told Ivy E. "It will mean so much to me to see you in the audience when I walk across that stage at graduation."

The psychologist in this case understood why her client was eager for her to attend the graduation. Ivy E. had been a major influence in Karen R.'s life and had provided her with unique sustained support. The psychologist was inclined to attend the graduation to provide her client with the emotional support she was requesting. Ivy E. understood the potential therapeutic benefit of her attendance at the graduation. She also sensed how hurt and disappointed Ms. R. would be if she declined the invitation and how this might undermine their therapeutic relationship.

At the same time, the psychologist was concerned about potential boundary issues. Although the client had not manifested major symptoms of boundary confusion in their relationship—which may be more likely to occur with some clinical syndromes than others, such as borderline personality disorder—Dr. E. was concerned that going to the graduation might communicate to Karen R. that their relationship, including their post-termination relationship, was moving in the direction of a friendship.

The psychologist raised her concerns with her clinical supervisor and with a colleague. The three agreed that the arguments in both directions were compelling. The psychologist's clinical supervisor encouraged her to think about Karen R.'s clinical issues and to speculate about the extent to which she had a history of boundary-related issues—for example, in Ms. R.'s relationships with family members or previous mental health counselors—that might be exacerbated by any boundary confusion in her relationship with the psychologist. Dr. E. truly believed, however, that this client had no such history and that, in this respect, attending the graduation was relatively low risk. After their lengthy consultation, the psychologist, her colleague, and her supervisor agreed that attending the graduation was reasonable. The supervisor, however, encouraged Dr. E. to take several steps to minimize the possibility of boundary-related problems. First, the supervisor encouraged her to document the invitation in the client's case record, the consultation process that Dr. E. engaged in concerning her decision about attendance, and the reason she decided to attend the graduation. The supervisor explained to the psychologist that this documentation would provide protection in the unlikely event that questions were raised about her decision to attend the graduation (for example, subsequent allegations that the psychologist was interested in having a personal relationship with the client). Such documentation would clearly show that Dr. E.'s decision was the product of professional judgment and decision making.

Second, the supervisor encouraged the psychologist to talk with Karen R. about her reasons for accepting the invitation—that the psychologist was eager to be supportive and believed that attending the graduation would be consistent with their therapeutic work together. The psychologist would ensure that the client did not misunderstand the meaning and significance of her attendance. The psychologist would also explain that she would need to avoid meeting and chatting with any of Karen R.'s friends or relatives who would be attending the graduation ceremony, so she could avoid compromising her client's privacy and any confusion regarding the nature of their relationship.

Finally, the psychologist would explain to the client that while she appreciates Ms. R.'s invitation to the graduation party, accepting it would be inappropriate. The psychologist would explain how the ethical standards in her profession discourage social relationships with clients and why. She would also document this conversation as further evidence of her attention to pertinent boundary-related issues.

Practitioners face comparable challenges when clients invite them to any social event, such as a wedding, baptism, confirmation, or bar mitzvah. We have ample evidence that practitioners disagree about the appropriateness of attending such events. For example, nearly half (46 percent) of the psychotherapists in the survey by Pope, Tabachnick, and Keith-Spiegel (1995) stated that attending a client's special event, such as a wedding, is ethical under many circumstances or unquestionably ethical. However, two-fifths of this group (39 percent) stated that doing so is unquestionably unethical or appropriate only under rare circumstances. Three-fourths (76 percent) of the sample reported having gone to a client's special event at least once. In these circumstances, practitioners must be vigilant in their efforts to avoid confusing the boundaries in their professional–client relationships.

Boundary issues that emerge because of practitioners' altruistic instincts are especially likely in programs that provide home-based services. Examples include intensive home-based intervention programs for families facing crises (for instance, as a result of substance abuse or allegations of child neglect) as well as those provided by hospices and visiting nurses. In these situations, practitioners must be careful to avoid boundary problems and inappropriate dual relationships, because they are working with clients in very personal, casual, somewhat intimate, and informal surroundings. Although formal office settings may have some drawbacks, they do convey to clients that what takes place within the office walls has a professional purpose, and this can help to reduce boundary violations and crossings. Home settings, however, do not automatically convey that message. In fact, the informality and intimacy of these settings can be the incubator for boundary confusion and problems. Some clients may experience any interactions in their homes as personal rather than professional, at least to a considerable degree.

Case 5.3. Malcolm B. was a social worker at a large family service agency. The agency sponsored a variety of programs, including services for families referred by the city child welfare agency following allegations of child abuse or neglect. Mr. B. worked in the family preservation program, which was designed to provide crisis intervention and supportive services to parents seeking to retain custody of their children.

Ordinarily, Mr. B. visited families in his caseload three to four times each week to monitor their status, respond to crises, and provide individual and family counseling. His arrival times varied according to his other commitments and the family's schedule. One day Mr. B. arrived at the family's home at noon on a Saturday, just as the family was about to have lunch. The father invited Mr. B. to join them. When Mr. B. hesitated, the father politely insisted that Mr. B. take a few minutes to eat with the family before they got down to their work together.

In this situation, the social worker may be tempted to accept the family's invitation to dine, not because the social worker is hungry (which may be true) but because he does not want to offend the family and wants to respond to the warm offer in a courteous way that signifies his regard for the family. Ultimately, the social worker may think, this will strengthen the therapeutic relationship and the effectiveness of his intervention approach.

At the same time, sitting with a family and breaking bread, as I noted earlier, may communicate to the family that its relationship with the social worker has moved to a new plane, one that involves a social as well as a professional relationship. This may be particularly problematic because the social worker's report and recommendations about the family's progress in treatment will have a direct bearing on the parents' ability to maintain custody of their children. Confusion about boundaries in this set of circumstances can be especially consequential, because the family may be upset with the social worker's recommendations. Family members may feel particularly betrayed if they had begun to sense that the social worker was their "friend," in part because the social worker socialized with the family during lunch. This is another example of a situation in which the practitioner may need to use great finesse to avoid insulting the family and avoid boundary confusion. One possibility would be for the practitioner to explain that he just ate or is not particularly hungry.

Offering Clients Favors

Now let's extend this example in order to make an additional point about the untoward consequences of altruistic actions that can result when practitioners offer clients favors. Let's suppose that about fifteen minutes before Mr. B.'s planned departure from the home, the mother takes a telephone call and finds out that her employer is insisting that she immediately come to work at her job at a nearby hospital to fill in for a colleague who called in sick. The family does not have a working car and, aware that the social worker is planning to head back to his agency, which happens to be located two blocks from the hospital, the mother asks the social worker whether he would be willing to give her a ride. The social worker wants to be helpful, yet he is also uncomfortable about establishing a precedent that involves spending informal time with a client outside the treatment context. The social worker is concerned that the mother—and perhaps other family members—will interpret this altruistic gesture as a sign that the social worker has a special relationship, resembling a friendship, with the family. Given the circumstances, the social worker is not in a position to consult with colleagues or a supervisor. He has to make a spontaneous decision.

Clearly, refusing the woman's request could be awkward and, in fact, doing so could ultimately undermine the social worker's therapeutic relationship with the family. In addition, the social worker's agency may prohibit staff members from transporting clients, which would provide the social worker with a convenient way out. Absent this convenient explanation and weighing all the competing factors, the social worker may feel the need to provide the woman with the ride. To prevent misunderstanding and to protect himself, however, the social worker should talk with the client about how this is an unusual situation and not a precedent. The social worker may want to consider entering a note along these lines in the case record as well, so his motives and reasons for offering the client a ride are clear.

Human service professionals may be tempted in a variety of circumstances to offer a client a favor for altruistic reasons. Here are several examples, some of which raise red flags:

Case 5.4. David A., a counselor in private practice, provided psychotherapy to a twenty-nine-year-old man who had a history of relationship
problems. Over time, the client resolved a number of emotional issues
that helped him sustain a long-term relationship for the first time in his
adult life. One day the client informed Mr. A. that he was planning to
marry and wanted Mr. A. to be in his wedding party.

Case 5.5. A psychiatrist in a mental health clinic, Dr. P., provided counseling services to a forty-two-year-old woman who had attempted to commit suicide. The woman was despondent after being accosted and
raped by a stranger. After more than two years of therapy, the client
decided to terminate her treatment. She told Dr. P. that she felt able to
live her life without sustained psychiatric treatment. Two months after
termination, the client stopped by Dr. P.'s office unannounced and said
she simply wanted to say hello and let her know that she was doing
okay. Dr. P. was inclined to accommodate the client's wish as a benev-
olent gesture but was unsure whether this informal encounter would
set a precedent that would be in neither the client's nor Dr. P.'s best
interest.

Case 5.6. Adam K., a social worker in a residential program for troubled
adolescents, provided services to a seventeen-year-old boy who had
been abandoned by his parents, both of whom had serious substance
abuse problems. Mr. K. helped the boy develop independent-living
skills. When the boy reached the age of majority, state regulations
required that he move out of the residential program. The boy moved
to a distant state to live with his mother's brother, whom he barely
knew. About six months later, the boy—now a young man—contacted
Mr. K. to explain that "things just aren't working out with my uncle.
This isn't the right place for me, but I have nowhere else to go." After
a lengthy discussion, Mr. K. offered to let his former client stay in a

vacant room in his large house until he found a more permanent residence.

Case 5.7. Anna P., a counseling psychologist who specialized in the treatment of anxiety disorders, received a telephone call from a former neighbor whom she did not know well. The acquaintance explained to Ms. P. that he had been having some problems lately, specifically related to feeling anxious when in a crowd. The acquaintance explained that he felt uneasy talking about his problem with a complete stranger and wanted to know whether Ms. P. would be willing to provide him with counseling.

Case 5.8. Tessa L., a social worker in private practice, provided counseling services to a college student who reporting feeling depressed after the death of her parents in a plane crash. The counseling lasted for about seventeen months while the client was in college. Following her graduation, the former client accepted a position as a case manager at a local domestic violence shelter. One year later, the client applied to graduate school in social work and eventually received her master's degree. Shortly thereafter, the former client contacted her former therapist, Ms. L., and asked whether she would be willing to provide the weekly supervision that the former client needed as she worked toward obtaining her license as a clinical social worker.

Case 5.9. Maria D., a marriage therapist, provided counseling to a couple who were having difficulty coping with their infertility. Several months after the counseling began, the wife was hospitalized following a miscarriage with serious complications. Ms. D. wanted to visit her client in the hospital to offer emotional support.

Case 5.10. Danielle M., a social worker, provided group counseling to clients who were dealing with self-esteem issues. The group had been meeting weekly for about three months. One client asked to speak with Dr. M. after a group session. The client then explained that she had been thinking for some time about converting to Judaism, knew that Dr. M. was Jewish, and wanted to know whether Dr. M. would be willing to talk with her about some aspects of the religion and help her find a local rabbi who might help her start the conversion process.

Case 5.11. Alma B., a psychiatrist, provided counseling and medication consultation to a ten-year-old boy with Tourette's syndrome. The client and his father arrived for their appointment one day, and the boy asked Dr. B. whether she wanted to purchase wrapping paper that the boy was selling to raise money for his school.

Each of these scenarios raises questions about the ways in which a human service professional's altruistic instincts may generate boundary issues. Some altruistic gestures toward clients are unlikely to create significant or problematic boundary problems. For example, the psychiatrist who decides to purchase a roll of wrapping paper from her client is not likely to stir up complex boundary problems that would harm the client or lead to an inappropriate dual relationship. Formulating an ambitious risk-management strategy in this situation would be gratuitous. In contrast, however, several of these situations are much more likely to lead to boundary problems. A counselor who agrees to be in his client's wedding party, a social worker who permits a former client to live in his home, a psychologist who agrees to counsel an acquaintance who is a former neighbor, and a social worker who agrees to actively help her client explore the social worker's religion are practitioners who are—perhaps inadvertently—creating greenhouse-like conditions for what could well become complex boundary problems. We can anticipate that the clients in these scenarios could easily become confused about the nature of their relationship with their practitioner. The line between professional and friend or social acquaintance is likely to seem blurry to both client and practitioner. In turn, this confusion could undermine the practitioner's ability to provide competent care and the client's ability to benefit maximally from the professional's services. Clients in these circumstances are likely to perceive and relate to their practitioners differently because of the extraprofessional contact. The former client who lives in the practitioner's home may see sides of the practitioner that are unnerving or disturbingly inconsistent with the client's earlier perception of the practitioner—for example, if the client were to observe the practitioner having difficulty handling conflict with his spouse or children. The social worker who counsels an acquaintance may unwittingly harm the client because of the social worker's reluctance to constructively confront an acquaintance on an important issue related to the therapy. The counselor who joins his client's wedding party may stimulate all manner of counterproductive fantasies in the client about their budding friendship.

Although some altruistic gestures are clearly benign or harmful, others are ambiguous. Practitioners may disagree, for example, about the appropriateness of a marriage therapist's decision to visit his hospitalized client, a psychiatrist's decision to meet briefly and informally with a former client who stopped by the office to "reconnect," and a social worker's decision to provide supervision to a former client who is now a colleague. Some would argue, for example, that a brief visit to a hospitalized client, or a brief informal encounter in the office with a former client, could have profoundly beneficial therapeutic consequences that far outweigh any associated risks. At the same time, others would argue that these apparently innocuous, altruistic gestures could be harmful. In these more ambiguous circumstances, practitioners should think carefully about the factors that may increase the risk of a misunderstanding, such as the client's clinical profile, the client's ability to handle boundary issues, the practitioner's personality, the strength of the therapeutic alliance, and the practitioner's experience (Simon 1999).

Accommodating Clients

In some instances, human service professionals encounter boundary issues because of their earnest attempt to accommodate a client's unique request or circumstances. These accommodations typically take the form of providing extraordinary service to the client (or former client) in an effort to be helpful. Here are several examples:

Case 5.12. Nora C., a counselor in a shelter for teenagers who have run away from home, was concerned about a particular client, a sixteen-year-old girl whose step-brother apparently had sexually assaulted her. The client had talked with Ms. C. about her profound despair. Ms. C. told the girl that she (Ms. C.) would be on vacation for one week. Ms. C. gave the girl her home telephone number and encouraged her to call if she was feeling desperate to talk.

Case 5.13. Bob K., a marriage and family therapist, provided counseling to a single man, a construction worker, who felt depressed after breaking up with his long-time girlfriend. After eight counseling sessions, the client's insurer refused to authorize payment for additional services. The construction worker told Mr. K. how eager he was to continue counseling, which he was finding quite helpful, but that he had no money to pay for the sessions. For about a year, the client had been using all his extra money to pay off an unusually large credit card debt and avoid having to declare personal bankruptcy. Mr. K., who was eager to be helpful to this unusually earnest client, agreed to provide the client with a number of free counseling sessions.

Case 5.14. Eric C., a social worker in a grade school, provided counseling services to a twelve-year-old sixth grader. The boy's teacher referred him to Mr. C. because the boy seemed withdrawn and socially isolated. Mr. C. spent time working with the student on self-esteem issues and relationship skills. In his spare time, Mr. C. volunteered to coach a basketball team affiliated with a local recreation center; Mr. C.'s son played on the team. Mr. C. considered inviting his client to join the team he coached, in an effort to help the boy make friends and have a positive social experience.

Case 5.15. Fran G., a counselor at Lutheran Family Service, was married to a prominent local minister. The minister occasionally referred church members to Ms. G. for counseling when members wanted to locate a mental health counselor who would understand and be sensitive to their religious values and beliefs. Ms. G. provided services to these individuals, many of whom she knew from the church.

As with offering clients favors, efforts to accommodate a client's unique circumstances require that human service professionals critically examine whether doing so is advisable. Some accommodations are clearly inappropriate, and some are relatively benign. For example, most practitioners would not object if a colleague agreed to provide a terminally ill, bedridden client with counseling in the client's home, even though all previous counseling sessions had occurred in the professional's office. This accommodation seems reasonable in light of the client's unfortunate circumstances. In contrast, accommodating clients who are acquaintances and members of the practitioner's husband's church could very well lead to harmful boundary issues. Circumstances may arise where the practitioner and her husband are unsure whether to share with each other critically relevant confidential information about the client—for instance, if the client shares information with the wife about illegal activities taking place in the church's business office. Also, clients who share deeply personal information with the minister's spouse may feel overexposed and worried about whether their minister will learn of these sensitive details.

Similarly, the sixth grader who plays on the basketball team coached by his social worker may encounter boundary problems. For example, suppose the boy and the coach's own son, who also plays on the team, become friendly, and the coach's son—who is not aware that his new friend is his father's client—invites the client to sleep over at his house. The social worker may end up in a situation in which one of his clients spends considerable social time at the social worker's home and participates in family events. This scenario is likely to confuse the client about the nature of his relationship with the social worker and could undermine his counseling experience. One might also wonder whether detrimental consequences might result if, for instance, the basketball team is not playing well and the coach (the social worker) benches his client "for the good of the team." The boy could be deeply wounded by being pulled out of the starting lineup and may experience this as a form of rejection by his social worker. Clearly, these situations can produce conflicts of interest for the parties involved.

Unique issues can also arise in relation to accommodating *former* clients. One particularly challenging case I encountered involved debate among community mental health center staff members about whether to hire former clients to work in their agency as case aides.

Case 5.16. The clinical director at the Lincoln County Community Mental Health Center decided that she wanted to create three new case aide positions. Her plan was to hire three former clients of the agency's outpatient counseling program for people with chronic mental illness. The three new staff members—all of whom were functioning at a high level—would be assigned to provide supportive and concrete services to current clients.

Several clinical staff members at the agency had concerns about this plan. They believed that this move might create boundary problems that would be difficult for the former clients and staff to manage. The clinical director and her immediate assistant, however, strongly believed in empowering people with histories of mental illness and that this hiring plan was consistent with that goal. Staff members agreed to schedule a meeting to provide an opportunity for all of the agency's professional staff to discuss the issue.

This agency's staff members asked me to facilitate their meeting and to help guide their discussion about the ethical dimensions of their disagreement. This experience provided me with an opportunity to explore for myself the pertinent boundary issues and the arguments for and against hiring former clients. The process the staff and I went through provides a good example of the benefits of sound procedures and decision making. At the beginning of the meeting, the staff was almost evenly divided on the issue—half were strongly opposed to hiring former clients, largely because of potential boundary problems, and half strongly favored hiring former clients, mainly because of the agency's empowerment approach to the delivery of mental health services. In an effort to address this issue thoroughly and comprehensively, I acquainted staffers with the concept of dual relationships and prevailing ethical standards in the relevant human service professions (psychology, social work, counseling, psychiatric nursing, and psychiatry). I then helped them identify arguments in favor of hiring former clients. First, as mentioned earlier, hiring former clients is a way to empower clients with mental illness and acknowledge the unique and valuable contributions they can make to others who are coping with somewhat similar issues; after all, who can better understand what current clients are experiencing in their efforts to cope with mental illness? Also, recognizing clients with mental illness as "equals" is a less elitist, paternalistic, and hierarchical way to provide mental health services and is more likely to promote client growth, self-esteem, and self-confidence than some traditional processes. In addition, hiring former clients can provide current clients with valuable role models—that is, constructive examples of colleagues who have struggled and coped well with their mental illness. Finally, staffers could not ignore the implications of the Americans with Disabilities Act, which prohibits discrimination in the workplace; certainly staff members would not want to refuse to hire former clients in a way that violated their legal rights.

The mental health agency staff and I then turned our collective attention to a variety of concerns associated with hiring former clients, related primarily to potential—although admittedly not inevitable—dual relationship and boundary problems. For example, staffers wondered whether former clients might encounter problematic transference issues as they attempted to relate to former treatment providers who are now colleagues. Would it be difficult for the former clients to relate to their former treatment providers as genuine colleagues, in light of their previous professional–client relationships? Of course, staff members might experience a comparable challenge, finding it difficult to relate to former clients as colleagues and, for instance, being unsure how candid they should be when expressing their views in staff meetings. Also, what would it mean for former clients to learn, as a result of their new employment status in the agency, that some staff members, including their former treatment providers, are not well respected or are involved in complex political feuds within the agency—that is, that the agency idealized by the clients is flawed in some important respects? Might this undermine the former clients' confidence in the services they had received? Also, what if personnel issues involving the former clients emerge that warrant critical feedback or discipline? What would it mean for the former clients to be "chastised" by their former treatment providers? As Doyle (1997) notes,

If a former client indeed begins work in the program in which a counselor treated him or her, issues relating to supervision, promotion, performance evaluation, and confidentiality may arise that can be problematic for one or both parties. For example, if the counselor were to become the former client's supervisor, objective supervision could be compromised by the circumstances of the previous relationship. Either positively or negatively, the counselor might find himself or herself recalling the new employee's previous behavior and responding accordingly to current situations. (431)

Further, what would happen if former clients who are now staff relapsed and wanted or needed to become active clients again? How would they, and their treatment providers, handle the shift away from a collegial relationship back to a professional–client relationship? Would the clients find this disconcerting and humiliating? Would they have difficulty resuming the role of client, and would this interfere with their therapeutic progress?

In addition, the mental health center staff and I discussed in what ways hiring former clients could have a detrimental effect on other clients, who might be discouraged when they realize they were not "picked" to become staff members and perhaps conclude that they have not progressed as well clinically. Current clients may also feel overexposed, fearing (perhaps unrealistically) that the former clients would have access to confidential information about them.

By the end of this protracted discussion and analysis of potential dual relationship and boundary issues, staff opinion clearly had shifted. Nearly all the staff had concluded that the potential risks outweighed any benefits from hiring former clients. Although all staff members embraced the virtues of empowering former clients, they concluded that the potential harm to them and to the agency's smooth functioning was a risk not worth taking. Instead, the staffers realized, they could accomplish much the same goal by working assertively with other social service agencies in the area in an effort to find comparable jobs for their former clients. In the staffers' opinion, finding jobs in other agencies for former clients would reduce the likelihood of boundary problems while achieving all the benefits associated with hiring former clients to work with active clients.

One other unique circumstance involves accommodating the wishes of relatives or acquaintances of deceased clients. In one unusual case on which I consulted, the parents of a deceased client asked the social worker to deliver a eulogy at the client's funeral. The parents understood how important the social worker had been to their son. After giving the parents' request considerable thought, the social worker was inclined to deliver the eulogy. The social worker consulted with her supervisor and several colleagues, all of whom supported her inclination; all the parties agreed, however, that the social worker should deliver the eulogy in a way that did not disclose the nature of her relationship with the deceased client. In addition, the social worker decided to obtain a signed, formal release form authorizing her to speak at the funeral; in this instance, the deceased clients' parents had the legal authority to sign the release. The social worker also documented the parents' request, the social worker's consultation with colleagues, and the reasons for the social worker's decision to deliver the eulogy.

As always, the most challenging circumstances involving dual relationships are those that are ambiguous, where practitioners can advance reasonable arguments both for and against accommodating clients' unique circumstances or requests. As with all ambiguous boundary issues, practitioners must weigh the competing arguments, being mindful of their ultimate responsibility to protect clients from harm.

Self-disclosing to Clients

In chapter 3, I discussed how a practitioner's inappropriate self-disclosure to a client often reflects the practitioner's unresolved emotional and dependency needs. In these situations, self-disclosure is often associated with the practitioner's unethical and harmful efforts to cultivate intimate relationships or friendships with clients.

In other circumstances, practitioners may self-disclose for more altruistic purposes, deliberately and *judiciously* choosing to share personal details — usually modest in scope — in an effort to empathize with clients, offer clients support, align with clients, and provide a constructive role model that clients may use in their efforts to address their own issues. Further, in some cultural or ethnic groups, a client may view the practitioner's self-disclosure as an important sign that the practitioner accepts the client and will not be patronizing. Here are several examples involving practitioner self-disclosure for altruistic purposes:

Case 5.17. Iris D., a counselor at a community mental health center, provided counseling to parents of a six-year-old boy whose teacher complained that his behavior in school was difficult to manage. According to the teacher, the boy behaved provocatively with other children by teasing them and playing tricks on them. The boy's classmates did not want to play with him, which increased the boy's negative attention-getting behavior. Ms. D., who was knowledgeable about child behavior management techniques and strategies, taught the parents how to use positive reinforcers at home and used role-playing techniques to help the parents learn how to communicate with their child effectively.

Ms. D. first learned many of these techniques when her own child was about six, and she and the child's teacher were having difficulty managing behaviors of his that were very similar to those engaged in by the child of the counselor's current clients. After explaining some of the rudimentary features of the behavior management protocol, Ms. D. told the parents that she has found them to be effective with many children, including her own child when he was younger. Ms. D. decided to share this personal detail as a way to let the parents know that she was able to genuinely appreciate their experience and frustration, that she had encountered similar challenges, and that hard work can produce positive results. In the counselor's judgment, this modest form of self-disclosure was likely to help her strengthen her therapeutic alliance with the parents and provide them with much-needed reassurance. Ms. D. did not feel overexposed and did not think this disclosure would compromise the professional–client relationship. In fact, toward the end of their successful work together, the parents told Ms. D. that her brief description of her experience with her own son was a turning point for them, that at that moment they began to have hope and knew that Ms. D. understood their frustration.

Case 5.18. Len J. was a psychologist at a student mental health center at a large university. One of Dr. J.'s clients was a student who sought counseling because her parents had just informed her they were divorcing. The student told Dr. J. that she felt deeply depressed and was falling way behind in her schoolwork. The student also explained that for weeks she had not felt like eating and had not been sleeping well. For about a month, Dr. J. provided the student with supportive counseling and referred her to the staff psychiatrist to determine whether psychotropic medication would be helpful. Despite these efforts, the student did not seem to progress.

Dr. J. was concerned about the student and consulted with colleagues about alternative treatment strategies. Dr. J. told his colleagues that the student often commented that no one, including Dr. J., could ever understand the intensity of what she was experiencing. In an effort to align with his client, Dr. J. told her that when he was in college, his parents also divorced and he found it very difficult to concentrate on his work and lead the life of a normal college student. Dr. J. disclosed this information deliberately and in a limited way. Almost immediately, the student seemed more responsive and eager to listen to Dr. J.'s comments during their counseling sessions. Dr. J. subsequently told his colleagues about the effectiveness of his strategy. Three of his four colleagues were complimentary; one, however, thought that Dr. J. had crossed a line, that such self-disclosure — even for entirely altruistic purposes — could confuse the client and lead to boundary complications. The one colleague was especially concerned that transference and countertransference could prove problematic. Dr. J. assured his colleague that he was well aware of these risks but felt that he had them under control. In the end, Dr. J. and his colleague agreed to disagree.

———

———

Case 5.19. Bob W. was a social worker in an outpatient substance abuse treatment program. Many of Mr. W.'s clients were alcoholic or addicted to cocaine. In addition to their treatment in the program, these clients regularly attended meetings of Alcoholics Anonymous or Narcotics Anonymous.

Mr. W. was also a recovering alcoholic. He had been sober for twelve years, and he attended AA meetings faithfully. One evening Mr. W. went to his customary AA meeting and on his way into the building encountered one of his current clients, who was also attending the meeting. Mr.

W. had to make a quick decision about whether to attend the meeting or leave. He was concerned that his presence at the meeting might confuse the boundaries in his relationship with his client. At the same time, Mr. W. realized that he could also serve as a constructive role model for his client—that he might actually perform a helpful service to his client by remaining at the meeting.

This last case involving a practitioner in recovery provides a valuable illustration of the complex issues related to a practitioner's self-disclosure for altruistic purposes. In fact, this is one of the relatively few dual relationship issues unrelated to sexual relationships that has generated significant discussion in the professional literature. This debate provides a valuable illustration of the complicated boundary issues that can emerge when professionals decide to disclose personal information about themselves to clients for apparently altruistic purposes.

Clearly, professionals in the substance abuse field disagree vehemently about the wisdom and appropriateness of self-disclosure that occurs when practitioners who are in recovery attend AA or NA meetings that clients also attend (Doyle 1997). One side argues that a practitioner's self-disclosure in this form provides a remarkably valuable service to clients who have substance abuse problems. The clients can view their counselors as role models who practice what they preach about the need to be earnest about recovery, attend AA and NA meetings, and so forth. This argument is especially significant in light of survey data showing that nearly three-fifths of the membership of the National Association of Alcoholism and Drug Abuse Counselors are in recovery themselves (Doyle 1997). In addition, practitioners who disclose their recovery status to their clients may establish instant credibility, particularly among clients who might be skeptical of counselors who have not experienced substance abuse and the challenges of recovery first hand.

In contrast are those who argue with equal passion that the blending of the personal struggles of practitioners with those of their clients—in the context of AA or NA meetings, for example—is likely to have profoundly detrimental consequences. Clients may have difficulty separating their practitioner's professional and personal roles. In addition, some clients may lose confidence in practitioners who display their own vulnerabilities, personal struggles, and personal failures; the result may be an undermining of the practitioner's authority and influence. Further, practitioners in recovery—like all people in recovery—run the risk of relapsing, at least in principle. Should relapse occur, the practitioner's clients may be devastated, disheartened, and disappointed, and this could jeopardize their recovery efforts. As Doyle (1997) notes,

> The issue of self-disclosure in the counseling session itself also raises dual relationship issues. If the counselor discloses that he or she is in recovery, a new element to the counseling relationship may be unwittingly introduced. Not only is the counselor's anonymity broken, but also, with this disclosure the relationship between the counselor and client now may become one in which they are co-members of the same A.A. group. The risk here is that the counseling relationship may no longer be an exclusively professional one, but one that has other features as well. The sharing of private information about one's recovery, its challenges, and its successes, while conceivably therapeutic, also may lead to the relationship becoming more personal than professional if caution is not used.
>
> Self-help group meetings provide attendees the opportunity to share their "experience, strength and hope" (Alcoholics Anonymous, 1984) with one another. Meetings typically last for an hour and may consist of one or two speakers or of a rotating discussion among those in attendance. Sharing such private information as the state of one's personal recovery program is certainly a risky proposition in any group setting. For the substance abuse counselor at a meeting with current (or former or future) clients in attendance, the ability to share fully might be compromised, thus lessening the benefit of attending at all. For example, what would be the impact on the counseling relationship if the counselor shared that he or she had nearly relapsed in the past week? Or, what if the counselor had relapsed recently and the client then realized that he or she had more time in recovery than the counselor? Other less dramatic examples exist as well that could include clinical considerations or dilemmas for the counselor. It is not difficult to imagine situations such as a counselor sharing dissatisfaction with his or her coworkers in the presence of clients of that facility, a counselor discussing thoughts of leaving the field, or a counselor revealing that he or she has difficulty maintaining positive feelings towards his

or her clients. Each of these hypothetical scenarios could significantly affect the counseling relationship should clients be in attendance at the self-help group meeting in which it was shared. (430)

In addition to these potentially detrimental clinical consequences, substance abuse counselors who are in recovery, who exercise some degree of control over their clients' lives—for example, providing progress reports to probation or parole counselors—and who interact with clients at AA and NA meetings may create conditions in which clients may feel exploited. According to Doyle (1997),

> The greatest potential for harm from a dual relationship, however, may result from the power held, or perceived as being held, by the counselor. Whereas the counseling relationship will eventually come to an end, the power differential may remain indefinitely, adversely affecting any future, nontherapeutic relationship between counselor and client (Haas & Malouf, 1989). In the substance abuse field, the counselor often holds a substantial amount of power over the client because of the frequency with which clients are involved with the court system. Often clients are required to participate in counseling as a condition of probation or parole, and violation of this requirement could result in their incarceration (Milam & Ketcham, 1981). Counselors thus hold a great deal of power over clients, power that can lead to exploitation. When exploitation appears in the personal interaction between counselor and client, serious dual relationship problems quickly arise. (429)

In the end, the debate about practitioners' self-disclosure to clients in recovery for altruistic purposes illustrates the difficulty of reaching consensus about some boundary and dual relationship issues. Because of the legitimate and complex debate that can arise—as this one issue demonstrates—practitioners would do well to grasp the critical importance of the *process* they should use to make sound decisions, recognizing that in the end reasonable people may disagree. This decision-making process should entail the elements outlined in chapter 1, especially the steps involving examination of conflicting professional obligations; identification of the individuals, groups, and organizations likely to be affected by the decision; identification of all viable courses of action and the participants involved in each, along with the potential benefits and risks for each; examination of the reasons in favor of and opposed to each course of action, considering relevant ethical principles and standards, practice theory and guidelines, and personal values; consultation with colleagues and appropriate experts (such as agency staff, supervisors, ethics committees); and appropriate documentation of these various steps.

6 Unavoidable and Unanticipated Circumstances

Another type of dual relationship involves circumstances that practitioners cannot easily anticipate or prevent—circumstances that, in most respects, are unavoidable. In these situations, practitioners encounter boundary crossings and dual relationships unexpectedly and need to manage the circumstances in a way that protects clients, colleagues, and practitioners to the greatest extent possible.

Boundary issues involving unavoidable circumstances fall into four major categories, including those that involve geographic proximity, conflicts of interest, professional encounters, and social encounters.

Geographic Proximity

The likelihood of unanticipated boundary issues increases in geographically small communities, especially in rural areas. Human service professionals in these settings often report how challenging it is when they encounter clients in, for instance, the local supermarket, community center, or house of worship (Ebert 1997). Practitioners often describe how they walk through their day wondering when—not if—they will encounter clients outside their work settings. They devote considerable effort to managing these encounters in a way that minimizes potential boundary confusion. As Smith and Fitzpatrick (1995) observe,

That dual relationships are inevitable in certain circumstances adds to the complexity of the issue. In small towns and rural communities, dual relationships are often unavoidable; denying help to a potential client because of a preexisting relationship could mean that the person gets no help at all. Moreover, in rural settings where mental health professionals might be regarded with suspicion, heightening one's visibility by way of involvement in community activities may defuse the suspicion and make the clinician appear more approachable (Gates & Speare, 1990). (502)

The following cases illustrate boundary issues and dual relationships that arise in small communities and rural areas:

Case 6.1. Alice S. was the only child psychiatrist in a rural town of about eighty-five hundred people. Dr. S. treated a number of children in the town and in the surrounding rural region. Dr. S.'s daughter, who was in the third grade at the local grade school, became friendly with one of Dr. S.'s patients and invited her over to their house to play. Dr. S. was unsure how to handle this predicament, particularly because she could not disclose to her daughter that her friend was Dr. S.'s patient.

Case 6.2. Brad O. was a social worker in a small rural community. Mr. O. had a contract with the county to provide mental health services for local police officers and fire fighters as part of the county's employee assistance program. One of Mr. O.'s clients was a police officer who was having marital difficulties. One day Mr. O. exceeded the speed limit as he drove to his son's high-school football game. The police officer who pulled Mr. O. over was his client.

Case 6.3. Melinda D. was a counselor at the community mental health center in a rural county. She provided clinical services to Albert K., an employee of the local gas department, who was having difficulty coping with his wife's death. Ms. D. and Mr. K. met weekly for about six months. One afternoon, Ms. D. answered her doorbell and found Mr. K. in his gas department uniform. He was covering a colleague's route and had arrived to record the reading on Ms. D.'s indoor meter. Mr. K. explained that he had no idea Ms. D.'s house was on this route.

Some unanticipated encounters in geographically small communities between practitioners and clients are innocuous and unlikely to pose significant problems. For example, the practitioner whose client visited her house to read her gas meter may have felt awkward having her client in her home, and her client may have felt awkward too; but, this brief, unplanned, and one-time encounter may not have significant, lasting repercussions. In contrast, the practitioner whose child has become friendly with the practitioner's client faces a more daunting challenge. As Brownlee (1996) notes,

> In almost all cases, living in a rural area means greater distances between people and communities. The relative isolation increases interdependence between residents and leads to multiple levels of relationships.
>
> Multiple levels of relationships in rural areas are often a significant factor affecting the services provided by mental health professionals (Brownlee, 1992). Such relationships are almost impossible to avoid when there is no choice but to shop at a client's store or when one's children are in school with or even friends with clients' children (Fenby, 1978). (499)

Dual relationships in small communities and rural areas take several forms, most commonly overlapping social relationships and overlapping business or professional relationships. An unusually ambitious study conducted by Schank and Skovholt (1997) explored these issues. The researchers interviewed sixteen psychologists in Minnesota and Wisconsin who lived at least fifty miles from major metropolitan areas. Ten research participants were in private practice, four were affiliated with community mental health centers, one was in a multidisciplinary group practice, and

one worked in a hospital setting. These interviews produced rich qualita-
tive data related to dual and multiple relationships in rural areas. The
respondents had a great deal to say about overlapping social relationships
that occurred in such settings as the practitioner's church, parties and social
gatherings, local restaurants, cultural events, school functions, and volunteer activities. The following are noteworthy and illuminating excerpts
from the research interviews:

> One of the things we have done in our church for the last 6 years is
> that we have taken a group of kids to Colorado skiing as part of the
> youth program. I feel some kind of tension about that sometimes. For
> example, one of my clients happened to be on the ski trip 3 or 4 years
> ago. Well, I thought, "Okay, we don't do anything socially with this
> family." But I don't think these pressures are so unusual. It's just that
> you have to keep those dual relationships clear in your mind. (Schank
> and Skovholt 1997:46)

> When I moved here, I got a membership to the YMCA to go to exercise
> classes. After running into a couple of clients in the locker room, I
> decided that this was just so uncomfortable for me. So I'm not going
> to continue my membership in the YMCA. It was just really awkward.
> It's not like there are a huge number of athletic clubs here that you
> can have a choice of which one you go to. (46)

Respondents in this study described three criteria they use to determine
whether they provide services to clients who pose potential boundary challenges: practitioners' own comfort level in traversing the overlapping relationships with clients; clients' opinions about the boundary issues and their ability
to handle them; and the type and severity of clients' presenting problems. Two
respondents described how they handle boundary issues with clients:

> I have this wonderful habit of just simply looking straight ahead when
> I go to the grocery store, and half the time I don't see people. So that
> has protected me. (Schank and Skovholt 1997:47)

> It is always establishing boundaries. I live on a very busy street in town
> and was doing some landscaping and working out in the front yard.
> One of my clients must have seen me and later said, "Oh, is that where
> you live? I saw you." I said yes, and she said, "Well, I noticed that the

house next to you is for sale. Wouldn't that be cool? You know, my parents are thinking of helping me buy a house." I said, "No, that would not be cool because you are my client—you are not a friend. If you moved in next door to me, it would be extremely uncomfortable. I know what you are saying—I listen to you, I care about you—but friends know about one another. You don't come in, and I sit and tell you about my problems and my life. I don't call you when I am hurting or need a friend for support." . . . She said, "Oh, yeah. I didn't even think about that." And so it's continually having to establish boundaries with a number of clients. (47)

The psychologists in Schank and Skovholt's sample also commented on unanticipated or unavoidable overlapping business or professional relationships with clients. The respondents said that while traveling to neighboring communities to transact business might be appealing, often this is not feasible; in such instances, practitioners must devise practical ways to manage the boundary issues.

I have clients who are locksmiths or electricians that have come to my house, with me not knowing that I was calling the electrical company that they work for. . . . It is hard to make small talk with someone who the day before was in your office talking about really powerful things. Sometimes clients will joke about it, which is kind of nice. They will break the ice. (Schank and Skovholt 1997:47)

When you do have business dealings with someone, I find it really hard. I won't bargain with them. Recently someone [who was a former client] worked on my car, and I thought the price was a little high. I trust the guy, but I felt awkward in asking him what the charges were for. If it were someone else, I would have had no problem asking. (47)

We have a nice, isolated building here in a beautiful, quiet place. So professionals many times will come here. Now, I have seen a lot of professionals in town [as clients], either for personal counseling or for their children. Then I refer [clients] to [those same professionals] because there is no one else. . . . If you read the rules about dual relationships, that is not allowed. (47)

I do consulting at a fair number of group homes. Sometimes I'm in that dilemma where there is someone [working there] that I've seen as a client. In fact, I can think of two instances where I currently was seeing people as clients and subsequently discovered that they had just obtained employment at one of the group homes. So I was dealing with them as clients, as well as in a professional relationship in terms of some of the consulting. (47)

Practitioners in small towns and rural areas often comment on the ways in which their professional relationships overlap, and sometimes interfere, with their family relationships. In these situations, practitioners typically find that their clients have independent relationships with members of the practitioner's family, which produces complex boundary issues. Here are several first-person accounts:

> I think there are a lot of variables. If I can avoid a situation, I will. Let's say it is a function like a hockey party. My kids are on the hockey team. The kids want to go, and they want the parents to go. So you are at this function [with clients]. You're not going to say to the kids, "Gee, I can't go to the hockey banquet." So you just go. . . . Sometimes you just kind of live with it. My older kids have friends who have been my patients in the past. I prefer that they not come over to our house, but you can't say to your kids, "Don't invite so and so." (Schank and Skovholt 1997:47)

> Young people that I've seen are becoming friends with my daughter through the school system. I was so surprised—one night I came home from work to discover that one of my clients was a good friend of my daughter's through school and was staying overnight with her. (47–48)

> I think the more difficult situation is interaction that my daughter has had. She is now away at college, but when she was here she would end up dating clients—only to find out and just be absolutely horrified and angry. That is probably the most difficult circumstance that we have been in. The confidentiality piece is really difficult because she would confront me with, "Is so and so your client?" She is real glad to be done with that. (48)

> My husband met another [colleague's] wife who wanted to socialize, and I had to say that I can't go to their house for dinner. . . . He was understanding but was still feeling curtailed by my practice because we couldn't socialize with people that he would have enjoyed because they had come to me for family counseling. (48)

Based on their extensive exploration of dual relationships that psychologists face in small communities and rural settings, Schank and Skovholt (1997) formulated a set of practical guidelines to help human service professionals manage boundary issues:

1. Nonsexual overlapping relationships are not a matter of "if" as much as "when" in the daily lives of small-community psychologists (Barnett & Yutrzenka, 1995). Ethical codes or standards are necessary but not sufficient and are tempered by experience and context (Barnett & Yutrzenka, 1995). Although it may seem obvious, knowledge of these codes and of state laws is essential in framing the background for small-community application. Continuing education in ethical issues adds to this framework.
2. Clear expectations and boundaries, whenever possible, strengthen the therapeutic relationship. This is especially important in situations where out-of-therapy contact cannot be closely controlled. Obtaining informed consent, sticking to time limits, protecting confidentiality (and explaining its limits), and documenting case progress (including being explicit about any overlapping relationships) diminished the risk of misunderstanding between client and psychologist.
3. Ongoing consultation and discussion of cases, especially those involving dual roles, provide a context for psychologists to get additional perspectives and decrease the isolation that sometimes accompanies rural and small-community practice. Each of us has blind spots—trusted colleagues can help us constructively examine them.
4. Self-knowledge and having a life outside of work lessens the chances that we as psychologists will use, even unknowingly, our clients for our own gratification. This also involves what Barnett and Yutrzenka (1995) have recommended in maintaining a constant interpersonal style and authentic presence with clients. (48–49)

Gottlieb (1995) offers a decision-making model designed to help practitioners conceptualize the degree of risk associated with such boundary challenges. The model focuses on three key dimensions: power, duration, and termination. According to Gottlieb, power refers to the amount or degree of influence that a practitioner has in relation to a client. Duration of the professional–client relationship is important because power increases over time. Clarity of termination refers to the likelihood that the client and the practitioner will have further professional contact. Gottlieb argues that dual relationships become more problematic as power increases and the length of treatment or services increases. In addition, vague or ambiguous criteria for termination of the professional–client relationship tend to complicate boundary issues.

Keeping these important dimensions in mind, human service professionals in small communities and rural areas would do well to anticipate the ways in which their professional lives may intersect with their personal and family lives and, where appropriate, talk with clients about how they might best handle these challenging circumstances. In some instances, practitioners and their clients can come up with relatively straightforward ways to manage the boundary issues. For example, a practitioner whose client works for the sole local plumber might talk about why it would be best for one of the client's colleagues in the plumbing company to handle visits to the practitioner's home. A practitioner who has an opportunity to chaperone an overnight class trip that includes both the practitioner's teenage child and the practitioner's client (that is, a classmate of the practitioner's child) can decide not to sign up to chaperone in order to avoid potential boundary confusion. Also, practitioners can talk with clients ahead of time about how they—the practitioners—will not approach clients they encounter in local stores in order to avoid boundary complications.

In contrast, however, are situations in which the potential or actual boundary issues are more difficult to manage. The practitioner whose client is employed at the same company as the practitioner's spouse may not be able to avoid encountering the client at a holiday party sponsored by the company for employees and their families. The practitioner whose client moves into a house near the practitioner's home cannot be expected to resolve the problem by moving to another location. The practitioner whose client is the one automobile mechanic in town cannot be expected to drive thirty-five miles to another mechanic. In these circumstances, it behooves the practitioner to broach the boundary issues with the client as early in their relationship as possible and discuss reasonable ways of handling potentially awkward circumstances in a manner that both find comfortable and in a way that protects the client's interests to the greatest extent possible. Practitioners should document these conversations to demonstrate their earnest efforts to handle these situations responsibly. In some situations, practitioners may feel the need to consult colleagues for advice or refer clients to other providers—if they are available—in an effort to avoid inappropriate or harmful dual relationships.

Conflicts of Interest

A constant theme in discussions of dual relationships and boundary issues is the concept of conflicts of interest. As I discussed earlier, some conflicts of interest arise when human service professionals knowingly enter into dual relationships—for example, when a practitioner receives a fee from a colleague to whom the practitioner refers clients or when a practitioner receives professional assistance from a client (such as a doctor or lawyer) who has specialized expertise from which the practitioner can benefit. However, in some instances conflicts of interest arise because of circumstances that are unavoidable or that practitioners could not have reasonably anticipated.

In my experience, such conflicts of interest take two forms. The first involves adversarial circumstances, in which practitioners unexpectedly find themselves caught between parties who are engaged in a dispute.

Case 6.4. Laura C. was a counselor who provided psychotherapy services for a twelve-year-old girl who was having difficulty maintaining friendships. During the course of the counseling, the girl told Ms. C. about problems that her parents—both of whom were schoolteachers—were having at home. The girl talked at length about her parents' incessant arguing and fighting. With the girl's consent, Ms. C. met with the girl's parents and talked about her distress concerning her parents' relationship. The girl's mother became enraged with Ms. C. and blamed her for meddling in the family's personal matters and upsetting her daughter. The mother then terminated the girl's counseling with Ms. C.

About five months later, when the next school year began, Ms. C. learned that the school had placed her son in a class taught by the former client's mother. Ms. C. was concerned that the mother would feel vindictive toward the boy and that his schooling would suffer as a result.

A common scenario with adversarial features involves practitioners who provide marital counseling. In some situations, the couple are unable to resolve their differences and decide to divorce. If the couple are not able to agree on child custody issues, the lawyer for one parent may subpoena the practitioner to testify about the emotional or psychiatric problems of the other parent that allegedly render the latter parent unfit. That is, one parent's lawyer may attempt to use the practitioner's testimony to impeach the other parent. Such practitioners, who would prefer to remain neutral and uninvolved in the legal dispute, then find themselves facing a subpoena that places them in a conflict-of-interest situation.

Case 6.5. Lorna S., a family therapist, provided counseling to Janice and Bob P. They were parents of eight-year-old twins and sought counseling to help them address chronic conflict in their relationship. After nearly a year of on-again, off-again counseling, the couple decided to divorce. Ms. P. was adamant that Mr. P. was emotionally unfit to parent their children. Ms. P. alleged that Mr. P. was a neglectful and emotionally abusive parent.

Ms. P.'s lawyer subpoenaed Dr. S. and her records in an effort to produce evidence of Mr. P.'s emotional and psychological impairment. Dr. S. felt uncomfortable because she was being forced to testify "for" one client and "against" the other.

Practitioners who provide couples or marital counseling should always anticipate the possibility (although not necessarily the probability) that the therapy will not resolve the couple's problems, that a serious legal dispute may continue after or arise from the therapy, and that one or both parties may try to involve the practitioner in the dispute. The practitioner should alert the clients to this possibility and of the practitioner's wish to avoid a conflict of interest. In fact, the NASW *Code of Ethics* (1996) highlights this specific phenomenon:

When social workers provide services to two or more people who have a relationship with each other (for example, couples, family members), social workers should clarify with all parties which individuals will be considered clients and the nature of social workers' professional obligations to the various individuals who are receiving services. Social workers who anticipate a conflict of interest among the individuals receiving services or who anticipate having to perform in potentially conflicting roles (for example, when a social worker is asked to testify in a child custody dispute or divorce proceedings involving clients) should clarify their role with the parties involved and take appropriate action to minimize any conflict of interest. (standard 1.06[a])

Similar guidance appears in the comparable standards in the American Psychological Association's *Ethical Principles of Psychologists and Code of Conduct* (1992):

When a psychologist agrees to provide services to several persons who have a relationship (such as husband and wife or parents and children), the psychologist attempts to clarify at the outset (1) which of the individuals are patients or clients and (2) the relationship the psychologist will have with each person. This clarification includes the role of the psychologist and the probable uses of the services provided or the information obtained. (standard 4.03[a])

As soon as it becomes apparent that the psychologist may be called on to perform potentially conflicting roles (such as marital counselor to husband and wife, and then witness for one party in a divorce proceeding), the psychologist attempts to clarify and adjust, or withdraw from, roles appropriately. (standard 4.03[b])

Human service professionals do receive subpoenas that place them in untenable conflicts of interest. In these situations, practitioners must understand the nature of subpoenas and specific strategies they can use in their effort to extricate themselves from these conflicts. Practitioners who are subpoenaed may face a special conflict-of-interest dilemma concerning the disclosure of confidential or privileged information. If the professional practices in a state in which laws grant clients the right of privileged communication, avoiding compliance with the subpoena may be easier because the legislature has acknowledged the importance of the privilege. Also, contrary to many practitioners' understanding, a legitimate response to a subpoena is to argue that the requested information should not be disclosed or can be obtained from some other source. A subpoena itself does not require a practitioner to disclose information. Instead, a subpoena is essentially a request for information, and it may be without merit. As Grossman (1973) has said, "If the recipient knew how easy it was to have a subpoena issued; if he knew how readily the subpoena could demand information when there actually was no legal right to command the disclosure of information; if he knew how often an individual releases information that legally he had no right to release because of intimidation—he would view the threat of the subpoena with less fear and greater skepticism" (245). Further, Grossman says, "In private discussions attorneys admit that the harassing tactic of using these writs is as important in court contests as the legal 'right to the truth'" (245).

Resisting disclosure of confidential information is appropriate, particularly when practitioners believe that the information is not essential or if they can argue that the information can be obtained from other sources. According to Wilson (1978),

> When data sought by the court can be obtained through some other source, a professional who has been subpoenaed may not have to disclose his confidential data. If the practitioner freely relinquishes his confidential though non-privileged data with little or no objection, the courts may not even check to see if the information can be obtained elsewhere. If the professional resists disclosure, however, the court may investigate to see if it can get the data from some other source. (138)

More specifically, practitioners can take several concrete steps to manage conflict-of-interest situations involving disclosure of confidential information:

1. Prepare a letter to the requester advising that the information is confidential and privileged and that absent the client's consent or a court order, the requested material cannot be released. Copies of any correspondence should be maintained in the file and may be necessary to present in a hearing on the matter.
2. File a motion to quash or objections to the subpoena based on the privileged nature of the communication between the client and practitioner. A request for a protective order may also be filed seeking to limit access to the records.
3. After writing a letter to the relevant parties in the case advising that the requested materials are confidential and privileged, it may be necessary to follow such a letter with written objections that

would be filed with the court or with a motion for a protective order that asks the court to deny access to the file because it contains privileged client information. Finally, a motion to quash the subpoena could also be filed. (Polowy and Gorenberg 1997:7)

Unanticipated conflicts of interest involving adversarial circumstances can also arise in nonclinical contexts. For example, human service administrators, researchers, or community organizers can find themselves in complicated boundary situations.

Case 6.6. Melinda T. was a social worker employed by a local community action program. Ms. T. was in charge of a grant-funded program to work with community residents and area developers to expand the supply of affordable housing for low- and moderate-income residents. Ms. T. also served on the board of the regional United Way, which provided partial funding for Ms. T.'s agency.

In her job as a program coordinator at the community action agency, Ms. T. learned that agency staff members were misspending United Way funds. She learned that approximately $20,000 of United Way money that was supposed to support staff salaries had been spent to refurbish the agency director's office. Ms. T. was unsure how to resolve her conflicting loyalties; she did not want to blow the whistle on her agency in a way that would jeopardize its viability, but she felt obligated to notify United Way officials of her agency's misappropriation of funds.

Case 6.7. Bonnie F. was the director of research in a large community mental health center. Her office was responsible for maintaining the facility's management information system and conducting program evaluations. The community mental health center received most of its funding from the state mental health department; Ms. F.'s husband was the assistant director of the division within the state mental health department that was responsible for funding her center and others throughout the state.

Ms. F. was reviewing agency data and was concerned about statistics showing a steady decline during the past six months in the number of clients served by the agency. Ms. F. knew that these data would pose a problem for the financially troubled agency, because the decline in clients served would translate into a reduction of state funding. Ms. F. decided to falsify some data about program use to inflate the service-delivery statistics. Ms. F.'s husband read his wife's report and realized that she had falsified the data. He felt caught between his loyalty to his wife and to his agency.

As these examples illustrate, some conflict-of-interest situations involve allegations or evidence of wrongdoing. In these dual relationship scenarios, practitioners feel caught between their duty to disclose misconduct of some sort and their loyalty to the agencies or organizations with which they are affiliated. As Barry (1986) observes with regard to whistle-blowing in agency settings,

> Truthfulness, noninjury, and fairness are the ordinary categories of obligations that employees have to third parties, but we can still ask: How are workers to reconcile obligations to employers or organizations and others? Should the employee ensure the welfare of the organization by reporting the fellow worker using drugs, or should she be loyal to the fellow worker and say nothing? Should the secretary carry out her boss's instructions, or should she tell his wife the truth? Should the accountant say nothing about the building code violations, or should she inform authorities? In each case the employee experiences divided loyalties. Resolving such conflict calls for a careful weighing of the obligations to the employer or firm, on the one hand, and of those to the third party, on the other. The process is never easy. (239)

The circumstances surrounding collegial misconduct and pertinent boundary issues are rarely clear-cut. The evidence of wrongdoing may be questionable, the effect of the misconduct may be equivocal, and the likelihood of resolving the problem satisfactorily may be small. Deciding whether to blow the whistle must be approached deliberately and cautiously. Human service professionals first should carefully consider the severity of the harm and misconduct involved; the quality of the evidence of wrong-doing; the effect of the decision on colleagues and the agency involved; the whistle-blower's motives (that is, whether revenge or a more noble purpose motivates the whistle-blowing); and the viability of alternative, intermediate courses of action (whether other, less drastic means might address the prob-lem—for example, directly confronting the alleged wrongdoer). As Fleish-man and Payne (1980) have argued, "There may be other ways to do right . . . than by blowing a whistle on a friend. A direct personal confrontation may serve both public interest and personal loyalty, if the corrupt practice can be ended and adequate restitution made" (43).

Codes of ethics can also provide conceptual guidance when practitioners find themselves in the midst of dual relationships and evidence of collegial misconduct. The NASW *Code of Ethics* (1996) provides a particularly good example of relevant standards that suggest an incremental approach, begin-ning with constructive collegial confrontation and ending, if necessary, with more formal notification of appropriate officials:

Social workers who believe that a colleague has acted unethically should seek resolution by discussing their concerns with the colleague when feasible and when such discussion is likely to be productive. (standard 2.11c])

When necessary, social workers who believe that a colleague has acted unethically should take action through appropriate formal channels (such as contacting a state licensing board or regulatory body, an NASW committee on inquiry, or other professional ethics committees). (stan-dard 2.11[a])

Of course, not all dual relationships involving conflicts of interest contain adversarial dimensions. Some conflict-of-interest situations involve people of goodwill who have only noble intentions, as in the following examples:

Case 6.8. Gary L. was a professor in a graduate program in psychology. He also served on the state parole board and several days per month conducted hearings for inmates eligible for parole.

One hearing Dr. L. conducted was for an inmate who was serving a seven-year sentence for drug possession and sales. Dr. L. and his col-leagues voted to parole the inmate, a college graduate who had been an enthusiastic and earnest participant in the prison's substance abuse treatment program.

One year after the inmate's parole, Dr. L. was surprised to find the man enrolled as a student in one of Dr. L.'s courses. The former inmate told Dr. L., with pride, that he was now working in the substance abuse treatment field and was pursuing a master's degree in psychology. Because the former inmate was still on parole—and was technically under Dr. L.'s jurisdiction during this period—Dr. L. was uncomfortable having the student in his class. Dr. L. talked with the student about transferring to another section of the course in order to avoid the dual relationship and potential conflict of interest.

――――

――――

Case 6.9. Cynthia W. was the executive director of a large psychiatric hospital that recently had merged with a nearby residential substance abuse treatment program. At the time of the merger, Ms. W.'s husband was the chief financial officer for the substance abuse treatment program. Under the terms of the merger, Ms. W. would retain her position as executive director of the new corporate entity. In principle, Mr. W. would have been appointed the new entity's chief financial officer. The new board was concerned, however, about nepotism and a conflict of interest, because Ms. W. would have direct supervisory responsibility for her husband.

――――

Whatever form unanticipated conflicts of interests take, human service professionals must take steps to minimize harm. As in the last case example, sometimes practitioners must be concerned about potential harm to colleagues and their employing organizations. In such instances, practitioners must take steps to protect these parties to the greatest extent possible. In the preceding example, for instance, the couple decided that the administration of the new corporate entity that resulted from the merger needed to be beyond reproach. Together they decided that Mr. W. would look for a new job in another organization.

Practitioners involved in potential or actual conflicts of interest that were unanticipated or unavoidable need to focus primarily on the need to protect their clients, whether the clients are individuals, couples, families, organizations, or communities. As the NASW *Code of Ethics* (1996) states,

> Social workers should be alert to and avoid conflicts of interest that interfere with the exercise of professional discretion and impartial judgment. Social workers should inform clients when a real or potential conflict of interest arises and take reasonable steps to resolve the issue in a manner that makes the clients' interests primary and protects clients' interests to the greatest extent possible. In some cases, protecting clients' interests may require termination of the professional relationship with proper referral of the client. (standard 1.06[a])

Professional Encounters

We saw in the discussion of dual relationships in small communities and rural areas that professional relationships sometimes produce overlapping and problematic boundaries. Such situations are not limited to small communities and rural areas, however. Dual relationships among professionals can occur even in the largest metropolitan areas. On occasion, practitioners who are involved in a professional relationship with a colleague will encounter that colleague unexpectedly in another professional context in a way that produces boundary issues. As with all dual relationships, practitioners must address the boundary issues in a manner designed to minimize potential harm.

Case 6.10. Professor S. was on the faculty of the graduate school of social work. She also served as a volunteer on a committee established by a prominent regional foundation with a large endowment to allocate funds for a wide range of human service endeavors. Twice each year, the committee solicited and reviewed grant applications.

The committee received applications from two of Professor S.'s colleagues at the university. One application was submitted by a colleague with whom Professor S. was working closely on another large research project. The second application was submitted by a colleague in the psychology department with whom Professor S. had only brief and superficial contact. In her effort to address the boundary issues, Professor

S. informed the chair of the grant review committee that she had decided it would be best to recuse herself from the deliberations concerning her research partner. Professor S. explained that she wanted to avoid any appearance of impropriety. However, Professor S. did not feel a need to recuse herself from the committee's deliberations about the application from her colleague in the university's psychology department, since her relationship with this colleague was superficial.

———

———

Case 6.11. A counselor, Margaret D., served on the ethics committee of her state's professional association. This committee reviewed and, when necessary, adjudicated ethics complaints filed against colleagues.

A long-standing client of Ms. D.'s, also a counselor in the community, was appointed to the ethics committee by the association's board of directors. Ms. D. was not comfortable serving on the ethics committee with her client, who was also her colleague. Ms. D. knew from experience that ethics committee members must engage in frank, sensitive discussion and debate about complicated ethical matters. On occasion, ethics committee members disagree with one another's judgments, sometimes vehemently. Ms. D. was concerned about the potentially harmful clinical implications for her client if they experienced conflict on the ethics committee. Ms. D. was also concerned that they might find dealing with each other in these two different contexts awkward and taxing. Ms. D. broached the issue with her client-colleague; together they decided that the potential downside was too great, and that Ms. D.'s client-colleague would not accept appointment to the association's ethics committee. Ms. D. was careful not to pressure her client-colleague to decline the appointment; rather, the two spent considerable time exploring the pertinent issues and reached a mutually satisfactory conclusion.

———

Social Encounters

One other form of unanticipated or unavoidable dual relationship involves social encounters with clients. Earlier I discussed practitioners' decisions when clients invite them to social events (such as a wedding, graduation, confirmation, or bar mitzvah) or when practitioners can reasonably anticipate encountering clients at community-based social events (for example, when a lesbian therapist in a relatively small community fully expects she will encounter a lesbian client at local social events).

In addition to these circumstances, human service professionals must also anticipate the possibility that they will encounter clients completely unexpectedly, in contexts in which neither party ever expected to encounter the other. Recognizing the frequency with which such unanticipated and unavoidable encounters occur, practitioners should have in mind how they will respond. In addition, practitioners would do well to raise the issue with clients in advance, in order to manage the situation as professionally and smoothly as possible, minimize harm that may result from the boundary crossing, and avoid bruising clients' feelings.

Case 6.12. A psychiatrist, Dr. F., had just begun providing clinical services to a thirty-two-year-old woman who had been diagnosed with posttraumatic stress disorder. She had been sexually abused as a child. Dr. F. provided psychotherapy and prescribed psychotropic medication.

On Thanksgiving Day, Dr. F. and her family went to her brother's home for their annual daylong get-together. Dr. F. was stunned to find that her brother's current girlfriend, whom he had invited to the Thanksgiving Day festivities, was Dr. F.'s client. Dr. F.'s brother had just started dating the client; she had not realized that her new boyfriend was Dr. F.'s brother, because they had different surnames and the identity of the woman's psychiatrist had not come up in her conversation with her boyfriend.

During the Thanksgiving Day get-together, Dr. F. tried tactfully to avoid sustained social conversation with her client. She also cut her visit short in an effort to avoid the awkward social encounter. During her next regularly scheduled appointment with the client the following week, Dr. F. broached the boundary issue in an effort to explore the various implications. The client said that she too felt uncomfortable, particularly because it appeared that she would continue to date Dr. F.'s brother. Dr. F. and the patient explored several options, including avoiding social contact at family events and the more drastic option of terminating their professional relationship. The client decided that because they had been working together for only a short period, it would not be too traumatic for her to locate a new psychiatrist. Dr. F. agreed with the plan and helped the woman find a new therapist.

Case 6.13. Kim T. was a clinical social worker. In her spare time, Ms. T. was a long-distance runner. She also worked out regularly at a local health club.

Ms. T. went to her health club one day and learned that one of her long-standing clients, David R., was working out in the weight room that Ms. T. frequently used. Ms. T. was very uncomfortable working out along with her client. She felt overexposed and was concerned that casual encounters with Mr. R. in this setting would complicate their professional–client relationship. Ms. T. was especially concerned about clinical ramifications because for several months she had wondered whether Mr. R. was feeling attracted to her; on a number of occasions, Mr. R. had made comments about how he wished he could find a girlfriend who was as sensitive and understanding as Ms. T. On two recent occasions, Mr. R. had asked Ms. T. whether she needed an escort to her car after their late-evening appointment, which was Ms. T.'s last appointment of the day.

Ms. T. discussed the issue with her peer supervision group. She and her colleagues decided that the situation was too uncomfortable and the clinical risks were too great for Ms. T. to continue encountering the client at the health club. Ms. T. explained to the client that she was concerned about the boundary issues and that she had decided to switch to another health club. Mr. R. denied that a problem existed and felt hurt by Ms. T.'s explanation and course of action. Ms. T. was not able to address the issue to Mr. R.'s satisfaction. Mr. R. eventually terminated the counseling.

This last case illustrates how even the most principled, conscientious, and thoughtful approach to boundary issues may not produce an entirely satisfactory outcome. Clearly, practitioners must do what they can to prevent and manage boundary issues in the most effective, ethical way possible. This includes discussing with clients, toward the beginning of their working relationship, how they will handle unexpected or unavoidable social encounters in the community. This approach does not guarantee satisfactory and uncomplicated outcomes, of course; however, a thoughtful, planned approach can substantially increase the likelihood that clients and other concerned parties will not be harmed.

Epilogue

I have examined a diverse array of dual relationship and boundary issues. Some issues that arise in the human services are relatively uncomplicated, and some are complex. Some involve practitioners who are motivated primarily by altruism, and some involve practitioners who violate clients' boundaries because of their own deep-seated pathology, emotional needs, or greed. Some boundary crossings serve a constructive purpose, whereas boundary violations are uniformly destructive.

Despite this remarkable variety, dual relationship and boundary issues share several key features. First, they contain the seeds for potential harm to others. Although serious harm is not inevitable—except in the most egregious violations, such as sexual involvement with a client—it is an ever-present possibility. Human service professionals must be vigilant in their efforts to minimize potential and actual harm to others.

Second, dual relationship and boundary issues pose risks to professionals themselves. At one extreme, practitioners who violate clients' boundaries and exploit their relationships with them run the very real risk of losing their license and destroying their career. Although some boundary violations occur in and remain in the dark, many eventually come to light. Even less egregious boundary crossings can sometimes trigger lawsuits and ethics complaints filed with licensing boards or other professional bodies, thus disrupting the careers of even the most noble practitioners. Given these possibilities, it behooves human service professionals to understand and follow sound risk-management strategies—primarily to protect clients but also to protect themselves.

Effective risk management concerning dual relationships and boundary issues should provide both conceptual guidance and practical steps that enhance protection of all parties involved. The following is a decision-making model, based on several available frameworks (Corey and Herlihy 1997; Gottlieb 1995; Reamer 2000), that practitioners can use when they encounter potential or actual dual relationships and boundary issues. This model incorporates various factors I highlighted throughout this discussion:

1. Attempt to set unambiguous boundaries at the beginning of all professional relationships.

2. Evaluate potential dual relationships and boundary issues by considering (a) the amount of power the practitioner holds over the client, (b) the duration of the relationship, (c) the clarity of conditions surrounding planned or actual termination, (d) the client's clinical profile (when involved in clinical work), and (e) prevailing ethical standards. How much power does the professional have over the client? How long has the relationship lasted? How likely is it that the client will return for additional services? In clinical relationships, to what extent do the client's clinical needs, issues, vulnerabilities, and symptoms increase the risk that the client will be harmed? To what extent does the dual relationship, boundary crossing, or boundary violation breach prevailing ethical standards? Relationships that entail considerable practitioner power, are long lasting, do not involve clear-cut termination, involve clinical issues that render clients vulnerable, and are not consistent with pertinent ethical standards are especially troubling and risky.

3. Based on these criteria, consider whether a dual relationship in any form is warranted or justifiable. Recognize that gradations exist between the extreme options of a full-fledged dual relationship and no dual relationship. For example, a practitioner may decide that attending a client's graduation from a substance abuse treatment program is permissible but that attending the post-graduation party at the client's home is not. A practitioner may decide to disclose to a particular client that he is a new parent without disclosing intimate details concerning his struggle with infertility. A human service grant administrator may decide to collaborate on a joint project with a private agency headed by her husband but recuse herself from all decisions at her agency concerning funding of her husband's program.

4. Pay special attention to potentially conflicting roles in the relationship or what Kitchener (1988) calls "role incompatibility." For instance, a clinical social worker should not agree to counsel her secretary. An administrator should not supervise her spouse. Of course, sometimes professionals do not

agree about the extent of role incompatibility, which entails divergent expectations and power differentials; among the best examples is the debate among professionals concerning whether practitioners in recovery should attend Alcoholics Anonymous or Narcotics Anonymous meetings at which a client is present and whether community-based mental health programs should hire former clients as staff members.

5. Whenever there is any degree of doubt about dual relationships or boundary issues, consult a thoughtful, principled, and trusted colleague. It is important to consult with colleagues who understand one's work, particularly in relation to services provided, clientele served, and relevant ethical standards.

6. Discuss the relevant issues with all the parties involved, especially clients. Clients should be actively and deliberately involved in these judgments, in part as a sign of respect and in part to promote informed consent. Fully inform clients of any potential risks.

7. Work under supervision whenever boundary issues are complex and the related risk is high.

8. If necessary, refer the client to another professional in order to minimize risk and prevent harm.

9. Document key aspects of the decision-making process, for example, colleagues consulted, documents reviewed (codes of ethics, agency policies, statutes, regulations), and discussions with clients. As Gutheil and Gabbard (1993) observe in reviewing the findings of Lipton (1977) with regard to clinical contexts, "It is ultimately impossible to codify or prescribe a personal relationship between therapist and patient in a precise manner. Perhaps the best risk management involves careful consideration of any departures from one's usual practice accompanied by careful documentation of the reasons for the departure" (195–96).

To prevent inappropriate dual relationships and to help practitioners manage complex boundary issues, human service professionals must mount an ambitious education and training agenda. This agenda should include four principal components. First, professional education programs in psychiatry, social work, psychology, marriage and family therapy, psychiatric nursing, and counseling must address these issues vigorously and comprehensively, in the context of both classroom education and internships. Discrete classroom courses devoted to professional ethics, and portions of other courses that include ethics as a key topic (for example, courses on clinical practice, administration, supervision), should incorporate readings about and discussions of dual relationships and boundary issues. Supervisors in internship settings should address this issue deliberately as well, with respect to interns' relationships with clients and with their supervisors and other staff.

Second, continuing education programs should highlight these issues regularly. Annual conferences of professional associations and continuing education seminars should routinely provide participants with workshops and seminars on dual relationships and boundary issues.

Third, human service administrators and supervisors should offer staff members sustained in-service training on these issues. In addition to traditional didactic presentations, the training should include opportunities for staff members to wrestle with complex case scenarios. In-service training facilitators can help staff members apply various guidelines—agency policy, pertinent laws, state regulations, codes of ethics—to this case material to help sharpen the staff's ethical judgment.

Finally, human service administrators and supervisors should develop and continually refine agency-based policies designed to provide staff with constructive guidance regarding boundary issues. Although formulating crystal-clear, unequivocal guidelines that address all boundary-related permutations is impossible, thoughtful, conceptually mature guidelines can communicate to staff members the core values and concepts they need to consider and help them enhance their critical thinking skills. Smith and Fitzpatrick's (1995) astute conclusion about the ambiguity of many boundary issues in clinical contexts has broad implications for the human services in general:

> In summary, boundary issues regularly pose complex challenges to clinicians. The effects of crossing commonly recognized boundaries range from significant therapeutic progress to serious, indelible harm. The issues are further complicated by the wide range of individual variation that exists in a field where what is normal practice for one clinician may be considered a boundary violation by another. Although setting appropriate boundaries is a professional imperative, flexibility in their maintenance is equally important. Clinicians should avoid setting simplistic standards that may create barriers to therapeutic progress. In the final analysis, ethical practice is governed less by proscriptions than by sound clinical judgment bearing on the therapeutic interventions that will advance the client's welfare. Given the

individual differences among clients, fine adjustments are required in every case. (505)

In the end, human service professionals who face difficult and challenging boundary issues must draw on their finely honed ethical instincts. Conceptual guidance is fine and important, but practitioners' handling of daunting circumstances ultimately must depend on their genuine and passionate determination to make ethically sound judgments.

References

Akamatsu, T. J. 1988. "Intimate Relationships with Former Clients: National Survey of Attitudes and Behavior Among Practitioners." *Professional Psychology: Research and Practice* 19:454–58.

American Association for Marriage and Family Therapy. 1998. *AAMFT Code of Ethics*. Washington, D.C.: American Association for Marriage and Family Therapy.

American Counseling Association. 1995. *Codes of Ethics and Standards of Practice*. Alexandria, Va.: American Counseling Association.

American Medical Association. 1996. *Principles of Medical Ethics*. Chicago: American Medical Association.

American Psychological Association. 1992. *Ethical Principles of Psychologists and Code of Conduct*. Washington, D.C.: American Psychological Association.

Anderson, Sandra C., and Deborah L. Mandell. 1989. "The Use of Self-disclosure by Professional Social Workers." *Social Casework* 70 (5): 259–67.

Austin, K. M., M. E. Moline, and G. T. Williams. 1990. *Confronting Malpractice: Legal and Ethical Dilemmas in Psychotherapy*. Newbury Park, Calif.: Sage.

Barker, R. L. 1999. *The Social Work Dictionary*. 4th ed. Washington, D.C.: National Association of Social Workers.

Barker, R. L., and D. M. Branson. 2000. *Forensic Social Work*. 2d ed. Binghamton, N.Y.: Haworth.

Barr, Derek. 1997. "Clinical Social Worker, Disciplined by State, Sued over Patient Relations." *(Harrisonburg, Va.) Daily News-Record*, November 14, p. 19.

Barry, Vincent. 1986. *Moral Issues in Business*. 3d ed. Belmont, Calif.: Wadsworth.

Bayles, M. D. 1986. "Professional Power and Self-regulation." *Business and Professional Ethics Journal* 5 (1): 26–46.

Berliner, A. K. 1989. "Misconduct in Social Work Practice." *Social Work* 34 (1): 69–72.

Bernard, John L., and Carmen S. Jara. 1986. "The Failure of Clinical Psychology Students to Apply Understood Ethical Principles." *Professional Psychology: Research and Practice* 17:316–21.

Bersoff, D. N., ed. 1999. *Ethical Conflicts in Psychology.* 2d ed. Washington, D.C.: American Psychological Association.

Besharov, D. J. 1985. *The Vulnerable Social Worker: Liability for Serving Children and Families.* Silver Spring, Md.: National Association of Social Workers.

Bissell, Le Clair, and Paul W. Haberman. 1984. *Alcoholism in the Professions.* New York: Oxford University Press.

Blackshaw, S. L., and J. B. Miller. 1994. Letter to the Editor. *American Journal of Psychiatry* 151 (2): 293.

Blythe, B. J., and T. Tripodi. 1989. *Measurement in Direct Practice.* Newbury Park, Calif.: Sage.

Bonosky, N. 1995. "Boundary Violations in Social Work Supervision: Clinical, Educational, and Legal Implications." *Clinical Supervisor* 13 (2): 79–95.

Borys, D. S., and K. S. Pope. 1989. "Dual Relationships Between Therapists and Clients: National Study of Psychologists, Psychiatrists, and Social Workers." *Professional Psychology: Research and Practice* 20:283–93.

Bouhoutsos, J. C. 1985. "Therapist–Client Sexual Involvement: A Challenge for Mental Health Professionals." *American Journal of Orthopsychiatry* 55:177–82.

Bouhoutsos, J. C., et al. 1983. "Sexual Intimacy Between Psychotherapists and Patients." *Professional Psychology: Research and Practice* 14:185–96.

Brodsky, A. M. 1986. "The Distressed Psychologist: Sexual Intimacies and Exploitation." In R. R. Kilburg, P. E. Nathan, and R. W. Thoreson, eds., *Professionals in Distress: Issues, Syndromes, and Solutions in Psychology,* pp. 153–71. Washington, D.C.: American Psychological Association.

Brownlee, Keith. 1996. "The Ethics of Nonsexual Dual Relationships: A Dilemma for the Rural Mental Health Professional." *Community Mental Health Journal* 32:497–503.

Bruni, Frank. 1998. "A Child Psychiatrist and Pedophile." *New York Times,* April 19, pp. 33, 36.

Bullis, R. K. 1995. *Clinical Social Worker Misconduct.* Chicago: Nelson-Hall.

Calfee, Barbara E. 1997. "Lawsuit Prevention Techniques." In *The Hatherleigh Guide to Ethics in Therapy,* pp. 109–25. New York: Hatherleigh.

Callahan, Daniel, and Sissela Bok, eds. 1980. *Ethics Teaching in Higher Education.* New York: Plenum.

Chapman, Charlotte. 1997. "Dual Relationships in Substance Abuse Treatment." *Alcoholism Treatment Quarterly* 15:73–79.

Cohen, C. B. 1988. "Ethics Committees." *Hastings Center Report* 18:11.

Cohen, R. J. 1979. *Malpractice: A Guide for Mental Health Professionals*. New York: Free Press.

Cohen, R. J., and W. E. Mariano. 1982. *Legal Guidebook in Mental Health*. New York: Free Press.

Coleman, Eli, and Susan Schaefer. 1986. "Boundaries of Sex and Intimacy Between Client and Counselor." *Journal of Counseling and Development* 64:341–44.

Commission on Employment and Economic Support. National Association of Social Workers. 1987. *Impaired Social Worker Program Resource Book*. Silver Spring, Md.: National Association of Social Workers.

Committee on Women in Psychology. American Psychological Association. 1989. "If Sex Enters into the Psychotherapy Relationship." *Professional Psychology: Research and Practice* 20:112–15.

Congress, E. P. 1996. "Dual Relationships in Academia: Dilemmas for Social Work Educators." *Journal of Social Work Education* 32 (3): 329–38.

Corey, Gerald, Marianne Corey, and Patrick Callanan. 1997. *Issues and Ethics in the Helping Professions*. 5th ed. Pacific Grove, Calif.: Brooks/Cole.

Corey, Gerald, and Barbara Herlihy. 1997. "Dual/Multiple Relationships: Toward a Consensus of Thinking." In *The Hatherleigh Guide to Ethics in Therapy*, pp. 183–94. New York: Hatherleigh.

"Counselor, Counseling Center Mishandle Transference Phenomenon." 1997. *Mental Health Law News* 12 (9): 6.

"Counselor Begins Sexual Relationship with Client." 1991. *Mental Health Law News* 6 (4): 1.

"Court Upholds Law Used to Convict Therapist for Sexual Misconduct." 1998. *Mental Health Law News* 13 (3): 2.

"Court Upholds Revocation of Psychologist's License Because He Had Sex with Patient." 1998. *Mental Health Law News* 13 (2): 6.

Cranford, R. E., and A. E. Doudera, eds. 1984. *Institutional Ethics Committees and Health Care Decision Making*. Ann Arbor, Mich.: Health Administration Press.

Deutsch, C. 1985. "A Survey of Therapists' Personal Problems and Treatment." *Professional Psychology: Research and Practice* 16:305–15.

Donagan, Alan. 1977. *The Theory of Morality*. Chicago: University of Chicago Press.

Dorland's Medical Dictionary. 1974. 25th ed. Philadelphia: Saunders.

Doyle, Kevin. 1997. "Substance Abuse Counselors in Recovery: Implications for the Ethical Issue of Dual Relationships." *Journal of Counseling and Development* 75:428–32.

Ebert, B. W. 1997. "Dual-Relationship Prohibitions: A Concept Whose Time Never Should Have Come." *Applied and Preventive Psychology* 6:137–56.

Elliott, Richard L., Greg Wolber, and Will Ferriss. 1997. "A Survey of Hospital Staff Attitudes Toward Ethically Problematic Relationships with Patients." *Administration and Policy in Mental Health* 24:443–49.

Epstein, Richard. 1994. *Keeping Boundaries: Maintaining Safety and Integrity in the Psychotherapeutic Process*. Washington, D.C.: American Psychiatric Press.

Epstein, R. S., and R. I. Simon. 1990. "The Exploitation Index: An Early Warning Indicator of Boundary Violations in Psychotherapy." *Bulletin of the Menninger Clinic* 54:450–65.

Feldman-Summers, Shirley, and Gwendolyn Jones. 1984. "Psychological Impacts of Sexual Contact Between Therapists or Other Health Care Practitioners and Their Clients." *Journal of Consulting and Clinical Psychology* 52:1054–61.

Fleishman, J. L., and B. L. Payne. 1980. *Ethical Dilemmas and the Education of Policymakers*. Hastings-on-Hudson, N.Y.: Hastings Center.

Frankena, W. K. 1973. *Ethics*. 2d ed. Englewood Cliffs, N.J.: Prentice-Hall.

Freudenberger, H. J. 1986. "Chemical Abuse Among Psychologists: Symptoms, Causes, and Treatment Issues." In R. R. Kilburg, P. E. Nathan, and R. W. Thoreson, eds., *Professionals in Distress: Issues, Syndromes, and Solutions in Psychology*, pp. 135–52. Washington, D.C.: American Psychological Association.

Gabbard, Glen O. 1990. *Psychodynamic Psychiatry in Clinical Practice*. Washington, D.C.: American Psychiatric Press.

Gabbard, Glen O., ed. 1989. *Sexual Exploitation in Professional Relationships*. Washington, D.C.: American Psychiatric Press.

Gartrell, Nanette, et al. 1986. "Psychiatrist–Patient Sexual Contact: Results of a National Survey." *American Journal of Psychiatry* 143 (9): 1126–31.

Gartrell, Nanette, et al. 1987. "Reporting Practices of Psychiatrists Who Knew of Sexual Misconduct by Colleagues." *American Journal of Orthopsychiatry* 57:287–95.

Gechtman, Lucille. 1989. "Sexual Contact Between Social Workers and Their Clients." In Glen O. Gabbard, ed., *Sexual Exploitation in Professional Relationships*, pp. 27–38. Washington, D.C.: American Psychiatric Press.

Gechtman, Lucille, and J. C. Bouhoutsos. 1985. "Sexual Intimacy Between Social Workers and Clients." Paper presented at the annual meeting of the Society for Clinical Social Workers, University City, Calif.

Gewirth, A. 1978a. *Reason and Morality*. Chicago: University of Chicago Press.

———. 1978b. "Ethics." In *Encyclopedia Britannica*. 15th ed. Chicago: Encyclopedia Britannica.

Gifis, S. H. 1991. *Law Dictionary*. 3d ed. Hauppauge, N.Y.: Barron's.

Goisman, R. M., and T. G. Gutheil. 1992. "Risk Management in the Practice of Behavior Therapy: Boundaries and Behavior." *American Journal of Psychotherapy* 46 (4): 532–43.

Gorovitz, Samuel, ed. 1971. *Mill: Utilitarianism*. Indianapolis: Bobbs-Merrill.

Gottlieb, M. C. 1995. "Avoiding Exploitive Dual Relationships: A Decision-Making Model." In D. N. Bersoff, ed., *Ethical Conflicts in Psychology*, pp. 242–43. Washington, D.C.: American Psychological Association.

Grinnell, R. M., Jr., ed. 1997. *Social Work Research and Evaluation*. 5th ed. Itasca, Ill.: Peacock.

Grosskurth, Phyllis. 1986. *Melanie Klein: Her World and Her Work*. New York: Knopf.

Grossman, Maurice. 1973. "The Psychiatrist and the Subpoena." *Bulletin of the American Academy of Psychiatry and the Law* 1 (4): 245–53.

Gutheil, T. G. 1989. "Borderline Personality Disorder, Boundary Violations, and Patient–Therapist Sex: Medicolegal Pitfalls." *American Journal of Psychiatry* 146 (5): 597–602.

Gutheil, T. G., and G. O. Gabbard. 1993. "The Concept of Boundaries in Clinical Practice: Theoretical and Risk-Management Dimensions." *American Journal of Psychiatry* 150 (2): 188–96.

Gutheil, T. G., and R. I. Simon. 1995. "Between the Chair and the Door: Boundary Issues in the Therapeutic 'Transition Zone.'" *Harvard Review of Psychiatry* 2:336–40.

Guy, J. D., P. L. Poelstra, and M. Stark. 1989. "Personal Distress and Therapeutic Effectiveness: National Survey of Psychologists Practicing Psychotherapy." *Professional Psychology: Research and Practice* 20:48–50.

Hancock, R. N. 1974. *Twentieth-Century Ethics*. New York: Columbia University Press.

Herlihy, Barbara, and Gerald Corey. 1992. *Dual Relationships in Counseling*. Alexandria, Va.: American Association for Counseling and Development.

"Improper Sexual Contact Blamed for Further Psychological Problems." 1997. *Mental Health Law News* 12 (6): 4.

Jamal, K., and N. Bowie. 1995. "Theoretical Considerations for a Meaningful Code of Ethics." *Journal of Business Ethics* 14:703–14.

Jayaratne, Srinika, and Wayne A. Chess. 1984. "Job Satisfaction, Burnout, and Turnover: A National Study." *Social Work* 29 (5):448–55.

Jayaratne, Srinika, Tom Croxton, and Debra Mattison. 1997. "Social Work Professional Standards: An Exploratory Study." *Social Work* 42 (2): 187–99.

Johnson, M., and G. L. Stone. 1986. "Social Workers and Burnout." *Journal of Social Work Research* 10:67–80.

Jonsen, A. R. 1984. "A Guide to Guidelines." *American Society of Law and Medicine: Ethics Committee Newsletter* 2:4.

Kagle, J. D. 1991. *Social Work Records*. 2d ed. Belmont, Calif.: Wadsworth.

Kagle, J. D., and P. N. Giebelhausen. 1994. "Dual Relationships and Professional Boundaries." *Social Work* 39 (2): 213–20.

Kilburg, R. R., F. W. Kaslo, and G. R. VandenBos. 1988. "Professionals in Distress." *Hospital and Community Psychiatry* 39:723–25.

Kilburg, R. R., P. E. Nathan, and R. W. Thoreson, eds. 1986. *Professionals in Distress: Issues, Syndromes, and Solutions in Psychology*. Washington, D.C.: American Psychological Association.

Kitchener, K. S. 1988. "Dual Role Relationships: What Makes Them So Problematic?" *Journal of Counseling and Development* 67:217–21.

Knutsen, E. S. 1977. "On the Emotional Well-Being of Psychiatrists: Overview and Rationale." *American Journal of Psychoanalysis* 37:123–29.

Koeske, G. F., and R. D. Koeske. 1989. "Work Load and Burnout: Can Social Support and Perceived Accomplishment Help?" *Social Work* 34 (3): 243–48.

Kultgen, John. 1982. "The Ideological Use of Professional Codes." *Business and Professional Ethics Journal* 1 (3): 53–69.

Kutchins, Herb. 1991. "The Fiduciary Relationship: The Legal Basis for Social Workers' Responsibilities to Clients." *Social Work* 36 (2): 106–13.

Laliotis, D. A., and J. H. Grayson. 1985. "Psychologist Heal Thyself: What Is Available for the Impaired Psychologist?" *American Psychologist* 40:84–96.

Lamb, D. H., N. R. Presser, K. S. Pfost, M. C. Baum, V. R. Jackson, and P. A. Jarvis. 1987. "Confronting Professional Impairment During the Internship: Identification, Due Process, and Remediation." *Professional Psychology: Research and Practice* 18:597–603.

Lipton, S. D. 1977. "The Advantages of Freud's Technique as Shown in His Analysis of the Rat Man." *International Journal of Psychoanalysis* 58:255–73.

Little, M. I. 1990. *Psychotic Anxieties and Containment: A Personal Record of an Analysis with Winnicott.* Northvale, N.J.: Aronson.

Loewenberg, Frank M., and Ralph Dolgoff. 1996. *Ethical Decisions for Social Work Practice.* 5th ed. Itasca, Ill.: Peacock.

McCrady, B. S. 1989. "The Distressed or Impaired Professional: From Retribution to Rehabilitation." *Journal of Drug Issues* 19:337–49.

Madden, R. G. 1998. *Legal Issues in Social Work, Counseling, and Mental Health.* Thousand Oaks, Calif.: Sage.

Millon, Theodore, Carrie Millon, and Michael Antoni. 1986. "Sources of Emotional and Mental Disorder Among Psychologists: A Career Development Perspective." In R. R. Kilburg, P. E. Nathan, and R. W. Thoreson, eds., *Professionals in Distress: Issues, Syndromes, and Solutions in Psychology*, pp. 119–34. Washington, D.C.: American Psychological Association.

Myers, W. A. 1994. Letter to the Editor. *American Journal of Psychiatry* 151 (2): 293–94.

National Association of Social Workers. 1996. *Code of Ethics.* Washington, D.C.: National Association of Social Workers.

Olarte, S. W. 1997. "Sexual Boundary Violations." In *The Hatherleigh Guide to Ethics in Therapy*, pp. 195–209. New York: Hatherleigh.

"Patient's Claims Against Psychiatrist Dismissed." 1998. *Mental Health Law News* 13 (12): 2.

Peterson, Marilyn R. 1992. *At Personal Risk: Boundary Violations in Professional–Client Relationships.* New York: Norton.

Polowy, Carolyn I., and Carol Gorenberg. 1997. *Client Confidentiality and Privileged Communication: Office of General Counsel Law Notes.* Washington, D.C.: National Association of Social Workers.

Pope, G. G. 1990. "Abuse of Psychotherapy: Psychotherapist–Patient Intimacy." *Psychotherapy and Psychosomatics* 53:191–98.

Pope, K. S. 1986. "New Trends in Malpractice Cases and Changes in APA's Liability Insurance." *Independent Practitioner* 6:23–6.

———. 1988. "How Clients Are Harmed by Sexual Contact with Mental Health Professionals: The Syndrome and Its Prevalence." *Journal of Counseling and Development* 67:222–26.

———. 1991. "Dual Relationships in Psychotherapy." *Ethics and Behavior* 1:21–34.

———. 1995. "Dual Relationships in Psychotherapy." In D. N. Bersoff, ed., *Ethical Conflicts in Psychology*, pp. 209–13. Washington, D.C.: American Psychological Association.

Pope, K. S., and J. C. Bouhoutsos. 1986. *Sexual Intimacy Between Therapists and Patients.* New York: Praeger.

Pope, K. S., P. Keith-Spiegel, and B. G. Tabachnick. 1986. "Sexual Attraction to Clients: The Human Therapist and the (Sometimes) Inhuman Training System." *American Psychologist* 41:147–58.

Pope, K. S., B. G. Tabachnick, and P. Keith-Spiegel. 1988. "Good and Bad Practice in Psychotherapy: National Survey of Beliefs of Psychologists." *Professional Psychology: Research and Practice* 19:547–52.

Pope, K. S., B. G. Tabachnick, and P. Keith-Spiegel. 1995. "Ethics of Practice: The Beliefs and Behaviors of Psychologists and Therapists." In D. N. Bersoff, ed., *Ethical Conflicts in Psychology*, pp. 72–84. Washington, D.C.: American Psychological Association.

Popper, Karl. 1966. *The Open Society and Its Enemies.* 5th ed. London: Routledge and Kegan Paul.

Prochaska, J. O., and J. C. Norcross. 1983. "Psychotherapists' Perspectives on Treating Themselves and Their Clients for Psychic Distress." *Professional Psychology: Research and Practice* 14:642–55.

"Psychiatrist Censured for Engaging in Commercial Transactions with Clients." 1996. *Mental Health Law News* 11 (3): 6.

"Psychologist Encourages Sexual Misconduct Between Patient and Psychiatrist." 1989. *Mental Health Law News* 4 (3): 2.

Rawls, John. 1971. *A Theory of Justice.* Cambridge, Mass.: Harvard University Press.

Reamer, F. G. 1979. "Fundamental Ethical Issues in Social Work: An Essay Review." *Social Service Review* 53 (2): 229–43.

———. 1980. "Ethical Content in Social Work." *Social Casework* 61 (9): 531–40.

———. 1982. "Conflicts of Professional Duty in Social Work." *Social Casework* 63 (10): 579–85.

———. 1983. "Ethical Dilemmas in Social Work Practice." *Social Work* 28 (1): 31–35.

———. 1984. "Enforcing Ethics in Social Work." *Health Matrix* 2 (2): 17–25.

———. 1987a. "Values and Ethics." In *Encyclopedia of Social Work*, 18th ed., pp. 801–9. Silver Spring, Md.: National Association of Social Workers.

———. 1987b. "Ethics Committees in Social Work." *Social Work* 32 (3): 188–92.

———. 1987c. "Informed Consent in Social Work." *Social Work* 32 (5): 425–29.

———. 1989. "Toward Ethical Practice: The Relevance of Ethical Theory." *Social Thought* 15 (3–4): 67–78.

———. 1990. *Ethical Dilemmas in Social Service*. 2d ed. New York: Columbia University Press.

———. 1992. "The Impaired Social Worker." *Social Work* 37 (2): 165–70.

———. 1993. *The Philosophical Foundations of Social Work*. New York: Columbia University Press.

———. 1994a. "Social Work Values and Ethics." In F. G. Reamer, ed., *The Foundations of Social Work Knowledge*, pp. 195–230. New York: Columbia University Press.

———. 1994b. *Social Work Malpractice and Liability*. New York: Columbia University Press.

———. 1995a. "Ethics and Values." In R. L. Edwards, ed., *Encyclopedia of Social Work*, 19th ed., vol. 1, pp. 893–902. Washington, D.C.: National Association of Social Workers.

———. 1995b. "Malpractice and Liability Claims Against Social Workers: First Facts." *Social Work* 40 (5): 595–601.

———. 1995c. "Ethics Consultation in Social Work." *Social Thought* 18 (1): 3–16.

———. 1997a. "Ethical Issues for Social Work Practice." In Michael Reisch and Eileen Gambrill, eds., *Social Work in the Twenty-first Century*, pp. 340–49. Thousand Oaks, Calif.: Pine Forge/Sage.

———. 1997b. "Ethical Standards in Social Work: The NASW *Code of Ethics*." In R. L. Edwards, ed., *Encyclopedia of Social Work*, 19th ed., suppl., pp. 113–23. Washington, D.C.: National Association of Social Workers.

———. 1998a. *Ethical Standards in Social Work: A Review of the NASW Code of Ethics*. Washington, D.C.: NASW Press.

———. 1998b. "Social Work." In Ruth Chadwick, ed., *Encyclopedia of Applied Ethics*, vol. 4, pp. 169–80. San Diego, Calif.: Academic Press.

———. 1998c. *Social Work Research and Evaluation Skills: A Case-Based, User-Friendly Approach*. New York: Columbia University Press.

———. 1999. *Social Work Values and Ethics*. 2d ed. New York: Columbia University Press.

———. 2000. "The Social Work Ethics Audit: A Risk Management Strategy." *Social Work* 45 (4): 355–66.

————. 2001. *Ethics Education in Social Work*. Alexandria, Va.: Council on Social Work Education.

————. in press. "Boundary Issues in Social Work: Managing Dual Relationships." *Social Work*.

Reamer, F. G., and Abramson, M. 1982. *The Teaching of Social Work Ethics*. Hastings-on-Hudson, N.Y.: Hastings Center.

Reaves, R. R. 1986. "Legal Liability and Psychologists." In R. R. Kilburg, P. E. Nathan, and R. W. Thoreson, eds., *Professionals in Distress: Issues, Syndromes, and Solutions in Psychology*, pp. 173–84. Washington, D.C.: American Psychological Association.

Rhodes, M. L. 1986. *Ethical Dilemmas in Social Work Practice*. London: Routledge and Kegan Paul.

Ross, W. D. 1930. *The Right and the Good*. Oxford: Clarendon.

Rubin, Allen, and Earl Babbie. 1997. *Research Methods for Social Work*. 3d ed. Pacific Grove, Calif.: Brooks/Cole.

St. Germaine, Jacquelyn. 1993. "Dual Relationships: What's Wrong with Them?" *American Counselor* 2:25–30.

————. 1996. "Dual Relationships and Certified Alcohol and Drug Counselors: A National Study of Ethical Beliefs and Behaviors." *Alcoholism Treatment Quarterly* 14:29–44.

Schank, J. A., and T. M. Skovholt. 1997. "Dual-Relationship Dilemmas of Rural and Small-Community Psychologists." *Professional Psychology: Research and Practice* 28:44–49.

Schoener, G. R. 1995. "Assessment of Professionals Who Have Engaged in Boundary Violations." *Psychiatric Annals* 25:95–99.

Schoener, G. R., and J. C. Gonsiorek. 1990. "Assessment and Development of Rehabilitation Plans for the Therapist." In G. R. Gonsiorek, J. H. Milgrom, and J. C. Gonsiorek, eds., *Psychotherapists' Sexual Involvement with Clients: Intervention and Prevention*, pp. 401–20. Minneapolis: Walk-In Counseling Center.

Schoener, G. R., et al. 1989. *Psychotherapists' Sexual Involvement with Clients: Intervention and Prevention*. Minneapolis: Walk-In Counseling Center.

Schutz, B. M. 1982. *Legal Liability in Psychotherapy*. San Francisco: Jossey-Bass.

Sell, John M., Michael C. Gottlieb, and Lawrence Schoenfeld. 1986. "Ethical Considerations of Social/Romantic Relationships with Present and Former Clients." *Professional Psychology: Research and Practice* 17:504–8.

Senger, H. L. 1994. Letter to the Editor. *American Journal of Psychiatry* 151 (2): 294.

Siegel, D. H. 1984. "Defining Empirically Based Practice." *Social Work* 29 (4): 325–31.

————. 1988. "Integrating Data-Gathering Techniques and Practice Activities." In

R. M. Grinnell Jr., ed., *Social Work Research and Evaluation*, 3d ed., pp. 465–82. Itasca, Ill.: Peacock.

Simon, R. I. 1995. "The Natural History of Therapist Sexual Misconduct: Identification and Prevention." *Psychiatric Annals* 25:90–94.

———. 1999. "Therapist–Patient Sex: From Boundary Violations to Sexual Misconduct." *Forensic Psychiatry* 22:31–47.

Sloan, Douglas. 1980. "The Teaching of Ethics in the American Undergraduate Curriculum, 1876–1976." In Daniel Callahan and Sissela Bok, eds., *Ethics Teaching in Higher Education*, pp. 1–57. New York: Plenum.

Smart, J. J. C. 1971. "Extreme and Restricted Utilitarianism." In Samuel Gorovitz, ed., *Mill: Utilitarianism*, pp. 195–203. Indianapolis: Bobbs-Merrill.

Smart, J. J. C., and Bernard Williams. 1973. *Utilitarianism: For and Against*. Cambridge: Cambridge University Press.

Smith, David, and Marilyn Fitzpatrick. 1995. "Patient–Therapist Boundary Issues: An Integrative Review of Theory and Research." *Professional Psychology: Research and Practice* 26:499–506.

"Social Worker Engages in Sexual Relationship with Patient." 1999. *Mental Health Law News* 14 (5): 2.

Sonnenstuhl, W. J. 1989. "Reaching the Impaired Professional: Applying Findings from Organizational and Occupational Research." *Journal of Drug Issues* 19:533–39.

Stake, Jayne E., and Joan Oliver. 1991. "Sexual Contact and Touching Between Therapist and Client: A Survey of Psychologists' Attitudes and Behavior." *Professional Psychology: Research and Practice* 22:297–307.

Stone, A. A. 1984. *Law, Psychiatry, and Morality*. Washington, D.C.: American Psychiatric Press.

Strasburger, L. H., L. Jorgenson, and R. Randles. 1995. "Criminalization of Psychotherapist–Patient Sex." In D. N. Bersoff, ed., *Ethical Conflicts in Psychology*, pp. 229–33. Washington, D.C.: American Psychological Association.

Strom-Gottfried, K. J. 1999. "Professional Boundaries: An Analysis of Violations by Social Workers." *Families in Society* 80:439–49.

Teel, K. 1975. "The Physician's Dilemma: A Doctor's View: What the Law Should Be." *Baylor Law Review* 27:6–9.

"Therapist Marries Patient with Multiple Personalities; Showcases Her While Treating Condition." 1996. *Mental Health Law News* 11 (12): 2.

Thoreson, R. W., M. Miller, and C. J. Krauskopf. 1989. "The Distressed Psychologist: Prevalence and Treatment Considerations." *Professional Psychology: Research and Practice* 20:153–58.

Thoreson, R. W., P. E. Nathan, J. K. Skorina, and R. R. Kilburg. 1983. "The Alcoholic Psychologist: Issues, Problems, and Implications for the Profession." *Professional Psychology: Research and Practice* 14:670–84.

Trice, H. M., and J. M. Beyer. 1984. "Work-Related Outcomes of the Constructive Confrontation Strategy in a Job-Based Alcoholism Program." *Journal of Studies on Alcohol* 45:393–404.

Twemlow, S. W., and G. O. Gabbard. 1989. "The Love-Sick Therapist." In Glen O. Gabbard, ed., *Sexual Exploitation in Professional Relationships*, pp. 71–87. Washington, D.C.: American Psychiatric Press.

VandenBos, G. R., and R. F. Duthie. 1986. "Confronting and Supporting Colleagues in Distress." In R. R. Kilburg, P. E. Nathan, and R. W. Thoreson, eds., *Professionals in Distress: Issues, Syndromes, and Solutions in Psychology*, pp. 211–31. Washington, D.C.: American Psychological Association.

Williams, Bernard. 1972. *Morality: An Introduction to Ethics*. New York: Harper & Row.

Wilson, S. J. 1978. *Confidentiality in Social Work: Issues and Principles*. New York: Free Press.

———. 1980. *Recording: Guidelines for Social Workers*. 2d ed. New York: Free Press.

Winnicott, D. W. 1949. "Hate in the Countertransference." *International Journal of Psychoanalysis* 30:69–74.

"Woman Blames Psychological Problems on Psychologist's Sexual Relationship with Her." 1997. *Mental Health Law News* 12 (8): 2.

"Woman Claims Improper Sexual Conduct by Psychologist." 1996. *Mental Health Law News* 11 (2): 3.

Wood, B. J., S. Klein, H. J. Cross, C. J. Lammers, and J. K. Elliott. 1985. "Impaired Practitioners: Psychologists' Opinions about Prevalence, and Proposals for Intervention." *Professional Psychology: Research and Practice* 16:843–50.

Woody, R. H. 1998. "Bartering for Psychological Services." *Professional Psychology: Research and Practice* 29:174–78.

Index

Accommodation of clients, 160–66
Act utilitarianism, 27–28. *See also* Utilitarianism
Actual duty (Ross), 24, 29
Additive goods (Gewirth), 30–31
Advice, receipt of, from clients, 133–35
Affectionate communications, 112–15
Akamatsu, T., 82
Alcoholics Anonymous, 48
Altruism, 16, 148–72
American Association for Marriage and Family Therapy, *Code of Ethics,* 32, 82, 146
American Counseling Association, *Code of Ethics,* 36–38, 53, 82, 126, 146
American Medical Association, *Principles of Medical Ethics with Annotations Especially Applicable to Psychiatry,* 6, 41–42, 82
American Psychological Association, *Ethical Principles of Psychologists and Code of Conduct,* 11, 13-14, 38–41, 82, 117–18, 125–26, 145–46, 183

Barry, V., 186
Barter, 122–28
Basic goods (Gewirth), 30–31
Bentham, J., 26
Blackshaw, S., 78
Bograd, M., 103
Borys, D., 66
Bouhoutsos, J., 74
Boundary crossing, 5, 6–7
Boundary violation, 5–6
Bowie, N., 31
Brodsky, A., 56, 59–60
Brownlee, K., 175
Business relationships with clients, 128–33

Calfee, B., 76
Codes of ethics, 31–42; American Association for Marriage and Family Therapy, 32, 82, 146; American Counseling Association, 36–38, 53, 82, 126, 146; American Medical Association, 6, 41–42, 82; American Psychological Association, 11, 13-14, 38–41, 82, 117–18, 125–26,

Codes of ethics (continued)
145–46, 183; National Association
of Social Workers, 6, 9–10, 10–11,
13, 31, 33–36, 43–44, 45, 46, 52–
53, 82, 87, 92, 117, 125, 146, 147,
182–83, 187, 189
Community-based contact with clients, 115–20, 151–56
Conflicts of interest, concept of, 5–6,
143–47, 181–89
Consultation, role of, in ethical decision making, 43–44
Corey, G., 5

Deontological theory, 24–25
Dependency needs, of practitioner,
14–16, 99–121
Deutsch, C., 49, 51–52
Documentation, importance of, in
ethical decision making, 44–46
Donagan, A., 29–30
Doyle, K., 164–65, 170–71
Duthie, R., 51

Ebert, B., 3–4
Egoism, 25–26
Emotional needs, of practitioner,
14–16, 99–121
Employment of former clients, 163–65
Epstein, R., 77–78
Ethical decision making, process of,
20–46
Ethical theory, 24–25
Ethics complaints, 18–19
Exploitation Index (Epstein and
Simon), 77–78

Favors: acceptance of, from clients,
135–43; offer of, to clients, 156–60
Financial relationships with clients,
128–33

Fitzpatrick, M.: on boundary issues in
small and rural communities, 173–
74; on influence of clinical ideology, 65; on physical contact, 97; on
risk management, 197–98; on self-
disclosure, 111–12
Fleishman, J., 187
Former sexual partner, counseling of,
11, 85–87
Freud, S., 2–3
Freudenberger, H., 99–100
Friendships with clients, 11–12,
101–3

Gabbard, G., 2, 67; on boundary cross-
ing versus boundary violation, 5; on
gifts for clients, 149; on risk man-
agement, 76–78, 96, 196; on self-
disclosure, 110; on sexual miscon-
duct, 72–73
Gartrell, N., 58
Geographic proximity, as source of
boundary issues, 173–81
Gewirth, A., 30–31
Giebelhausen, P., 2
Gifts, 11; for clients, 148–51; from
clients, 135–43
Goisman, R., 66
Good-aggregative utilitarianism, 26.
See also Utilitarianism
Goods and services (barter), 12–14.
See also Barter
Gottlieb, M., 179–80
Grossman, M., 184
Gutheil, T., 2, 65–66; on boundary
crossing versus boundary violation,
5; on gifts for clients, 149; on risk
management, 76–77, 96, 196; on
self-disclosure, 110; on sexual mis-
conduct, 72–73
Guy, J., 49, 50

Herlihy, B., 5
Hippocratic Oath, 57
Home-based services, 154

Impaired practitioners, 47–54
Impropriety, appearance of, 7–8
Institutional ethics committees, 44
Intimate gestures, 11–12
Intimate relationships, 9–12, 55–98

Jamal, K., 31
Jorgenson, L., 75

Kagle, J., 2
Kant, I., 25
Kaslow, F., 50
Keith-Spiegel, P., 49
Kilburg, R., 50
Kitchener, K., 195
Klein, M., 3
Krauskopf, C., 49

Lamb, D., 48, 49, 79
Lawsuits, 19–20
Lawyers Concerned for Lawyers, 47
Little, M., 3
Locus-aggregative utilitarianism, 26.
    See also Utilitarianism

Malpractice, claims of, 19–20
Meals with clients, 138–40, 155
Metaethics, 24
Mill, J. S., 26
Miller, J., 78
Miller, M., 49
Monetary gain, incentive of, 12
Myers, W., 64

National Association of Social Work-
    ers, Code of Ethics, 6, 9–10, 10–11,
    13, 31, 33–36, 43–44, 45, 46, 52–
53, 82, 87, 92, 117, 125, 146, 147,
    182–83, 187, 189
Natural duties, 28
Negative utilitarianism, 29. See also
    Utilitarianism
Nonsubtractive goods (Gewirth),
    30–31
Normative ethics, 25

Olarte, S., 78; on incidence of sexual
    misconduct, 57–58; on profile of
    offending therapists, 59; on situa-
    tional offenders, 68
Oliver, J., 57, 58

Payne, B., 187
Personal benefit, incentive of, 12–14,
    122–47
Physical contact, 10–11, 92–98
Poelstra, P., 49, 50
Pope, G., 59, 67, 74
Pope, K., 49, 58, 66
Popper, K., 29
Prima facie duties (Ross), 24, 29
Professional encounters with clients
    (clients as colleagues), 189–90
Professional ethics, growth of, xi–xii, 2,
    23–24
Psychologists Helping Psychologists,
    47

Quinlan, K., 44

Randles, R., 75
Rawls, J., 28–29
Recovery, practitioners in, 169–72
Reeves, R., 60
Referral fees, 145–46
Risk management, guidelines for,
    17–20, 194–98
Ross, W. D., 24, 29, 116

Rule utilitarianism, 27–28. *See also* Utilitarianism
Rule worship (Smart), 25

Schank, J., 175–79
Schoener, G., 57, 67–69, 80–81
Self-disclosure, 108–12, 166–72
Senger, H., 108–9
Services, receipt of, from clients, 133–35
Sexual misconduct. *See* Sexual relationships
Sexual relationships, 9–12, 55–74; causes of, 63–73; with clients' relatives or acquaintances, 87–90; with colleagues, 90–92; consequences of, 73–75; with former clients, 81–85; and practitioner rehabilitation, 79–81; and risk management, 75–79; with students, 90–92; with supervisees, 90–92; with trainees, 90–92
Simon, R., 75–76; on patterns in sexual misconduct, 69–72; on risk management, 77–79; on transference and countertransference, 64, 65; typology of sexual contact devised by, 57
Skovholt, T., 175–79
Smart, J.J.C., 25, 29
Smith, D.: on boundary issues in small and rural communities, 173–74; on influence of clinical ideology, 65; on physical contact, 97; on risk management, 197–98; on self-disclosure, 111–12
Social encounters with clients, 190–93

Social Workers Helping Social Workers, 47
Solicitation of clients, 146
Sonnenstuhl, W., 79
Stake, J., 57, 58
Stark, M., 49, 50
Strasburger, L., 75
Supererogatory duties, 28

Tabachnick, B., 49
Teleological theory, 24–26. *See also* Egoism; Utilitarianism
Thoreson, R., 49, 51
Twemlow, S., 67

Unanticipated circumstances, as source of boundary issues, 17, 173–93
Unavoidable circumstances, as source of boundary issues, 17, 173–93
Unconventional interventions, 104–8
Undue influence, concept of, 6, 65, 127, 146
Utilitarianism, 25–29; act, 27–28; good-aggregative, 26; locus-aggregative, 26; negative, 29; rule, 27–28

Values, role of, in ethical decision making, 43
VandenBos, G., 50, 51

Whistle-blowing, 186–87
Williams, B., 29
Wilson, S., 184
Winnocott, D., 3
Wood, B., 49, 50–51
Woody, R., 124, 126, 127–28